Sir Harry Hamilton Johnston

Livingstone and the exploration of Central Africa

Sir Harry Hamilton Johnston

Livingstone and the exploration of Central Africa

ISBN/EAN: 9783337120719

Printed in Europe, USA, Canada, Australia, Japan

Cover: Foto ©Andreas Hilbeck / pixelio.de

More available books at **www.hansebooks.com**

LIVINGSTONE

AND THE

EXPLORATION OF

CENTRAL AFRICA.

BY

H. H. JOHNSTON, C.B., F.R.G.S., F.Z.S., ETC.

(H.M. COMMISSIONER FOR NYASALAND AND CONSUL-GENERAL
FOR PORTUGUESE EAST AFRICA.)

AUTHOR OF "THE RIVER CONGO," "KILIMANJARO EXPEDITION,"
"HISTORY OF A SLAVE," ETC. ETC.

WITH

*TWENTY-TWO ILLUSTRATIONS FROM PHOTOGRAPHS OR
DRAWINGS BY THE AUTHOR, AND SEVEN MAPS
DRAWN BY E. G. RAVENSTEIN, F.R.G.S.*

LONDON:

GEORGE PHILIP & SON, 32 FLEET STREET;

LIVERPOOL: 45 TO 51 SOUTH CASTLE STREET.

1891.

PREFACE AND DEDICATION.

WHEN I was about to set forth on a journey which would cover much of the lands, lakes, and rivers that had been first revealed to us by Livingstone (I had further visited at different times scenes connected with his life and travels in Angola and South Africa), the editors of this series of the "Lives of Great Explorers" asked me to write the Life of Livingstone in its especial connection with Central Africa.

This little book is the result of that request—whether an unfortunate -one or not the reading public must decide. To the author its compilation has been a source of increasing interest and education, for until he travelled in Livingstone's footsteps and entered minutely into the recorded details of Livingstone's work in Africa, he realised but feebly the debt which African civilisation owes to that great man, and the permanent and solid value of his careful researches into the physical conditions and natural history of the Dark Continent. That the author should have been chosen by chance or design to be the agent in placing "Livingstone's land" under the protection of the British Crown has tended to increase his appreciation of the zeal with which Livingstone worked with the same end in view, as the only effectual means

of assuaging the evils which perpetually desolate Negro
Africa and render useless to humanity at large these
fertile plains, these noble lakes and broad rivers, these
wealthy mineral deposits, and the grandest mammalian
fauna which remains on any continent.

This work is to be regarded more in the light of a
sketch of Livingstone's life as an African explorer. It
does not pretend to be a regular biography, which,
indeed, would be somewhat superfluous after the works
of Dr. Blaikie and Mr. Hughes. The author, however,
has striven to write as accurately as possible, and above
all to be impartial and unprejudiced in the treatment
of his subject. With this end in view, he has caught
eagerly at every legitimate opportunity for blaming,
criticising, and even sneering at Dr. Livingstone's character and actions, in the dread lest his writing should
become a mere monotonous eulogy; and if these oppor-
tunities are so few that the general estimate of this book
is that of nearly unmitigated praise, the conclusion to
be drawn is, that Livingstone was a really great and
good man, and that it is impossible to belittle him by
recounting the truth, the whole truth, and nothing but
the truth.

The author must express his grateful sense of obliga-
tion to Alexander Low Bruce, Esq., and Agnes Livingstone Bruce (the son-in-law and daughter of the great
explorer) for the loan of Dr. Livingstone's private
letters; to William Snell Anderson, Esq., of Dalfruin,
for his kind assistance in obtaining views of the scenes
of Livingstone's early life at Blantyre; for much elucidatory information derived from William C. Oswell, Esq.,
the distinguished and well-known sportsman and explorer, and one of the few staunch and true friends

whom Livingstone found out of the crowd of flattering, self-advertising acquaintances and patrons who sprang up around him; to J. Scott Keltie, Esq., of the Royal Geographical Society, one of the editors of this series, who has been superbly patient under much provocation from a querulous writer, hard to please; and, lastly, to Ernest G. Ravenstein, Esq., the accomplished cartographer, whose maps confer on this book the chief value it possesses, and whose revision of the proof-sheets has ensured accuracy in all geographical details.

To Mr. E. G. Ravenstein I dedicate this work on Livingstone and the exploration of Central Africa; for if Livingstone be first among African explorers, Ravenstein is the best of African cartographers, and Ravenstein was an authority on African maps contemporaneously with Livingstone's work as a practical surveyor of Unknown Africa.

CONTENTS.

—⊷—

x CONTENTS.

LIST OF ILLUSTRATIONS AND MAPS.

FULL-PAGE ILLUSTRATIONS.

ILLUSTRATIONS IN TEXT.

ILLUSTRATIONS IN TEXT (*Continued*).

MAPS, &c. (*Printed in Colours*).

MAPS IN TEXT.

LIVINGSTONE AND CENTRAL AFRICA.

—••—

CHAPTER I.

CENTRAL AFRICA—NATURAL HISTORY.

THE history of the southern half of the African continent has widely differed from the northern portion as regards the manner and period in which it has been explored and made known by races higher than the Negro. More than that, the Negroes inhabiting the long half of the Dark Continent which lies to the south of an irregular border-line commencing at the Cameroons on the West Coast, and passing across the continent to the East Coast at Mombasa, present two[1] very distinct language-stocks, which are totally unrepresented in the northern half of Africa. For convenience, I shall call this line dividing Northern from Southern Africa the "Bantu Border-line," because it coincides exactly with the northern limit of the Bantu[2] language-field.

[1] The Bantu and the Hottentot-Bushman.

[2] *Bantu* is the name now given to that remarkably homogeneous family of prefix-governed South African languages to which belong the dialects of the Cameroons, the Congo and Zambezi basins, the Great Lakes, the Zanzibar coast, and, in fact, all Southern Africa except the western part of Cape Colony and Namakwa-land.

A

It is remarkable that in Africa north of the Bantu border-line the progress of almost all exploration has been from the north southward, while south of this irregular limit its general direction has been from the south upwards to the north; and in spite of the rapid progress of African exploration at the present time, there still remains a narrow zigzag ribbon of unknown country lying between the extreme reaches of the northern and southern waves of discovery. It is true that this unexplored belt no longer extends unbroken in its continuity. Speke and Grant were the first to cross it in 1861 in their journey from Zanzibar to the Victoria Nyanza, and thence down the Nile to Egypt; but for some twenty-six years afterwards the Nile Valley remained the only travelled passage for Europeans from North to South Africa overland.[1] The next cut through the ribbon (I except the journeys made by Dr. Schweinfurth and Dr. Junker when they passed from the Nile basin to the upper waters of the Welle, because it is not certain that they reached the Bantu border-line) was performed by a not sufficiently known German traveller, Dr. Zintgraff, who succeeded in 1889, after repeated plucky attempts, in crossing from the northern limits of the Cameroons watershed to the south bank of the Benue. Stanley's recent journey from the Aruwimi to the Albert Nyanza was a more abrupt, decided passage from the Congo to the Nile basin than was Dr. Schweinfurth's, but he did not, so far as I can learn, actually cross the Bantu border-line, though in

---

[1] Speke and Grant were succeeded in their passage across the Bantu boundary in the Nile basin by Sir Samuel and Lady Baker, by Colonel Chaillé Long, M. Linant de Bellefonds, Messrs. Chippindall, Wilson, and Felkin, Mason Bey, Gessi Pasha, Colonel Gordon, Emin Pasha, and Signor Casati.

some places he skirted it very closely. In the real centre of Africa, Dr. Henry Barth [1] had pushed southwards as far as that still mysterious river the Shari in the year 1854; but although his researches in that direction were subsequently amplified by Dr. Nachtigal, and although Dr. Junker, coming from the Nile, and Mr. Grenfell (the well-known Baptist missionary) and Captain Van Gèle, travelling up from the Congo, have carried the course of the Welle-Dua-Mubangi River, and with it the Bantu border-line, to a little beyond the fourth parallel of north latitude, there still remains an unexplored gap of some four hundred miles in width between the two limits of exploration in that direction—the Shari and the Dua-Mubangi. Then, again, in Eastern Africa, in spite of the great journeys up from the south, through Masailand, of Joseph Thomson and Count Teleki (the latter reaching as far as 5° north latitude), and of Borelli, down from the north through the almost unknown lands southward of Abyssinia, and the plucky attempt of the James Brothers and Mr. Lort Phillips to pass through Somaliland, there remains yet in Eastern Africa an unexplored belt nearly as wide as that which lies between the Upper Nile and the Cameroons.

Curiously enough, this "divide" in the direction of European exploration is almost exactly followed by the manner in which the Mohammedan propaganda has attacked the great savage continent. By the Mohammedan propaganda I mean the slave-making, ivory-hunting raids of Arabs, semi-Arabs, or Arabised races

---

[1] One of the greatest names in African exploration. He was of German nationality, but (after the death of Consul Richardson, whom he accompanied) entered the employ of the British Government, at whose expense his truly remarkable journeys were made.

such as the Berbers,[1] Fulahs,[2] Hausa, Nubians, and Wa-swahili. Propaganda it no longer is, in the religious signification of the word, although certainly in the northern half of the continent this rush of Mohammedan conquerors was originally started by the successive inroads of proselytising Arabs which occurred during six centuries after the death of Mohammed.

The Fulahs and the Hausa; the armies of Bornu, Baghirmi, Wadai, and Darfur; the Arabs and Nubians of the Nile Valley and the Eastern Soudan; the Abyssinians and Gallas (whose preposterous Christianity offers 'no real distinction from the nature of their Mohammedan neighbours) : all these peoples have for centuries raided and ravaged Tropical Africa up to, but not beyond, the Bantu border-line. The Hadhramaut and Persian Gulf Arabs, who have been settled on the Zanzibar Coast ever since the early centuries of the Christian era (if not before), have by degrees, and of late by leaps and bounds, penetrated the interior of Central Africa in a north-westerly direction, starting from Zanzibar, till they have at length reached, as the northern limits of their extension, the country of Buganda, the Upper Congo, and even the Ituri River (Aruwimi), and possibly the south shores of the Albert Nyanza; and with these Zanzibar Arabs may be practically identified the remarkable Swahili people, the race

---

[1] "Moors," Tuaregs, Tamasheq—peoples speaking languages of the Libyan or Hamitic type, inhabitants of the great Sahara Desert.

[2] Or, as they should properly be called, "Ful-be," which is the plural form of Pul-o, a "Ful" man. The Fulbe, like the Tibu of the Central Sahara, the Nubians, Gallas, Somalis, and perhaps to some extent the Mandingo, are Negroids rather than Negroes, with finer features and longer hair. The Hausa are Negroes, but speak a language with Semitic-Hamitic affinities.

formed by the mingling of Arab and Negro. But in all their slave-raids or trading journeys, these Arabs and Wa-swahili have never yet, to our knowledge, crossed to the north of the Bantu border-line, except in the company of Europeans. Neither is it known to us that any Mohammedan invaders have passed to the south of the Bantu border-line coming from the north, though there are reported to have been one or two doubtful cases contingent on the journeys of Europeans. Practically speaking, the Mohammedan, like the Christian explorers, have halted at this meandering line, which runs across the continent from the estuary of the Rio del Rey on the West Coast to—let us say—the mouth of the River Tana on the East Coast. The Zanzibar Arabs, who travel as far north as the country of Bunyoro and the Victoria Nile, do not yet meet their co-religionists from Khartum; the Mohammedans from Bornu and Wadai have not yet penetrated from the upper waters of the Shari to the banks of the Mubangi, that great northern affluent of the Congo; no Swahili trader has succeeded in reaching Abyssinia from the Masai country, nor has any Abyssinian slave-dealer been known to come overland across the Galla countries to the Zanzibar dominions.

What has caused this remarkable break in the relations between Northern and Southern Africa? Between the Africa of the Egyptian, the Nubian, the Libyan, the Hausa, the Fulah, the Niam-niam, and the Africa of the Bantu and the Hottentot? Between the Nigritia, the Libya, the Ethiopia, the Bilad-as-Sudan, the Land of the Blacks, which was known to the old Egyptians, the Phœnicians, the Carthaginians, the Greeks, the Romans, and the Saracens, and which, in spite of the intervening

Sahara Desert,[1] held far-off relations with the ancient Mediterranean peoples, and that great southern half of Africa which was first made known to us by the Eastern Arabs and the Portuguese?

There is seemingly no line of natural obstacles stretching across Africa to account for this division in its history. It is true the dense forests of the Congo basin may have arrested the advance of the Mohammedan raiders from the Benue and the Shari, for these people ride horses and prefer a more or less open country for their operations ; but to the eastward of the Congo watershed the country on both sides of the Bantu border-line appears to be the same in character. Why then should the Nubians, who have reached the Monbutu country, stop short at Burega, or the Swahili Arabs who visit Bunyoro not continue their journey to Gondokoro ? Perhaps the real explanation may lie in several causes combined : in the dense forests of West Central Africa, in the difficulty of penetrating this unknown tract from the east or west, owing to the harsh deserts and savage people of Somaliland and the pathless woodlands of the Cameroons, and in the fact that exploration coming from the north and south has about spent its force when it has reached the Bantu border-line.

It is of that Bantu half of Africa which lies to the south of this zigzag but well-defined language-limit that I propose to treat in the present volume, more especially in conjunction with a review of the life and work—and

[1] The Sahara quite possibly was less arid two or three thousand years ago than it is now. We know from the remarkable rock-paintings discovered by Richardson and others in Fezzan that in ancient times bullocks were employed for transport across the Sahara. The camel only came into use quite recently, perhaps about the eleventh century of our era.

results which have followed on the work—of that great traveller, David Livingstone, who may be said to have initiated the scientific exploration of Central Africa by the European race. I think fit to apply to that portion of the African Continent which was illumined and affected by Livingstone's discoveries the designation of Central Africa, in contradistinction to the Temperate South Africa already known to us in its main features before Livingstone's day, to the great mass of Mohammedan North Africa, and to those eastern and western extensions of the Dark Continent that are practically unconnected in the history of their exploration and development with that Bantu Africa which will for all time be associated with Livingstone's name.

Central Africa may be roughly subdivided into the East and West Coast-lands; the Lake Region, and the basins of the Congo and the Zambezi. Draw a line down through its middle, and you will find that the eastern half contains nearly all the great lakes and high mountains, while the western portion, except for the coast-range marking the edge of the central basin, is mainly flat, and most abundantly watered by innumerable streams. The western half belongs to the "Forest" Region,[1] while the eastern section exhibits that park-like, savannah country which is so characteristic of the

[1] Wallace's "West African" sub-region. This definition is now chiefly restricted to a narrow strip of coast-land stretching from the River Gambia on the north to the River Kwanza on the south, with a vast inland extension over nearly the whole of the Congo basin, up to the western shores of Lakes Albert Edward and Tanganyika. This *West African* or "Forest" country, which offers a curious parallel to the forest regions of the Amazon basin in South America, was once, I believe, characteristic of the greater part of Tropical Africa, but largely through the action of man during many centuries in destroying the trees by fire and axe, the forest region is now confined to the West Coast and the

greater portion of Tropical Africa. The forest region
has a richer flora, but in some respects a poorer fauna,
than the park country, and from the protection afforded
by its dense forests to feeble forms of life and unsuccessful species, it presents a more primitive and truly
African aspect in its characteristic types than the
eastern, northern, and southern parts of the continent—
something, in fact, suggesting a slight resemblance to
Madagascar, which island represents to a great extent
the character of the African fauna of the period ante-
cedent to the irruption into Africa from the Mediterranean countries and Western Asia of the larger and
more striking types of mammalia which occupy the main
part of this continent at the present day.

Among such mammalian forms as are peculiar to West
Central Africa, I may cite the three or four species of
anthropoid apes,[1] which approach more nearly to mankind in their structure than their Asiatic congeners;
two most extravagantly - developed baboons, the drill
and the mandrill; the Mangabey monkeys (*Cercocebus*);
eleven or twelve kinds of *Cercopithecus*, among which the
most remarkable are the Diana and Pluto monkeys;
two remarkable lemurs (*Arctocebus* and *Perodicticus*);
two bats; the otter-like insectivore, *Potamogale ferox;*
two peculiar civets (*Nandinia* and *Poiana*); a red tiger-
cat; a species of manatee; a curious pig - like little
ruminant, *Hyomoschus;* a red-haired buffalo; a large

Congo basin, where the much greater rainfall and consequent moisture
sustains a vegetation too exuberant to be easily coped with, and too
damp and full of sap to afford much scope for bush-fires.

[1] The gorilla, the common or white-skinned chimpanzee, the bald-
headed chimpanzee, and possibly the Bam-chimpanzee from the Welle
district, and the Soko, found by Livingstone in Manyema, though these
two latter animals may be the same species as the common chimpanzee.

Cephalophus antelope with a white back, and a smaller species with a back strangely barred with black stripes; and the red river-hog (*Potamochœrus penicillatus*).

Among remarkable or peculiar West African birds are a tit (*Parinia*), four flycatchers, four shrikes, a swallow (*Waldenia*), several finches and weaver-birds; a peculiar crow (*Picathartes*), a starling (*Onychognathus*), a ground-thrush (*Pitta africana*), a genus of woodpeckers (*Verreauxia*), three peculiar genera and several species of barbets; a remarkable genus (*Myioceyx*) of kingfishers, and one or two peculiar species of hornbill; that handsome bird the great blue plantain-eater (*Schizorhis gigantea*), and two or three other species of Turacu; the celebrated grey parrot, and possibly several species of *Pœocephalus* parrots, a love-bird (*Agapornis*), and a West African form of *Palæornis;* two very remarkable genera of guinea-fowl,[1] and two peculiar species of the common genus *Numida;* a slaty egret (*Ardea*

---

[1] *Phasidus niger* and *Agelastes meleagroides*, the former with dull black-grey plumage, but head nearly bare, except for a few isolated plumules and a crest of black feathers along the occiput [naked skin of head a reddish colour]; and the latter with the bulk of its plumage a bluish-grey, speckled—"*saupoudré*"—with tiny white spots, and the feathers of the neck and breast white, while the upper part of the neck and the head are bare. Both these birds possess spurs, which distinguishes them from all the other guinea-fowl (except the Vulturine species, which has a rudimentary spur in the male), for these African *Phasianidæ*, unlike their congeners in Asia, Europe, and North America, have no spurs on the tarsus.

The Guinea-fowl form an interesting group of Pavonine birds, which are the peculiar appanage of the African region throughout which they extend, even to Madagascar and Western Arabia. They are indigenous nowhere else, though they have become naturalised by man in the West Indies and Central America. Their nearest allies are the Tragopans, the Peacocks, the Polyplectrons, and the Turkeys. The turkey is simply an aberrant peacock which has found its way through Eastern Asia to North America, just like the wild goat and wild sheep

gularis), a tiger bittern, a white-bellied stork (*Abdimia sphenorhyncha*), a Tantalus stork (*Pseudotantalus*); two peculiar genera of hawks (*Urotriorchis* and *Dryotriorchis*), and an interesting form of fishing vulture (*Gypohierax angolensis*, also found on Upper Zambezi); a rail (*Hydrornia alleni*), and a peculiar fruit-pigeon (*Treron macrorhyncha*).

Twelve genera of snakes are supposed to be restricted in their range to the West African sub-region, and a few species of other genera—among them two specially venomous vipers—*Vipera nasicornis* and *V. rhinoceros*—are also, as far as we know, confined to this portion of the continent. Three genera of lizards, two of tortoises, and two of tree-frogs are said to be peculiar to West Africa, as also ten genera of butterflies and fifty-three genera of beetles; but, of course, with the lower forms of vertebrates, and still more with insects, it is not so

of the Rocky Mountains, which are the only ring-horned ruminants in North America, and have their nearest allies in Asia.

As the region of Central Africa under description possesses nearly all the genera and species of Guinea-fowl, it may be of interest to append a complete list of the members of this sub-family of Pheasants:—

	Habitat.
Phasidus niger	West African forests, from Old Calabar to Congo.
Agelastes mcleagroides	West African littoral, Liberia to Niger Delta.
Numida vulturina	East Equatorial Africa.
,, *ptilorhyncha*	Abyssinia.
,, *meleagris*	All Tropical Africa.
,, *cornuta*	South Africa.
,, *coronata*	East Africa.
,, *mitrata*	Madagascar.
,, *cristata*	West Africa.
,, *rendalli*	West Africa.
,, *pucherani*	East Africa.
,, *plumifera*	East Africa.

easy to prove their restricted range as it is with the more readily discernible mammals and birds, so that many of these butterflies, beetles, frogs, and lizards, which are at present considered to be restricted in their range to the West African forests, may ultimately be found in other parts of Africa, as that continent comes to be more carefully searched.

. The same condition applies not only to the fresh-water fishes of the West African rivers, but in a still greater degree to the flora of this sub-region, which, in spite of its much greater luxuriance of growth, possesses but few genera or species which are absolutely confined to this district in their range and denied to the rest of Tropical Africa. A few kinds of ferns perhaps, two genera of palms [1] (*Podococcus* and *Calamus*), several genera of arums, one or two orchids, a certain number of Rubiaceous plants (*Psychotria*, for instance, and a good many species of *Mussænda*), the genus *Begonia* (which, so far as it is distributed in Africa, is confined to the western sub-region), a few papilionaceous shrubs and herbs, such as *Camoensia* and *Leucomphalus*, one or two genera of *Connaraceæ* and *Ochnaceæ*, nearly all the species of *Cola* (some of which yield the cola-nut of commerce), the handsome monotypic genus *Omphalocarpum*, several species and genera of the *Guttiferæ*, such as many of the *Sarciniæ*, and the peculiar genera of *Pentadesma* and *Allanblackia;* [2] also four or five species of *Anona* are believed to be restricted in their *habitat* to the West

[1] *Elais Guinëensis*, the oil palm, although thought to be peculiar to the West African sub-region, has been discovered by Sir John Kirk growing wild on the island of Pemba (Zanzibar), and on the mainland of East Africa ; and I have found it at the north end of Lake Nyasa.

[2] Professor Oliver is responsible for this very cacophonic name. What causes botanists to compose such ill-sounding, unclassical names

African forest regions. But, as I have already stated, West Africa differs from the eastern side of the continent, in respect to its flora, rather in greater exuberance of growth and individual abundance of forms than in generic or in strong specific character. What may be a poor starveling shrub on the east coast of Tanganyika may be, owing to greater moisture of climate and richer soil, a fine bushy tree on the west shore of that lake. Some plants that are deciduous in the drier parts of the Zambezi basin are evergreen in the rainy lands of Lunda. The difference in the aspect of the flora which Schweinfurth and Junker noticed when they passed from the basin of the Nile to that of the Congo, which Cameron observed when he crossed from one side of Tanganyika to the other, and Livingstone when he passed from the park-lands of the Zambezi to the forests of the Upper Liba and the Kasai, and which the present writer has also witnessed in his journey from Angola to the Congo, and Nyasa to Tanganyika, arose less from the difference of species and genera than from the more luxuriant character of the vegetation, the profuse display of plants and trees, which are practically unknown to the traveller coming from the east side of the continent; not because they are absent from that region— for their range probably extends all over Tropical Africa —but because in the drier atmosphere of the eastern versant of the continent they are hidden away in restricted localities, where special conditions of moisture and soil favour their growth or their perennial greenery. For an example to explain this, let us take an imaginary

for new orders and genera of plants ; as, for instance, *Ternstrœmiaceœ*, *Kosteletzkya, Chailletiaceœ, Wormskioldia, Smithia, Smeathmannia, Goodenovieœ ? !*

journey from Mombasa, on the east coast of Africa, to
the edge of the great Congo Forest, just beyond the
Semliki River, travelling *viâ* Mount Kilimanjaro and
Lake Victoria Nyanza. From the coast to near the
base of the big snow mountain, we shall pass through a
country of scanty vegetation, varied by a little pleasing
growth of flowering shrubs and clumps of acacias,
baobabs, and fan-palms; still, nothing whatever which
comes up to the ideal tropical forest, with its dense
glossy-green foliage, its ferns, mosses, lichens, fungi,
creepers, which are delicate lace-like veils of verdure,
parasitic orchids, epiphytic arums, and trees with smooth,
white, column-like stems running up seventy feet above
the leaf canopy of the lesser shrubs before they deign to
expand themselves into a crown of foliage. But some
thirty miles from the snows of Kilimanjaro, along the
course of the little River Lumi, which drains the eastern
slopes of the mountain, you will pass from out of the
glaring sunburnt plains into the dense forest of Taveita,
where, from the character of the vegetation, you may
reasonably fancy yourself in West Africa. This little
district of Taveita is some thirty square miles in extent,
and the River Lumi, for ever fed by the snows of
Kilimanjaro, trickles through it into Lake Jipe beyond,
and, because of its sluggish flow and several branches,
keeps the soil always moist, and thus maintains this
extravagant growth of forest. A botanist dropped into
Taveita from a balloon, and told to guess where he was
by the character of the vegetation, would say, "West
Africa." Very well; let us leave Taveita, and, skirting
the north side of Kilimanjaro, strike straight for the
Victoria Nyanza, cross the lake, and march overland
ill you have passed the Semliki and entered the great

West African forest which stretches from the edge of the Congo watershed to the Atlantic. Herein we shall see just the same kind of forest and the same trees, flowers, creepers, ferns, and fungi which were characteristic of Taveita; and yet, if we have followed the route indicated, we shall not have seen the like assemblage of vegetation elsewhere between Taveita and the Congo basin. In fact, it may be said that East Africa, from the borders of the Somali Desert to the Zambezi, is dotted in places, where the water-supply and components of the soil are propitious, with patches of "West African" forest.

Western Africa, however, with all its wealth of flora and its peculiar and recondite forms of animal life, lacks not a few of the higher vertebrates—beasts and birds— which are so characteristic of the more open park-lands, grassy plateaux, and arid steppes of the Ethiopian sub-region.[1] It possesses the elephant and hippopotamus in numbers,[2] but not the rhinoceros or the wart-hog. The giraffe, the kudu,[3] the common variety of eland, and

[1] The Ethiopian sub-region really includes the whole of Africa within the tropics, except the Congo basin, the Cameroons, the Lower Niger, and a narrow strip of coast-land from the mouth of the Kwanza River in 9° S. latitude to the mouth of the River Gambia in 14° N. latitude. It is the "East African" sub-region of Wallace, but I prefer to call it the "Ethiopian," as "East African" is too restricted a term to apply to a subdivision of the African region which includes Senegal, Lake Tshad, and Benguela within its limits.

[2] Besides the common hippopotamus, which is found abundantly in West Africa, there is another species, the pigmy hippopotamus, which is restricted in its distribution to the rivers of Liberia.

[3] The place of the true kudu appears to be taken by two large Tragelaphs, the *Tragelaphus gratus* and *T. Euryceros*. The striped or "Derbian" eland is found in parts of Western and West Central Africa, but not the common dun-coloured species, which is peculiar to South, East, and East Central Africa. The *Tragelaphinæ* are an interesting group of purely African ruminants, analogous to the guinea-

nearly all the great antelopes, except those of the genus *Cobus*, are also absent; neither is there any zebra or

fowl among the pheasants, and equally muddled, misnamed, and badly classified by many naturalists. It may therefore be well to append here a little synopsis of the known species and genera and their distribution over Tropical Africa. I would further premise that it is as incorrect to call the Tragelaphs "antelopes" as it would be to apply that term to the *Bovinæ*. "Antelopes" should be reserved to designate the ring-horned ruminants, such as the Cephalophines, the Rupicaprines, the goats, sheep, and gazelles. The nearest ally of the Tragelaphs is the Nylgaie (*Boselaphus tragocamelus*), which is a generalised Tragelaphine form that has been developed in every direction but in length of horns. After the Nylgaie, the oxen come nearest to the Tragelaphs. The leading features of the latter ruminants are the tendency to spiral growth in the horns (which are not ringed as in the antelopes), and the white spots and stripes on the hair of the head and body. These white markings are evidently characteristic of the primitive ruminants, and even of the original *Artiodactyla*. They reappear in young pigs, in the deer, and in the Tragelaphs and some of the oxen. The Anoa (a small buffalo in Celebes) and the Nylgaie are both spotted with white on the face :—

TRAGELAPHINÆ.

Habitat.

Tragelaphus scriptus (Harnessed antelope) } .	Western Africa.
T. sylvaticus (Bush buck) } · · · · {	Ethiopian sub-region : principally South and East Africa.
T. gratus . . . . . . {	Marshy districts of West African littoral from mouth of Congo to mouth of Niger.
T. Spekii (Setshire) } · · · · {	Marshy districts of Ethiopian sub-region.
T. Angasii	South Africa.
T. euryceros	Mountains of Gaboon and Cameroons.
T. strepsiceros (Kudu) } · · · {	Ethiopian sub-region (except Somaliland) and South Africa.
T. imberbis (Dwarf kudu) } · ·	Somaliland down to River Tana.
Oreas canna (The eland) } · · ·	Ethiopian sub-region and South Africa.
O. canna var. *Derbianus* (Striped eland) }	The less forested parts of West and West Central Africa.

other wild equine species. The place of the great buffaloes [1] of East and South Africa is taken by the smaller,
weaker, red buffalo (*Bubalus brachyceros*). Over the
greater part of West Africa the lion (so abundant in
the Ethiopian sub-region) is practically absent, though
the leopard ranges impartially over the whole of Africa,
West, East, North, and South, excepting the uninhabitable parts of the Sahara and Kalahari deserts,
and the over-inhabited districts of Algeria, Egypt, and
South Africa. The cheetah, on the other hand, is confined to the Ethiopian sub-region, and never enters West
Africa, where, however, its near ally, the serval, is found.
Hyenas, so abundant in all other parts of Africa, are
almost absent from the true West African sub-region ;
but if any species of this scavenger does enter the fringe
of that district, it is the striped hyena, and not the
spotted. The hunting-dog (*Lycaon*) is also absent from
West Africa, and confined in its range to the Ethiopian
sub-region, while that most primitive of all living dog
forms, *Otocyon*, is confined to South Africa, and the
various desert foxes (the Fennecs — *Canis cerdo* and
C. chama) keep to the north-east and south of the
continent in their range. The only wild dogs in West
Africa are the black-backed and side-striped jackals.
Many of the rodents, so abundant in East Africa, do not
extend their range to the western districts. The four
genera of mole-rats (*Spalacidæ*) are unrepresented there ;
so are many of the *Muridæ*, and all the jerboas, the
octodonts, and the hares. Yet these animals range
over all the Ethiopian sub-region, as do the *Orycteropus*

---

[1] *Bubalus caffer*, which is found all over the Ethiopian region, and
B. æquinoctialis, which is restricted to Abyssinia and part of the
Egyptian Sudan. This latter animal, by the shape of its horns, is an
interesting link between the Asiatic and African buffaloes.

edentate and the *Hyrax* or rock-coney, which are also absent from West Africa. The manatee is not found in East African river estuaries, but an allied animal, the dugong, takes its place.

There is no ostrich in West Africa, no secretary-bird,[1] no bustard, no sand-grouse, and no lark. Many species of eagle[2] and vulture are absent, as are the Vulturine guinea-fowls, the Stanley and Demoiselle cranes, the great-billed ravens, and several genera of starlings (such as *Buphaga, Amydrus,* and *Spreo*), all of which birds are numerously represented in East and South Africa.

If the grandeur of West Africa lies in its superb forests, which recall in their extravagant development of vegetation the long-past geological epochs of the Coal measures, it is the special glory of East Africa to possess still, and despite the vigorous slaughterings of British sportsmen,[3] the finest collection of large and striking mammals of any district in the world. Besides the elephant, the hippopotamus, and the river-pig (*Potamochœrus*), the Tragelaphs, and the Cobus antelopes, the leopard and the serval, which it shares with the western half of the continent, Eastern Africa still harbours the remarkable Gelada monkey, with its bare breast and huge mane, the large Tshakma baboon, and the culminating species of Colobus monkey, with its white-plumed tail; the lion, the cheetah, the spotted and the brown hyenas, the rhinoceros, the zebra and other wild asses, the giraffe, the buffalo, the oryxes, hartebeests, gnus, pallahs, and gazelles. Eastern Africa has, in fact, been the refuge of

---

[1] *Serpentarius reptilivorus.*

[2] Those of the genera *Aquila, Helotarsus, Spizætus,* and *Circætus.*

[3] The most inexcusable, and ordinarily the most unintelligent, of destroyers, in that they neither kill for food, as do the natives, nor for science, but merely for sport.

the great carnivorous and herbivorous mammalia which developed into specialised forms in Eastern Europe and Western Asia, and were driven thence into the Dark Continent through Syria and Arabia by the rise and rapid increase of mankind, who crowded these beasts out of their feeding-grounds; it may also be by the cold touch of some glacial epoch.

By the same road, no doubt, through Syria and Arabia [1] came the first human immigrants into Tropical Africa. It is the most reasonable solution of the problems raised by the contemplation of the existing varieties of mankind and their present distribution over the land surface of the globe to imagine that, in whatever part of the world our species first originated, it was in Asia that the human tribe effected its first decided concentration. From its centre of distribution in this continent it sent forth horde after horde of emigrants, north-east into America, west into Europe, south-east into Malaysia, Australia, and the Pacific Archipelagoes, and south-west into Africa. No doubt the earliest type of man had fine, long, silky hair on his head, with just a slight kink or crimp in it. [2] In his Asiatic home, however, there soon sprang up two distinct variations from the primal stock—the men with short, curly hair, and the men with long, coarse, straight hair. The latter spread more to the north, and in long ages differentiated into the red American, the yellow Mongol, and the white European; the former turned more to the south, settled in India perhaps, and in that hive of nations developed itself into a Nigritic type, which overflowed

[1] The Red Sea is supposed to have been at different times reduced to an isolated lake by a slight rise of its shallow bed near Perim.
[2] This is much the character of the head-hair in the Chimpanzee.

Khartum BEJA Red Sea Danakil

be shr
AI El Fasher Kordofan ABYSSINIA Aden
DARFUR El Obeid Zeila
Blue Nile

Shilluk Harrar

Bongo D Kafa GALLA S
NIAMNIAM Welle Bari O
Duu Je Mangbattu Medi Turkan M
Lotka Akka A Mandishu Banwa
olo Anwunga Bu-ganda Busoga L
Kavirondo Kenia I
Victoria Nyanza Jub
Batwa Kilimanjaro Lamu
songo Manyema Mumbasa
Baluba WANYAMWEZI Zanzibar INDIAN
BARUA OCEAN
ko UNDA Bahemba 10°
Babisa
luvale Maravi Yao Rovuma C.Delgado Comoro Is
Baloi or Kaonga Johanna
Ba Rotse Sulumbwe Banrai Mozambique
Makololo Batoka Tete Barue
Mashona Kwama or Zambezi
Kayeye Matabele Bateve Sofala
L.Ngami BETSHUANA
BUSHMEN
Limpopo
Delagoa B.
Griku Zulu
Basuto

G. Philip & Son

The Range of the Peoples
speaking
BANTU
Languages.
By H. H. Johnston
Scale 1: 80,000,000

Bantu Africa
A dotted line round border indicates
slight uncertainty as to actual local limits

to the south-east over Malaysia and Polynesia, and as far away as to Australia, Tasmania, and even to New Zealand (and there gave rise, by further changes and by intermixtures with the fringe of the long-haired type,[1] to Negritos, Papuans, Australians, Tasmanians, and Maories), and westwards into Arabia,[2] where probably the true Negro variety of man was first initiated. A Nigritic influence is distinctly traceable among the autochthonous tribes of Eastern Arabia, Mesopotamia, and Balutshistan, which is not to be sufficiently explained by a supposed intermixture with Negro slaves. The classical geographers and historians also make mention of dark-skinned peoples inhabiting the shores of the Persian Gulf. It must not be forgotten, indeed, that, as regards race and language, there are quite sufficient links existing to connect the Arab and the Negro with a chain of intermediate types.

The original Nigritic stock in Western Asia developed three leading types—the ascending Hamite and Semite, and the somewhat retrograding Negroes and Hottentot-Bushmen. The first immigrants from Asia into Africa were no doubt the lowest Negro forms, the ancestors of the present Bushmen and other dwarf races of Central Africa. To them succeeded the Hottentots (a slightly higher type, with Hamitic affinities in their language), and probably for many centuries the Bushmen-Hottentot tribes monopolised the whole southern half of Africa,

[1] The Malays and Polynesians, on the other hand, are the long-haired type which has mingled slightly with the Negrito ; so are the Dravidian peoples.

[2] We have reason to believe, from the deeply-cut beds of its dried-up rivers, and from other signs and traditions, that Arabia, like the Sahara, has suffered from a continued and increasing desiccation, and that it was once a better watered, more fertile country, able to support a varied fauna and a large population.

leading an unprogressive existence among its woods and mountains. Other Nigritic invasions occupied a great band of North Central Africa from east to west, and here the typical dark-skinned, burly Negro became more emphatic in his development. In the meantime, the Hamites were advancing considerably in the scale of humanity. They were acquiring longer and more bushy, less kinky hair than their Negro relations, and their intelligence was sharpening. They had in them the impulse to progress while the Negro remained stationary, and the Bushman-Hottentot retrogressed. The Hamites settled in the lower valley of the Nile (whence they developed into that marvellous Egyptian race, the first civilised people in human history). They extended across the Sahara Desert to the Atlantic, the Mediterranean, and the Canary Islands, while other and earlier branches of their stock had established themselves along the Red Sea coast, round the flanks of Abyssinia, the eastern versant of the Nile, and over Somali and Galla lands.

The Semites, in the meantime, had acquired still lighter complexions and straighter hair than their Hamitic brethren, though even with them the "kink" in the hair is not wholly lost.[1] They probably branched off from the Hamites in North-Eastern Africa, and spread out over Palestine, Syria, the Euphrates Valley, Arabia, and both sides of the Persian Gulf. In the two last-named districts (Arabia and Southern Persia) increasing drought had probably the effect of driving away (into Africa chiefly) most of the old Nigritic inhabi-

[1] It reappears among the Arabs still, and even among the modern Jews occasionally, in a certain "waviness" of the hair of the head, which has a crimped appearance.

tants who had been the prior occupants of the land: the remainder were absorbed by the Semites, and much intermixtures produced races like the Elamites. In the north and west and east the Semite invasion was ultimately checked, and its border types much modified and "whitened" by the descent of Aryans[1] and Mongols.[2]

The earliest types of man which invaded Central and South Africa from Arabia were probably (as I have already pointed out) the ancestors of the Bushmen and Hottentots.[3] It is possible these pygmy, yellow-skinned, low-type Negroids spread even over nearly all the African continent, but were earlier and more completely effaced or absorbed by superior races in the northern than in the southern half of Africa. At the present day they are only represented by the Bushmen and the Hottentots in the countries south of the Zambezi and by the scattered pygmies in the great Congo Forest.[4] These latter people are of a much less definite type than the Bushmen-Hottentots; and although reported to possess a language of their own, are only known to speak the dialects of the Bantu or Nilotic-Negro tribes among whom they dwell.

The true black Negro, who entered Africa somewhere about Abyssinia, spread right across the continent to the west in a broad band, bounded on the south by the

---

[1] Early Greeks, Armenians, Persians.

[2] Hittites, Accadians, Turks.

[3] The modern Hottentot has been greatly modified in physical characteristics by Bantu intermixture.

[4] The only sections of these Central African dwarf races at present known are the Akka or Batwa of the eastern basin of the Congo, the Ba-yaka of the Mubangi, and the Obongo of the Gaboon forests. Krapf professed to have discovered a dwarf race, the Doko, to the south of Abyssinia, but we know too little about this tribe to be able to classify it.

Congo basin, but on the north only limited and kept in check by the uninhabitable nature of portions of the Sahara Desert, and by the haughty repulse of the superior Hamitic race, which had occupied North Africa from Egypt to Morocco. It is probable that at one time the Negroes sent little offshoots of their race northwards across the Sahara Desert to the southern slopes of the Atlas Mountains and the verge of the Mediterranean, though these invasions were finally checked and their results absorbed by the Hamites. But the main stem of the Negro race—the "right down, regular" Negroes, so to speak—had pushed steadily across Africa from the Red Sea coast to the Atlantic shores in a belt lying more or less between the 10th and 5th degrees of north latitude, though commencing and ending farther to the north. Another subsidiary Negro embranchment occupied the country northward of the main stock, and a third branch spread out over the Upper Nile basin. Somewhere about the very centre of the continent, in some forest district midway between the watersheds of the Nile, Lake Tshad, the Benue, and the Congo, there diverged and developed from the main Negro stock that great southern section of the race which we call the Bantu. The obstacles, whatever they were,[1] which had hitherto checked the big black Negroes from invading

[1] Though it is not clear what prevented a superior type of black man from invading Southern Africa from the eastern portion of the Nile basin, it was no doubt the belt of dense forest stretching from the Lower Niger to the Congo watershed and the Nile sources which was the main obstacle, extending over three-quarters of the breadth of Africa. The Bushmen-Hottentots appear to have kept pretty much to the eastern side of Africa in their descent, and the great western forest region before the Bantu invasion was probably only penetrated by a few bands of Pygmies. It was at that time mainly given up to those incomplete men, the anthropoid apes.

Diagram showing the
ORIGIN
and Degrees of
RELATIONSHIP
of
NEGRO, HAMITIC & SEMITIC RACES.
By H.H. Johnston.

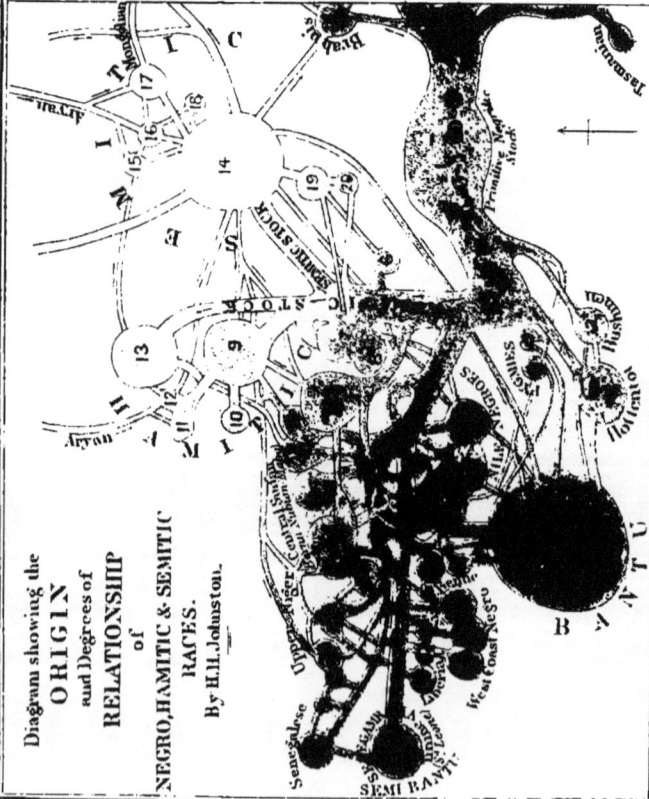

Explanation.

The degree of tone indicates the colour of the Race, ranging from the White Semitic to the Black Negro.

The main origin of each group is indicated by the thickest connecting stem. Intermixtures with other groups are shown by connecting branches or filaments which are graduated in thickness according to the lesser or greater extent of the intermixture. The arrows indicate the direction which the intermixture has taken. Where there is no arrow it means that reciprocal intermixture has taken place.

The relative length of the main stems indicates degree of divergence. The arrangement of the groups is mainly but not entirely in accordance with geographical distribution.

1. Central Negritic Stock.
2. Bushmen.
3. Hottentot.
4. Akkas & Batwa.
5. Obongo.
6. Beja or Bishari (Hadendowa & Danakil)
7. Galla. Somali.
8. Turban or West? Galla
9. Lybians (Tuareg Immashaq Berbers)
10. Canary Islanders (Guanches)
11. Shluh & Riff.
12. Kabail.
13. Egyptians (Ancient & Copt.)
14. Arabs.
15. Phoenicians Canaanites.
16. Jews.
17. Assyrians.
18. Aramaeans.
19. Abyssinians.
20. Harrar.
21. Hausa.
22. Tibbu.
23. Nubians.
24. Maba (Darfur, Wadai, Baghirmi)
25. Fulah or Pul-be.
26. Kanuri (Bornu)
27. Sonyai or Central Niger
28. Mandingo-Susu.
29. ?
30. Peoples of the Niger Senegal.
31. ?
32. Wolof.
33. Senegambian Tribes (Biafada Timni Bulom)
34. Kru Tribes.
35. Peoples behind country behind Liberia
36. Gold Coast (Kru?)
37. Ijo (Bonny & Bras?)
38. Gold Coast (Ashanti Accra)
39. Dahome (Ewe)
40. Yoruba Nupe.
41. Ibo Efik.
42. South Benue people (Mishi &c)
43. Lower Cross River people Lochadi Camaroon?
44. Bantu.
45. Musgu.
46. Num Num.
47. Manghattu.
48. Madi.
49. Bongo.
50. Dinka, Shilluk.
51. Bari Masai.

Southern Africa were now overcome, and the Bantu, who had probably, in the fertile regions of their primal home, increased and multiplied extraordinarily, burst, as might a dammed-up lake, through the weakest portion of the barrier, and swept over the southern half of Africa with a rush, driving the Pygmies, Bushmen, and Hottentots before them, licking them up, absorbing them, killing them, or leaving isolated fragments of those inferior races to subsist in the densest forests or the dreariest deserts. This important change in the history of African man has occurred in comparatively recent times, not much more than two thousand years ago, probably. This is shown by the extraordinary similarity of all the Bantu languages one towards another, a similarity which exceeds that of the various members of the Aryan family, and is the more remarkable—and thus the more evident proof of the recent dispersal of the Bantu Negroes—from the known tendency of unwritten tongues to vary speedily from the primal stock. Further and more definite reasons in support of this theory of the relatively recent expansion of the Bantu are given in my work on the "Kilimanjaro Expedition" (pp. 483, 484), to which I would refer the very few (alas!) among my readers to whom this question is of any interest. For the purpose of more clearly understanding the views which I have ventured to express in the foregoing pages as to the origin and intricate relationships of the African races of man, the reader is advised to study the accompanying diagram.

CHAPTER II.

CENTRAL AFRICA—HUMAN HISTORY.

AFTER these ages of continual race-movements between Asia and Africa, wherein the foundations of the leading types of African peoples were laid down, there was, no doubt, a kind of lull, during which the Negroes and the Hamites settled down to colonise the northern half of the Dark Continent, and the Semites concentrated themselves in Western Asia and Arabia. Perhaps the gradual depression of the bed of the Red Sea, and the consequent intervention of a gulf of water between Africa and Arabia, may have had something to do with the isolation of Africa which ensued on the first great invasions and migrations of the primitive Negroes and Negroids.

Some ages passed—many thousand years perhaps—and then the dawn of History arose in Egypt. In the valley of the Nile, as almost simultaneously in the far east of Asia, man had finally quitted the beast in becoming able to turn round and consciously review his position, in transforming the disconnected pictures he had hitherto drawn [1] of the objects round him into conventional characters which recorded his thoughts, his beliefs, his wars, and the names of those who ruled over him. No doubt

[1] Drawing is really an extremely low art, possessed by the lowest races of man, past and present.

24

man was man long before writing was invented, but
that organised scheme of representing sounds by figures
which we call "writing" was the first means to his
hand of convincing future generations that the human
species had definitely left beasthood. We may yet find
the osseous remains of anthropoid apes so extremely
human in their appearance, so high in their development, that the osteologist who examines them will be
puzzled to say whether they represent the most advanced
species of ape or the lowest type of man. The border-
line between the genus *Homo* and other mammals never
becomes strongly marked until men are able to put
history in writing. Oral traditions go for nothing.
They are simply Instinct not yet crystallised, not yet
stamped on the convolutions of the brain, or added to
the primal impulse of the germ. Man is not the only
mammal who manufactures, remembers, ponders, communicates his thoughts to others, acts in concert, weeps,
sings, laughs,[1] or reasons. There is, however, a certain
degree of mental development which we are generally
agreed marks the confines of humanity, and as this can
only be attested by written records in the case of ancient
races who passed away before the science of compara-
tive anthropology began, the earliest papyrus, the oldest
inscribed tablet, the most anciently scribbled rocks are
the first reliable landmarks of the existence of real
humanity.

Progress in development is by no means uniform,
whether it be in man and the things of men, or in the
mute, stupid, blundering operations of Nature. It is
an affair of long pauses, apparent stagnation, quiet,

[1] All the higher old-world monkeys grin and laugh, while the
anthropoid apes cachinnate like man.

gradual accumulation of causes, and then, suddenly, a
rise, a revolution, a rush of development, a catastrophe
lasting ten minutes or ten months, which changes the
condition of ten thousand square miles of land and
water, or ten millions of people. For countless centuries the Zambezi flowed down through South Central
Africa into a great lake which covered much of Northern
Betshuanaland and the Kalahari Desert ; then there was
a volcanic disturbance in the rim of high land which
separates the lower part of its course from the basin of
the Kafue and the watershed of the Indian Ocean : a
rent was made, a zigzag crack—possibly in an hour of
earthquakes—in the bed of the Zambezi, and the great
river was deflected in its course, hewed its way through
the cliffs of basalt, and flowed henceforth to the Indian
Ocean, leaving the once great lake to slowly evaporate
till its bed becomes the Kalahari Desert, and its deepest
hole the trivial Lake Ngami.

For two hundred years and more chemists in their labo-
ratories made experiments as to the nature of electricity
without clearly foreseeing whither their gropings were
leading them. At length their discoveries converged to
a combination, in which the parts of the puzzle were
fitted together, and then, all at once, electricity became
a practical force placed ready for use in our hands, and
in a few years the lands of Europe were criss-crossed
with telegraph wires, while successive developments of
the initial discovery have since begun to revolutionise
the conditions of civilised existence. In this century of
unexampled inventions the same thing may be said about
the history of steam-power, the development of photo-
graphy, the success of automatic machines at railway
stations ; of all sudden results coming after long, patient,

unapparent experiments ; the amazingly rapid spread of new ideas and the bursting of social reservoirs.

A million years and more man spent in emerging from the brute; another five hundred thousand, it may be, were passed in attaining to the level of the Australian savage ; but it is quite likely that civilisation in the valleys of the Nile, the Euphrates, the Ganges, and the Yang-tse-Kiang sprang up suddenly out of savagery, and was developed with a marvellous quickness compared to the tardy and almost imperceptible rate of man's previous progress. In some trees the bud grows on the branch for months slowly, slowly swelling, and perfecting itself within, but showing in its outer aspect scarcely any visible change from day to day ; then, all at once, in one warm night, the sepals part, the petals expand, and in a few hours the dull-coloured, sulky-looking bud has become a radiantly beautiful flower.

So in the same way, perhaps, a hundred years sufficed for the emergence of the Hamitic savages of the Lower Nile into the historical period, into the astonishing civilisation of ancient Egypt ; just as the same short course of time in this unsurpassed nineteenth century has raised the higher types of civilised man into beings with the powers of demi-gods.

For many, many centuries, no doubt, after the first great incursions of Negroid men from Arabia, Tropical Africa was left pretty much to itself to develop its Bushmen and black Negroes without outside interference ; but as soon as Hamitic Egypt had attained to that degree of comfort and prosperity which permitted and incited it to interfere with the concerns of its neighbours, besides invading Syria and Cyprus, and raiding

Canaanites and Hittites,[1] it turned round on Black Africa and sent its forces up the Nile to Nubia and Ethiopia, and round by sea to the Land of Put—the aromatic country—modern Somaliland. I do not think the explorations of the ancient Egyptians extended far into Tropical Africa. They probably knew a little about the rivers, lakes, and mountains of Abyssinia, and if they thought or cared about the question of the Nile sources, they probably attributed them to the latter country. Nubian and Nile-Negro slaves possibly brought tales of the White Nile and the Bahr-al-ghazal or Western Nile, but I cannot believe that the Egyptians themselves were sufficiently animated by a love of geographical exploration to venture far up the Nile valley, away from the comforts of Egypt, in a land of intense heat, and among savage, brute-like people.

The first impulse to explore Central Africa in an intelligent way (other, I mean, than a mere blind, un-reasoning race-movement, such as the unrecorded Semitic invasion of Abyssinia) came from the Phœnicians. This restless, enterprising branch of the Semitic stock appears to have first originated on the western shores of the Persian Gulf, but it soon afterwards reappeared in little colonies on the Mediterranean littoral of Syria. The Persian Gulf, the Mediterranean, the Red Sea, and the Atlantic and Indian Oceans soon became the resort of the galleys and daus of the first bold navigators of human history ; for the deliberate and repeated voyages of the Phœnicians to India, Africa, Spain, and Britain were very different from the occasional outings of wind-

---

[1] It would be an interesting question for Egyptologists to solve why Egypt, with all its vigour, never turned its forces westwards. It could conquer northwards as far as Asia Minor, and southwards to Dongola : why did it not invade Tripoli and Mauretania ?

driven junks in the China seas. The Phœnicians, by agreement with the Egyptian monarchs, launched their ships on the Gulf of Suez, and sailed down the Red Sea round the great Somali promontory, and along the East Coast of Africa, attracted by the gums and spices of Somaliland and Southern Arabia, possibly also by the gold of the Zambezi valley, though this I doubt. I fancy there was no gold worked in South-Eastern Africa much before the Christian era. The land was considerably more forested in ancient days than when subsequently invaded and settled by the pastoral Bantu tribes, and at the time of the Phœnicians' visits to the Zambezi (if they made any), the only inhabitants would be timid, spiteful, half-animal Bushmen or Hottentots, who would know and care nothing about gold, they not being metal-workers like the Bantu. It was not likely, therefore, that they would indicate its presence to the Phœnicians, who would further have to go some distance up-country, and reside some time in the land, to find out the existence of gold for themselves.

The Ophir of the Bible, whence the Phœnicians brought gold, ivory, monkeys, and peacocks to the Jewish king, was probably the West Coast of India.

However, it is possible that these bold mariners, these Portuguese of antiquity, not only coasted East Africa and (starting from their Carthaginian colony) West Africa as far as Sierra Leone, but that a Phœnician navigator in Egyptian employ actually effected the circumnavigation of the continent.

When the Phœnician power had died away, the Egyptian Greeks and the Persians made a few half-hearted attempts to explore East Africa; but although certain Greek and Persian settlements were formed respectively

on the coasts of Somaliland and Socotra, and on the
Zambezi littoral, no known attempts were made to
explore the interior. The Romans, when they became
the masters of Egypt, did something towards discovering the source of the Nile, but were soon discouraged by the heat and the savage tribes of the
Sudan.

The first thoroughgoing exploration and colonisation
of Black Africa was undertaken by the Arabs of South-
West, South, and East Arabia, both before and after
Mohammedanism added a powerful incentive to emigration and conquest. During the first ten centuries of the
Christian era, Arab colonies, growing into Arab sultanates, had been founded all along the East Coast of
Africa, from the south of Somaliland to Sofala, and up
the Zambezi as far as Sena. In some cases these Arab
settlements were founded on a foregoing Persian basis,
for it must not be forgotten that under the Khozru
dynasty, and even before that period, Persia had established trading depots, and even colonies, at different places
along the Zangian[1] coast, such as Lamu, Zanzibar,
Kilwa, and Moçambique. (At the two former places
Persian influence was so strong that it created, especially
at Lamu, quite a local civilisation and distinct race of
people, which to this day is light coloured, owing to
its far-off Persian ancestry. A few Persian words are
found in the Ki-swahili language, and a Persian festival,
the *Nairuz*, or "New-year," still lingers among the customs of Zanzibar.) The Arab invasions of Africa north

---

[1] The very terms "Zangian," "Zangibar," "Zanzibar," are derived
from the Persian word *Zang* or *Zanj*, "a black man." The termination *bar* is, I believe, also Persian or Arabo-Persian, and means
"country." This word has, in the form *barra*, been adopted into
Ki-swahili, where it means "wilderness."

of the Bantu border-line [1] have little to do with the scope
of this book, and indeed proceeded more from the north
and north-west of Arabia than those which have brought
at different times so much of Eastern Africa under Arab
sway.

I believe it was the early Arab settlers in South-East
Africa who first discovered and worked the gold existing in Zambezi-land.   To them I attribute the building
of those strange stone walls, forts, and towers in the
countries of the Mashona and Matabele.   At the end
of the fifteenth century the Arabs had created a strong
Sultanate at Kilwa,[2] to which the subsidiary states or
minor Sultanates of Sofala, Sena (Zambezi), Moçambique, Zanzibar, Mombasa, Malindi, and Lamu (properly spelt Al-Amu) were more or less tributary.   They
had also greatly influenced the Comoro (*Kamar* = full
moon) Islands and the north end of Madagascar.   This
latter island had apparently been peopled at a very
distant period with men of Bushmen race, who in turn
were followed by some Bantu tribe from the opposite
coast (the traditional Va-zimba); and later still the
great island was invaded and occupied by a Malay
people coming across from the Eastern Archipelago.

Although the Zanzibar Coast, the Lower Zambezi, and
Sofala were long occupied by the Arabs, they nowhere ad-
vanced far into the interior (except possibly in Southern
Africa) till the beginning of this century, when there was

---

[1] Namely, the different Arab invasions of Egypt, from time imme-
morial to, say, the end of the twelfth century of this era ; the Arab
incursions into North and North-West Africa, principally in the
seventh and twelfth centuries ; and the Arab settlements formed in
North Central Africa (Kordofan, Darfur, Wadai, and part of Bornu)
from the twelfth to the eighteenth centuries.

[2] A place on the coast in lat. 8° 50′ S.

a recrudescence of Arab activity and immigration at Zanzibar and on the opposite coast-line, and similarly a large
increase in the slave-trade. To supply their own wants
and keep up the huge demands for Negro slaves which
came from Turkey, Arabia, Persia, and the United
States of America,[1] the Zanzibar and 'Omani Arabs, and
their black half-breed children, the Wa-swahili,[2] penetrated farther and farther inland, till they were established on the shores of Nyasa and Tanganyika, and
until they even met and joined hands and trade with
the half-caste Portuguese of the West Coast. In our
own day they have become masters of the Upper Congo
and the Aruwimi, and extend their influence to the
Victoria and Albert Nyanzas.

But while these Arab movements enter into the
history of Bantu Africa, they can scarcely rank as acts
of geographical discovery. No individual stands out
from among the crowd of illiterate slave-traders or
ivory merchants who rambled over parts of Africa south
of the Equator. Beyond certain vague rumours of lakes
or a lake in the interior, they told the outer world
nothing about African geography. It was different
with the more cultured Arabs of North Africa—men
like Ibn Batuta, Muhammad at Tunsi,[3] and Muhammad
Bu-al-Moghdad[4]—whose itineraries can be to some extent

[1] Until the cessation of slavery in North America in the earlier
"'Sixties," the Moçambique Channel, the Zanzibar and Madagascar
coasts, used to be haunted by piratical American slave-ships.

[2] *Swahili* is believed to be derived from the Arab word (in the
plural) *Sawahel*, *i.e.*, "coast-lands." *Wa-sawahel* or *Wa-swahili* =
"coast-people." In the singular this word is *Sahel*.

[3] Who travelled in Darfur at the end of the last century. He was
a native of Tunis.

[4] Travelled across the Western Sahara from Senegal to Morocco.
He was an Algerian.

traced on the map, and whose information is reliable and of value; but still these men, to a great extent, were Europeanised; that is to say, partook of the Mediterranean civilisation, and the last two of them explored Africa in relatively recent times. The first people who really gave the modern world any glimpse of the great southern half of Africa were the Portuguese. Marco Polo brought back from the Persian Gulf tales of Madagascar and Zanzibar, and possibly was shown by the Arabs the dry, grey, plume-like frond of the Raphia palm (brought from the east coast of Africa), which he took to be a feather of the "Rukh" or "Roc," but he did not, as far as we know, himself visit Bantu Africa. A few Dieppe navigators and whalers are said to have found their way for some distance along the West African coast in the twelfth century, but they are hardly worth mention, because even if they did get farther south than the coast of Morocco, Europe was none the wiser for their ignorant voyagings. No; the first intelligent explorers, worthy of the name, who mapped out the coast of Bantu Africa, sailed from the ports of that remarkable little kingdom of Portugal while Castile and Aragon were still fighting their last battles with all that remained of Moorish power in Spain, and Columbus, the Genoese, was planning and preparing his discovery of the New World lying beyond the only ocean which was known to European civilisation.

During the fourteenth century the Canary Islands had been rediscovered [1] by Aragonese ships; then, in the early part of the century that followed, the Portuguese lit upon Madeira, and voyaged bit by bit along the West

[1] I write "rediscovered" because they were dimly known to classical geographers—Pliny, for example.

African coast till they had found the Senegal River, rounded Cape Verde, and Fernão do Pôo had discovered the first bit of Bantu Africa which (as far as we know) had been reached by Europeans on the west coast—the island which bears his name.[1] In 1484 Diego Cam [2] reached the mouth of the Congo River, and put up a stone pillar at the promontory of Sant' Antonio on its southern bank. In 1487 Bartolomen Diaz landed at Angra Pequena (which name means a "little narrow bay"), and erected a stone cross to commemorate his visit, which cross endured there more than three hundred years, till some English or Dutch vandals threw it down.[3] Shortly afterwards he rounded the Cape of Good Hope, and coasted along South Africa as far as the great Fish River, where his officers and men insisted on returning. On his way back he saw the Cape of Good Hope (or, as he called it, "Cabo Tormentoso " = the " Stormy Cape "), which he had passed unknowingly on his outward voyage.

In the meantime the Portuguese paid considerable attention to the kingdom of the Congo and its southern province, Angola, where they obtained a footing at the place they named São Paulo de Assumpção de Loanda, and on the River Quanza (Kwanza) ; and when, in 1495, Vasco da Gama passed round the Cape of Good Hope and landed in Delagoa Bay, he was struck with the resemblance which the Bantu tribes of that district bore in race and language to the natives of Angola.

Vasco da Gama passed on from Delagoa Bay to the Arab settlements at Sofala and Moçambique, and so on

---

[1] Fernando Po, as it is usually written, was discovered in 1471.

[2] Cam or Cão, pronounced the same way, "Cowng." This name means nothing more or less than "dog" (Latin, *Canis*).

[3] It is now in the Museum at Lisbon.

up the east coast to Malindi, whence he obtained an Arab pilot to take him across to India. A few years afterwards, Albuquerque had snatched from the Arabs Sofala, Moçambique, Kilwa (Quiloa), Zanzibar, Mombasa, Malindi, Barawa (Brava), Magdishu (Magadoxo), on the East African coast; and Aden, Maskat, and Ormuz in Arabia and in the Persian Gulf. In 1569 an expedition under Francisco Barreto, with three ships, nearly a thousand men, and many horses, asses, and camels, set out from Lisbon, reached the Zambezi[1] the following year, and ascended it (in boats, I presume) as far as Sena, where they found the Arabs strongly established as traders. From Sena they set out, over five hundred strong, to discover the gold-mines of Manika; but the tsetse-fly killed most of their horses, the natives attacked them, and the unhealthy climate of the Zambezi valley laid so many of them low with fever that they had to return to their ships and abandon the search for gold.

In 1616 a Portuguese gentleman, named Jaspar Bocarro, formerly in the service of the Marquez de Ferreira, offered to carry samples of Zambezi silver overland to Malindi without going near Moçambique. He really journeyed overland from Tete to the Shire River, through the country then ruled over by the Maravi, crossed that stream near the Ruo junction, passed through the Manguru or Anguru country, then northwards down the Lujenda valley to the Rovuma River (which he spells Rufuma), and after crossing this stream, reached the coast at or near Mikindani, whence he took ship to Kilwa (Quiloa).

---

[1] Vasco da Gama had already discovered the Zambezi Delta, and had called one of its branches the "Rio dos bons Signaes"—the "River of good indications."

Previous to this, however, Jesuit priests had ascended the Zambezi, and had established themselves as far as the confluence with the Loangwa (Zumbo), and at other places between that limit and Sena. As a rule they had succeeded in winning the friendship of the turbulent Zambezians; but one priest at least was martyred, no doubt more from political suspicion than from any bigotry against Christianity. The dominant chief of the countries of the Lower Zambezi in those days, who went by the name of the "Lord of Motapa" (Monomotapa), was responsible for this murder of one of the earliest Jesuit propagandists, and the name of the Bishop Hannington of his day was Gonçalo da Silveira. The work of the Jesuits on the Zambezi will be for ever commemorated by the introduction into these countries of the mango, the orange, the lime, and other useful fruit-trees. On the Lower Congo, and especially to the south of that river, in West Africa, the Jesuits had, some few years earlier, commenced the same good work of civilisation as they initiated on the Zambezi. They rapidly Christianised the kingdom of the Congo, and introduced into West Africa, as they had done into the eastern part of the continent, the orange and the lime, with the addition of fruits derived from Brazil, such as the pine-apple and the cashew.

From these devoted men, the less cultured, less known, inglorious Livingstones of their day, was learnt almost all that little knowledge which Europe possessed of the interior of Bantu Africa before the beginning of this century. The Jesuits are said to have travelled up the Congo River as far as the vicinity of the modern station of Manyanga. It is likely, also, that they knew of the existence of Stanley Pool (or "Mpumbu," as the natives

S. Thome · I. de Corisco · Equinotialis · Quiola R. · Mombacha

C. de lopo Gusalues · Fontes Nili · Quiola

C. Primo · Mone Lune

Haec pars Aphricae antiquioribus mansit incognita.

Rio de Manicogo · Elesia · Meguales · R. de Fern del Velloso · Moncobi qui

R. de Magdalena · Carnia · Sagaea · Mechinarica · Charagassa · Saber de alilo

Angra · Copia auri

C. Nigram · Hengi · Zedaici · Padro de S. Raphael · Rio de Bon Suraes

G. dos Areas · Bali · P. de S. Vincisa

Plaia Verde · MARE PRASSODUM

C. da Padrom · Capricorni Circulus · das Tareasu

Angra da tementa · Rio de Lago

P.ta de Sabra · G. de S. Thome · Serramas · P. de S. Lucia

C. das Voltas · Rio de Infante

G. de S. Helena · G. dos Quemadas · G. de Sambras

C. de Bona Speranza

HYLACOMILUS. 1522.

Nubia · Merye · Cano chin · Hamarich · Mocana · Mer

Ad del Rey · R. del campo

Nubia deserta · Astabo · Prete Ianni · Delaca · Zeila · Melindeo · Opim · Afim

Zoqala · Gunagona · Maguiazo · Zarzella

C. de Lopo Goncalez · Bardi M. · Zediaba · Huba Coloa p. · C. Braña

Betolina · Gjala · Ceigra · Mombaca

C. primero · Manicogo · Heicer · Bozos · Pendu

Murama · Rava dos Raphael · Zenzibar

Galilu · Talu del Nilo · Zdeana · Quiloa · Monfia

C. Ledo · S. Lazaro · Mabrue · Gil · F. del Comoro

C. de los bos nuga · Moti de Luna · Mocabique

Aigesa · Dera · Baf

Mote negro · S.ta de S. Lazaro · Bariu · Ciera · Sofala

Negro · Adia · Enggi · C. Piget · S. Apolonia

C. del padron · Garnia · Maputa

Plaia fria

P.ta de las concepcio · Damot · R. del Rey · Corientes

A.ta de S. Antonio · C. Feriera

Angra de las buelias

M.te de los bramidos · R. de S. Xynal

R. de l'infante · C. Arecife

C. de buena speranza · C. del Infante

G.º GASTALDO. 1545.

George Philip & Son.

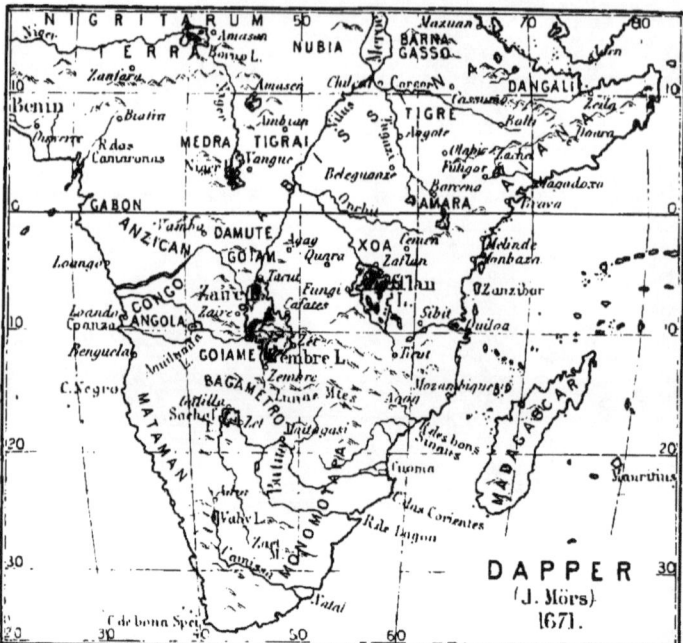

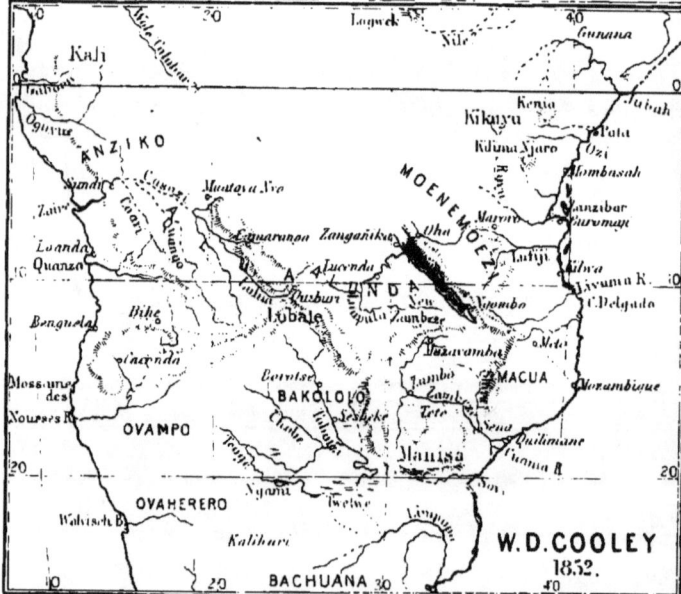

DAPPER
(J. Mörs)
1671.

W.D. COOLEY
1852.

call it), that lake-like expansion of the Upper Congo before its last falls, either by the reports of the natives or their own rambles, and that this, in a much exaggerated form, is one of the lakes through which or from which the Congo is made to flow in the old Portuguese maps. The other Jesuits on the Zambezi no doubt heard and transmitted rumours of the existence of Lake "Maravi" (Nyasa), and those priests, who like Father Lobo travelled far to the south of Abyssinia, brought back hearsay information of yet other large inland seas : possibly Lake Samburu or the Victoria Nyanza. In fact, until the first scientific journey into South Central Africa made by Dr. Lacerda in 1798, European geographers relied chiefly on the information supplied by the Jesuits for such paltry attempts as they might make to lay down the geography of Inner Africa south of the equator, just as, until some thirty years ago, we knew nothing of the interior of China and Tibet but through the hands of Jesuits and other Roman Catholic missionaries.

In the middle of the eighteenth century, however, the Jesuits were expelled from all the Portuguese dominions by order of the Marquez de Pombal, and after their retreat from the Congo kingdom and from the Central Zambezi, those countries rapidly fell back into barbarism.

At the end of the last century the Portuguese Government was stirred up to do something towards exploring South Central Africa, and, curiously enough, the English appear to have been indirectly the cause of this action on the part of the Portuguese ; for in 1795 England had seized Cape Town from the Dutch East India Company, lest it should fall into the hands of the French ; and the Portuguese shrewdly surmised that England would stick to South Africa, and that British enterprise might drive

a wedge northwards between the colonies of Angola and
Sena (*i.e.*, Lower Zambezi). These, at least, are the arguments employed successfully by the learned Dr. Francisco
José Maria de Lacerda e Almeida, a native of Brazil, a
doctor of mathematics of Coimbra University (Portugal),
and the first scientific explorer who set foot in Bantu
Africa; and Dr. Lacerda so far convinced the Portuguese
Government on the subject that he was made Governor
of the Rios de Sena (Zambezi),[1] and appointed to conduct
an expedition "á contracosta "—across Africa to Angola.

Previously to Dr. Lacerda's journey two Goanese of
the name of Pereira, father and son, had gone gold-
hunting to the north of the Zambezi, and had eventually
pushed on with their armed slaves till they reached
the Kazembes' country, near Lake Moero. The reports
they gave of the wealth and power of the Kazembe (a
lieutenant or satrap of the Muata Yanvo of Lunda) decided Dr. Lacerda to proceed thither on his way across
to Angola. His expedition numbered seventy-four or
seventy-five white Portuguese and the two Goanese,
Pereira and son, who were to serve as guides. Dr.
Lacerda made a careful but uninteresting journey as far
as Kazembe's capital, in about 8° 30′ S. latitude, but
avoided, as did the two other Portuguese expeditions
which followed along that route, all those big lakes which
Livingstone afterwards discovered. Unfortunately, Dr.
Lacerda died untimely on October 18, 1798. After
many wrangles and much double-dealing and secret
opposition to their plans shown by the Kazembe, the
disorganised expedition had to give up the idea of continuing the journey to Angola and return to Tete on the
Zambezi.

[1] A post answering to the modern government of Tete.

Subsequently two half-caste Portuguese, the Pombeiros,[1] P. J. Baptista and Amaro José, crossed from Kasanji on the Kwango River (Angola) to the Kazembes' country, and thence to Tete, on the Zambezi. This journey occupied them from 1802 to 1811, and left geographers almost as much in the dark as to Inner African geography as if it had never been undertaken. The same thing may be said about the journey of Major Monteiro and Captain Gamitto, who, in 1831, conducted a second mission from the Portuguese Government from Tete to the Kazembe. Neither of these gentlemen were scientific observers, and therefore the map of Africa profited but little by their expedition.

What is noteworthy, however, about all these Portuguese travellers of earlier days, and of Silva Porto,[2] who succeeded them, and who journeyed for trading purposes over much of South Central Africa, is not what they discovered, but what they missed. They picked their way among great lakes, and saw none of them. They lit on interesting rivers and never followed them up in an intelligent manner, so as to arrive at some understanding of the hydrography of these countries, which remained an inexplicable enigma until the subsequent journeys of Livingstone, Cameron, Serpa Pinto, Capello, Ivens, Selous, and Arnot. In the Portuguese visual discovery of any of the great lakes I scarcely believe.[3] All that we can attribute to them is having gathered a

[1] *Pombeiro* means a vassal, a serf; a superior, trustworthy slave.
[2] Silva Porto was an old Portuguese colonist who lived in Bihe, at the back of the Benguela district, and who travelled chiefly between the years 1849 and 1889. He committed suicide a few months ago in chagrin at his services being ignored by the Portuguese Government.
[3] Unless we may credit Senhor Candido do Costa Cardoso with having sighted the south-west corner of Lake Nyasa in 1846.

few vague rumours of these lakes which pointed to their existence and site. The utmost they actually *saw* was probably limited to the little salt lake, Shirwa, and to the lake-like expansions of the Shire river, now reduced to vast marshes.[1] They reported a large lake existing in the direction of Lake Nyasa which they called "Zachaf," but Zachaf is a very un-Bantu-like word, and hardly likely to be derived from a local name. Lacerda heard that to the east of his route there was a large "water" or river called "Nyanja" (in Portuguese spelling, Nhanja), and the same "water" was more commonly known by the name of Lake Maravi, after the Maravi people who dwelt to the west of it. The *Pombeiros* make one or two doubtful allusions to Tanganyika as a big river or lake to the north of Kazembe's country, but of Bangweolo or Moero we hear nothing.

Between the end of the fifteenth century and the middle of the nineteenth the Portuguese had explored much of the West African coast from Morocco to the Cape of Good Hope, and had named nearly every important river, lagoon, and headland. They never, however, attempted to exercise rule elsewhere than in Angola, between 7° S. latitude and 18°. In this district they concentrated their dominion on the River Kwanza (Coanza), and from the end of its navigable channel struck across to the Kwango, near which stream they established the "fair" or market of Kasanji. On the east coast of Africa they simply held a few isolated spots— little fortified islands and islets in most cases—from the north shores of Delagoa Bay to Malindi and Magadoxo; and nowhere extended their rule inland, except along

[1] The Elephant and Morambala marshes.

the Zambezi banks (up which stream they possessed forts and trading stations as far as Zumbo) and a short distance up the Loangwa (or Aroangoa) River, which flows into the Zambezi near Zumbo. A little gold-mining was done in the Maravi country to the north of Tete and south of the Lower Zambezi in Manika.

Portugal had as much intended at one time to keep all Africa, or, at any rate, all Bantu Africa, to herself, as Spain had endeavoured to monopolise Tropical America. But other rivals soon appeared in the new field, and of all the ospreys which swooped on little Portugal and tried to tear from her beak or make her disgorge from her pouch part or the whole of her big fish, none was fiercer than Holland. The Dutch seized places on the Gold Coast and made desperate attempts to take Angola from the Portuguese during the enfeeblement of Portugal which resulted from its unwilling subjection to the Spanish throne.[1] About the same time, too, the Dutch settled at the Cape of Good Hope, which, although not actually a Portuguese possession, was still a place of constant call for Portuguese Indiamen, and a part of South Africa which Portugal looked on as hers by right of discovery, although she might not choose to occupy it.

However, although the Dutch collected and collated much geographical information from the Portuguese, and compiled some of the best maps of Africa during the seventeenth and eighteenth centuries, they did but little original work themselves as explorers. In South Africa they extended their colonisation along the coast from the Elephant (Oliphant) River to the Great Fish River, and

[1] A little later on, also, they attacked the Portuguese on the east coast at Moçambique and elsewhere, and took Mauritius from them. The Portuguese, after a hard struggle, regained Moçambique as they regained Brazil, which the Dutch had also seized.

inland as far as the second range of mountains, called in
different parts the Roggeveld, Nieuwveld, and Sneeuw-
bergen; and they made several journeys of exploration
in a northerly direction at a short distance from the
south-west coast. In 1685 Commander Van der Stel
went up through Namakwaland to within a very short
distance of the lower course of the Orange River (then
and long afterwards known as the Groote Rivier = Great
River). The chief bait which led to persistent ramblings
of the Dutch through Western Namakwaland was the
desire to find the gold and copper mines (above all, the
latter) reported to exist by the Hottentots, who backed
up their reports by, at any rate, producing samples of
the copper, if not of the gold. It was not, however, till
the middle of the eighteenth century that a Boer elephant-hunter reached and crossed the Orange River.
His reports led to the despatch of a well-equipped expedition in 1761, led by Captain Hop, and accompanied
by a botanist, mineralogist, and surveyor.[1] The expedition found and crossed the Orange River, and with
much difficulty, owing to the scarcity of water to the
north of that stream, struggled on as far as the latitude
of Angra Pequena; after which they returned, bringing
back but little information excepting vague reports of
the Damakwa,[2] a big, black people dwelling to the

[1] Great, very great credit must be given to the Dutch for the help
they rendered science during the eighteenth century by the manner
in which they encouraged and helped naturalists of all nations in
acquiring a knowledge of the South African *fauna* and *flora*. Especially noteworthy as a patron of science was Governor Ryk Tulbagh,
a truly great man in every respect. Captain Hop's expedition obtained
several giraffes, and Governor Tulbagh sent home the skin of one of
these to Leyden, the first giraffe ever sent to Europe from South Africa.

[2] The Hottentot name for the *Ova-herero* or *Damara*. Damara is
a contemptuous feminine form of the same word in the dual number.

north of the Hottentots, and the Birikwa,[3] a goat-keeping nation to the west. In 1791-92 Willem van Reenen journeyed along Captain Hop's route, but extended his exploration as far north as the verge of the Damara country, at the back of Walfish Bay; and in 1793 a large party of Dutchmen sailed to Walfish Bay and Angra Pequena, explored the vicinity of those harbours, and took possession of them in the name of the Dutch East India Company. Pieter Pienaar travelled inland from Walfish Bay to the Damara country, a journey of about 120 miles.

I cannot find recorded any other remarkable explorations on the part of the Dutch, though during the latter days of Holland's possession of South Africa several foreign explorers did good work under the Dutch ægis. Notable among these was Captain Robert Jacob Gordon, a Scotchman in the service of the Dutch East India Company, who in 1777 discovered the Orange River at its junction with the Vaal, 600 miles from its mouth. Lieutenant William Paterson, an Englishman, and one of the first real, *bonâ fide* British explorers in South Africa, accompanied Captain Gordon part of the way; but in 1779 both these gentlemen made another journey overland through the Little Namakwa country to the mouth of the Great River, which they ascended in a boat they had brought with them for thirty or forty miles. It was Captain Gordon who named this stream the "Orange River," after the Dutch Stadhouder. About the same period there travelled in various parts of South Africa (not very far from the coast) the Swedish naturalists, Sparrmann and Thunberg, and the celebrated

---

[3] *Birikwa*, from *Biri*, a goat (an unknown domestic animal to the Hottentots), was the name given by the Hottentots to the Betshuana.

French zoologist, Le Vaillant. They all three added markedly to our knowledge of the botany, the birds, and beasts of Cape Colony.

The French nation had paid very little heed to Africa till the eighteenth century, and French explorers of Bantu Africa are not heard of till the afore-mentioned Le Vaillant travelled over a small portion of Kaffirland. But in the early decades of the eighteenth century France began to take an interest in South Africa, which arose from two causes: the successful colonisation of some parts of Cape Colony by Huguenots, and the growth of the French East India Company. The desire to possess India impelled France to obtain a foothold in South Africa and the Southern Indian Ocean. She accordingly seized and colonised Mauritius (then Dutch) and Bourbon (afterwards called Réunion); attempted to make a settlement at Delagoa Bay ; was finally ousted thence by mingled clamour and force on the part of Portugal ; and, lastly, cast longing eyes on Cape Colony, where her trade had become very large, and her ships [1] constituted about one-half of the total shipping of all nations trading with the South African ports. Through the friendliness or weakness of the Dutch Government, Cape Colony had become in the latter part of the eighteenth century a powerful basis of supplies, and a safe refuge for the French fleet when at war with England. In 1781 it was resolved by the British Government that the Cape of Good Hope must be seized and occupied, to prevent it from becoming a powerful base of action to the French, who would thus command the route to India. War had broken out between Holland and France on the one side, and England on the other,

[1] In 1781-84.

so that all compunction in seizing a Dutch colony (which had hitherto restrained the British Government from dislodging the French from their growing hold on South Africa) was at an end, and a fleet of forty-six vessels, with 3000 troops on board, was despatched under Commodore Johnstone to take possession of Cape Colony. Unfortunately, this secretly planned expedition was revealed to the French Government by a spy in London, Delamotte by name, who was afterwards hanged for his pains, and the British were forestalled. The French Government despatched Admiral Suffren to the Cape with seven ships-of-war and eight transports carrying troops. Suffren overtook the English fleet in Porto Praya (Cape Verde Islands), attacked them unexpectedly, destroyed three ships, and although not without damage to his own vessels, sailed away and got to the Cape before Captain Johnstone, who, on his arrival, found the place so strongly garrisoned that he could not attempt to take it. In revenge, he destroyed or captured all the Dutch East Indiamen and other ships lying in Saldanha Bay.

Nevertheless, the British Government kept its eye on the Cape. It was tacitly understood that South Africa must either fall to France or England. Holland was too weak a power to maintain her hold on such a great stake in the game of political supremacy. Accordingly, as soon as the French marched into Holland in 1794, and the Prince of Orange, the Stadhouder, fled to England, the British Government obtained from the fugitive Prince an authorisation to occupy Cape Colony until he was restored to his position of chief magistrate in the United Provinces. A powerful fleet and a large body of troops (eventually increased to nearly 4000)

were sent out under Admiral Elphinstone and General
Craig, and Cape Colony was invited to place itself under
British protection and control until the Prince of Orange
should be restored to his rights. The Cape Government declined, and opposed a half-hearted resistance
to the British occupation ; a few skirmishes took place,
but at length an amicable arrangement was come to,
and the forts and Government offices of the Dutch
East India Company were handed over to the British
officials.

Having thus been frustrated and forestalled in the
occupation of South Africa, France—or rather her great
and far-seeing ruler, Napoleon Bonaparte—resolved to
secure what was then considered the secondary route to
India, that through Egypt and the Red Sea. Hence
the Egyptian expedition of 1798. Here, too, fate was
unkind to France. British naval victories compelled
her to leave Egypt, which she has never since reoccupied.
For a while her African aspirations were relentlessly
nipped in the bud, even Senegal being taken from her ;
but at the conclusion of peace in 1815, she regained the
island of Réunion and a feeble foothold in Senegambia.
During the earlier decades of this century she rapidly
extended her sway over the Senegal Basin, she occupied
Algeria, founded establishments on the Gold Coast and on
the Gaboon, and nibbled at Madagascar and the Comoro
Islands. Finally, she has found ample compensation for
the loss of Egypt in a vast North African empire which
extends from Tunis to the confines of Liberia and the
rivers of Senegambia. Her South African aspirations
are surely satisfied in her Madagascar protectorate ; she
has the Comoro Islands, Obock, and a province of the
Congo which alone is larger than her own home terri-

tory in extent.   France at the present day has a bigger African empire than any other European power.

The first British occupation of Cape Colony lasted from 1795 to 1803, when, on the conclusion of the peace of Amiens, it was somewhat unwillingly restored to the Batavian Republic.   War broke out again, however, between England and Napoleon (who had drawn Holland into his circle of subsidiary kingdoms), and the British Government again seized the Cape of Good Hope, this time never to give it up.   The possession of the colony was confirmed to Great Britain in 1814.

After the addition of South Africa to the British Empire, exploration went on apace.   Campbell, a Scotch missionary, in 1812 laid down on the map, pretty accurately, the course of the Orange River, and discovered the sources of the Limpopo; Moffat and other missionaries extended our knowledge of Bechuana-land; Angas illustrated Zululand; Major Vardon explored the Limpopo; Lieutenant Farewell (in 1824) opened up what is now the colony of Natal;[1] and Captain Owen, who was the first to survey with any care the east and west coasts of Bantu Africa, made a careful examination of Delagoa Bay and its vicinity.   The emigration of the dissatisfied Dutch farmers across the Orange and the Vaal Rivers, and their settlement in what are now the Transvaal and Orange River States, also added considerably to the area of explored South Africa.

The systematic exploration of Africa by the British may be said to have commenced in 1788 by the founding of the African Association.[2]   Before that period, however, the attention of our Government had been turned

---

1 Founded as a colony in 1843.
2 Afterwards developed into the Royal Geographical Society.

towards Africa, partly with a view to regulating or
suppressing the slave-trade and opening up fresh fields
for legitimate commerce, and partly (as was seen in the
abortive attempt to seize the Cape of Good Hope in
1781) for securing convenient points of vantage on the
ocean route to India.[1] For the first or second of these
motives, the settlement of Sierra Leone had been founded
in 1787 ; and later on, the irregular trading stations of
the Gambia and Gold Coast were erected into colonies.
At the end of the last and commencement of the present
century, Mungo Park had explored the Gambia River
and the Niger from near its source to the rapids of Busa,
where he was killed. On his second journey to the
Niger he went at the expense of the African Association,
which body was influential in urging the Government to
undertake the exploration of the Sahara, the Central
Soudan, Lake Tshad, and the Lower Niger and Benue.
In 1816, Captain Tuckey was sent out to examine the
Congo and attempt to trace its course upward from its
mouth. He surveyed the river as far as the Yellala
Falls, and carried his exploration inland above these
rapids to near the modern station of Isangila. Captain
Tuckey and most of the members of his expedition died
from fever, but his journey resulted in considerable
additions to our knowledge of Bantu Africa, its people,
languages, and *flora*.

The Cross river which skirts the north-west corner of
the Bantu language-field was ascended by Consul Beecroft
as far as its rapids in 1841 ; the same gentleman explored the Benin River and a portion of the Cameroons
Delta.

[1] With this view St. Helena Island had been taken from the Dutch
in 1673.

Our very limited knowledge of Bantu Africa before the advent of Livingstone is well illustrated in the accompanying maps by Mr. Ravenstein. From this it will be seen that, beyond the southern extremity of the continent, the Portuguese province of Angola, and a narrow strip of country from Kazembe's town to the Lower Zambezi, the interior of South Central Africa from the Bight of Biafra to the Orange River, from Somaliland to Delagoa Bay, was either a mere blank or a bewildering maze of false and nonsensical geography until the Apostle of Africa commenced those explorations which incited others and yet others to explore, and sent forth ever-widening circles of knowledge; so that, in less than fifty years from the commencement of Livingstone's career, Central Africa, in its main geographical features, its marvels, its riches, and its horrors, has been completely laid bare to the contemplation of the white man.

D

CHAPTER III.

On the 19th March 1813 David Livingstone was born, the second son of Neil and Agnes Livingstone. This event took place at the little manufacturing town of Blantyre, on a beautiful part of the River Clyde, where, even up to the present time of writing—the year 1890—man has been unable wholly to obliterate the natural loveliness of the scenery. The Clyde here winds between steep banks which are surmounted and overhung by umbrageous trees, oaks and ashes, birches and haw-thorns. In places, the broad, calm mirror of the reflect-ing stream is marred by weirs and rapids which break up the glassy duplication of houses, chimneys, wharves, trees, banks, and sky with bars of white foam and stretches of swirling, hurrying, frothing water. Round the rim of half the horizon, looking southwards, are richly-wooded heights interspersed with slender red shafts of chimneys which belch out wreaths of white, grey, and black smoke. Northwards, round the great green shoulder of a hill, is a peep of Glasgow, eight miles distant, with its thousand-and-one furnace chim-neys dimly discernible through that iridescent mist of smoke, sunshine, and rain which is the normal atmosphere of Blantyre. In the nearer distance, between the confines

of the great city and the outskirts of Blantyre, lie strips
of murdered country, fields of rye alternating with fields
of baking bricks. This description of Blantyre scenery,
though written in the present tense, is applicable, with
scarcely any alteration, to what Livingstone must have
seen in his childhood from the front and back of the
house in which he was born ; for no great or easily discernible change has, I am told, taken place in the surroundings of Blantyre since the early part of the century :
that is to say, the river and hills have not altered, the
trees are not much diminished, and though Glasgow may
have trebled its extent since the "twenties," still there
were smoking chimneys in Livingstone's youth, and that
is what you chiefly see of Glasgow from Blantyre. The
house in which Livingstone was born remains, according
to local opinion,[1] practically unchanged in its exterior
appearance from that very early part of the nineteenth
century—1810—when Livingstone's father and mother
first settled down here, after a brief residence in Glasgow.
The building in question is situated on one side of a
little blind-alley (closed in with a paling and densely-
foliaged trees), near the summit of a small hill overlooking the river, with cotton-spinning factories below it and
between it and the Clyde. It is a large house, built very
solidly of stone, and flanked in front with great circular
bastions which screen the outer staircases communicating with the different floors ; for I need hardly say this

[1] It should be mentioned that Livingstone's two surviving sisters
assert that their father's original house at Blantyre was burned down
after they left it in 1839, and another one built on its site exactly like
it ; but local opinion and tradition is positive in averring that, while
some of the surrounding houses and part of the factory have been
burnt or pulled down and rebuilt since Livingstone's boyhood, his old
home remains unaltered.

building is, and always was, divided into a number of
separate tenements, one of which was occupied by Livingstone's parents.   On the opposite side of the court or
alley is a curious whitewashed turret like a low, angular
dome.   " What is that place used for ? " I asked a bright-
faced boy in tatters, who had attached himself to me as
cicerone when I went to visit Blantyre.   " That's whar'
they keep the 'doos,'"[1] he replied.   From the old
appearance of this building, no doubt the progenitors of

BIRTHPLACE OF LIVINGSTONE.

the pretty blue-rock pigeons which were strutting about
the ground at my feet inhabited this same "colum-
barium" in Livingstone's boyhood.   At the back of the
house, after being led through an evil-smelling, dirty
archway, and past a common wash-house, you are shown
the dull-looking, small-paned window of Livingstone's
room on the second floor.   But though this room is

[1] Doves, pigeons.

small and poky and ill-lit, it is by no means a dreary
lodging for a studious, contemplative boy, and the view
from the open window has a certain suggestive charm of
quiet screened-in industry which recalls to you vaguely
the saw-mills at work in some tranquil Swiss valley.
There are factories, it is true, in the foreground and
middle distance ; indeed the air is full of the subdued
roar of their machinery mingled with the noise of the
falling Clyde ; but the bricks of which they are made are
a pleasant red in tone ; and these buildings, with their
slender furnace-chimneys, suggest in a far-off way the
palaces, monasteries, and *campanili* of an old Italian
town.   Beyond the factories, with the invisible Clyde
rushing over weirs in the gorge between, is a high ridge
of wooded down ; and above all, that strange, opalescent
heaven, with its rainbows and curtains of vapour, its
wreaths and rolling masses of cloud, its mists and films
of smoke, its watery sunshine ; or its lurid glare of
fire when night falls, and the smoke-pall which daylight
has rendered so dull-coloured and opaque becomes one
vast shimmer of rosy flame.

Livingstone's grandfather was a Highlander of the
Isle of Ulva, off the west coast of Mull in Argyleshire.
He could, as can most Highlanders, trace his ancestry
back for six or seven generations, and boasted proudly
that there had never been a dishonest man among his
forbears.   The honesty of the Highland Livingstones
(whose Gaelic name, by-the-bye, was M'Leay [1]) was no
doubt more of the limited and tribal character than is

---

[1] How this came to be translated into "Livingstone" as its English
version, is not very clear, because "M'Leay" appears to mean "The
Son of the Grey-headed."

our modern and wider understanding of that quality in
the nineteenth century. That is to say, they were loyal
to their chiefs, followed them eagerly to the field of
battle (one of Livingstone's ancestors was killed at
Culloden fighting for Prince Charlie), and probably no
bribe of any kind would have induced them to betray
a member of the clan; but I dare say, all the same, they
robbed and raided and ravished on the lands of other
clans with hearty self-approval. However, in 1792, the
grandfather of Dr. Livingstone, together with most of
his relations, left the Island of Ulva for more profitable
countries. Some of these Livingstones emigrated to
Canada, Prince Edward's Island, and the United States;
but the grandfather of the great David settled at Blantyre, where he found employment in a cotton factory.
This emigrant from Ulva left a reputation for the
same sterling, rugged honesty that he claimed for
his ancestors; and having served his cotton-spinning
employer with just such unswerving fidelity as his
forefathers would have accorded to their bandit chiefs,
he eventually retired on a pension. All his sons, with
one exception, fought in the army and navy during the
Napoleonic wars, and seem to have died mostly in the
prime of life, either in battle or the sicknesses of
camps. The one exception was Neil Livingstone (the
Doctor's father), who remained at home and became a
tea-dealer. He was fervently religious in temperament
and in the whole tenor of his life—almost oppressively
so (though he was no hypocrite), if we may judge by his
son David's frankly-recorded reminiscences, wherein the
father, in his misdirected zeal for the attainment of his
ideal of godliness, is shown as endeavouring to prevent
his son from reading scientific works or books of travel

in order that he might give his attention to weary, un-
profitable disquisitions on theology. "The difference of
opinion between father and son," says David Livingstone,
in his brief review of his early life, "reached the point
of open rebellion on my part, and his last application
of the rod was on my refusal to peruse 'Wilberforce's
Practical Christianity.'" "This dislike to dry, doctrinal
reading and to religious reading of every sort," writes
Livingstone of himself, "continued for many years
afterwards."

It would seem, however, as though, in the composition of David Livingstone's character, the religious
zeal of the father had been mingled with the more
tolerant, kindlier nature of the mother; for Livingstone, from his boyhood to the very end of his days,
was never for one moment a bigot, nor exhibited
the least shade of hypocrisy, sanctimoniousness, or
ostentation of religious feeling. The father, as I have
already stated, was a tea-dealer, but he seems to have
had such a distinctly "missionary" bent that his worldly
business apparently somewhat suffered by his devotion
to the affairs of a Sunday-school and a Missionary
Society, the promotion of prayer-meetings, and the
spread of teetotalism. "He had indeed the very soul
of a missionary," says Dr. Blaikie, who also tells us that,
when travelling through the neighbouring parishes in
his vocation of retail tea-merchant, Neil Livingstone
acted at the same time as *colporteur*, "distributing tracts
and encouraging the reading of useful books." But
whether this devotion to religious teaching interfered
unduly with the profitable pursuit of his business as a
tea-merchant, or whether that trade in itself was in those
days a poor one on which to support and educate a

family of five children, is not to be clearly determined
from the scanty records we have of David Livingstone's
early years ; but it would seem, from all we know, that
the Livingstone family for some time found it difficult to
maintain a comfortable existence, the mother well-nigh
wearing herself out in her struggle to make both ends
meet, and David himself, like both his brothers, having
to begin work at a very early age in order to contribute
to the support of the home.   In fact, he was only ten

FACTORY AT BLANTYRE.

when he was sent to work in the cotton-spinning factory
close by, belonging to Monteith & Company, the same
wherein his grandfather had occupied a position of trust.
Here, working as a "piecer," and afterwards as a cotton-
spinner, Livingstone laboured day after day during the
six days of the working week, from six o'clock in the
morning till eight o'clock at night, with only slight
intervals for breakfast and dinner.

Although, of course, the eulogistic biographies of Livingstone already published are bound to make him out under all conditions a model of good behaviour, it would seem, from the local traditions which I have gathered up at Blantyre, Livingstone was not a hearty worker at the cotton-spinning factory. His passionate and all-absorbing love of reading made him an absent-minded and even careless workman; and although it gives the reader of his reminiscences a glow of sympathy to learn from his own description how he so arranged a book on a portion of a spinning-jenny that he could manage to read during his work by snatching a sentence minute after minute as he passed backwards and forwards, still, no doubt, this devotion to study somewhat tended to abstraction and slowness in his work. At least such was the opinion of some of his old acquaintances at Blantyre, and of others still working in the same factory, one of whom told the writer that "Dr Livingstone was no thocht to be a by-ordinar'[1] laddie; just a sulky, quiet, feckless sort o' boy."

From his earliest years David Livingstone was an ardent and omnivorous reader, and although he received that good general education which, even in those early days, was acquired by the very poorest in Scotland, by attending night-classes supported by the subscriptions of himself and a number of other lads from the factory, he practically taught himself the half of what he knew by his private studies at home, and by the reading which he snatched during his long hours of work at the factory. Out of his first week's earnings, when he was only ten years old, he purchased Ruddiman's "Rudiments of Latin," at which he would work till far into the night.

[1] Extraordinary, out of the way.

In this way he acquired such a knowledge of Latin that he had mastered many of the classical authors while still it his boyhood.

Brought up in different surroundings, and with different influences reacting on him, or rather no influences at all, it seems likely that David Livingstone, with his intense love of nature (which manifested itself in early botanical and geological studies in the fields and on the hills) and his tendency to reason and theorise from his observations, might have become a second Darwin; but it would seem as though the pressure brought to bear on him by his father's teaching and preaching succeeded in giving his mind just a sufficient religious warp to make him a missionary of religion instead of an emissary of science. We can gather, by a careful perusal of his frank statements as regards the evolution of his religious ideas, that he was not naturally disposed to concern himself much with supra-mundane questions; but the natural imitativeness of youth, the desire to feel as those around him felt, or affected to feel, and the real, earnest goodness in the lad, which regretted that it could not find orthodox expression in conformity with the sectarian bigotry of his parents, pastors, and masters: these various causes produced the usual effect of making his thoughts run to some extent in the same groove as that in which the average feeling around him was directed. About his twelfth year he was worried into reflecting " on his state as a sinner." During his early adolescence the native originality of his inquiring mind indisposed him to go through the stereotyped course of religious development; "his convictions were effaced," we are told, "and his (religious) feelings blunted." However, as everybody in those days professing that class of evangelical Christianity had to "experience conversion"—that is to say, at some period of their lives undergo a spasmodic change in their religious feelings which brought before them a clearer sense of their own innate wickedness and unworthiness, and sank them to the depths of spiritual despair in inducing the belief that they were eternally lost, before the almost hysterical revulsion took place in the more definite realisation that through the atonement of Christ they were saved, in spite of their sins—so Livingstone, insensibly affected by the religious routine of his parents and companions, himself imagined, after an intervening period of callousness, that he had attained "grace" and been converted. He speaks but sparingly of this change in his nature—which was really no change at all, but simply a faint, unconscious simulation of the religious hysteria of those around him—partly because the man had such a loathing of humbug and gush that he afterwards avoided as far as possible any parade of devotional feeling, and partly, I think, because he felt conscious that this crisis had not been a very marked one in his life. Some mention of it he had to make in his early writings, because in those sanctimonious times it was expected of him. No real godliness could be seen in a man unless he could accurately precise the time and occasion in which he had experienced conversion. People in those days still believed in Original Sin. In fact, when presenting himself to the Directors of the London Missionary Society for entrance into mission-work, he had to satisfy them as scrupulously as to the details of his conversion as a modern missionary would be required to convince the successors of the same Directors of his practical knowledge of medicine and hygiene. The exploration fever

in his blood, the love of research in natural history,
combined with the religious impress given to his mind,
directed David Livingstone's thoughts towards the career
of a missionary as one calculated to satisfy these longings
for travel and evangelisation. The writings of Gützlaff,
a German missionary,[1] gave point to his aspirations, and
made him resolve to go out as a medical missionary
to China. He accordingly, with the assistance of his
parents and elder brother, proceeded to Glasgow in
his twenty-third year, and entered himself as a student
at the University, where he studied Greek, theology,
chemistry, and medicine. He offered himself to the
London Missionary Society in 1837, being attracted
towards that body from the unsectarian nature of its
Christianity; for Livingstone even in those days held
broad views as to creeds and formulas, and detested what
he called "geographical Christianity" and the sharply-
drawn differences of dogma. By the London Missionary
Society he was somewhat cautiously and hesitatingly
accepted as a probationer. In 1838 he proceeded, at
their invitation, to London, where his sweet, simple disposition and quiet enthusiasm made him many friends.
After passing two examinations, he was so far accepted
by the Society that he was sent to pursue his studies
under the Rev. Richard Cecil at Chipping Ongar, in
Essex, with whom he read Latin, Greek, and Hebrew.
It is not clear who supported him at this time and
defrayed the cost of his education,—whether his parents,
his brother, or the London Missionary Society. At the
end of three months' study with Mr. Cecil, the first
report sent in to the Directors of the Society was unfavourable, on account of Livingstone's utter failure as a

[1] Born in Pomerania, 1803.

preacher, his hesitating manner in conducting family
worship, and his lack of fluency in extempore prayer ;
and the result of this was very nearly being the closure
of Livingstone's missionary career ; but, fortunately, the
Directors decided to give him another chance, and during
the next three months which ensued he became sufficiently conversant with the glib phraseology of common-

DR. ROBERT MOFFAT.
(*From a Photograph by Elliott & Fry.*)

place prayer to scrape through his examination.   Then
he was definitely accepted, and threw himself heart and
soul into his medical studies.   For nearly two years he
worked thus in London, walking the hospitals, while his
ultimate destination as a missionary vacillated between
the West Indies, China, and Africa.   To the West Indies

he objected to go, because, as he very rightly argued, there was no good opening for a medical missionary, inasmuch as the islands were already well provided with qualified doctors. China was closed to him on account of the opium war ; so, sick of this period of indecision, he persuaded the Directors of the London Missionary Society to send him to South Africa. His thoughts were directed towards that Dark Continent, which he afterwards did so much to enlighten, by his future father-in-law, Mr. Moffat, one of the greatest of African missionaries, whom he met in London in 1840, at a time when Exeter Hall had gone mad over African missionaries and Mrs. Jellyby ruled supreme. He returned once more to Glasgow, passed an examination in medicine, and received his diploma as a Licentiate of the Faculty of Physicians and Surgeons, bade good-bye to his parents, returned to London, was ordained a missionary in Albion Chapel on the 20th November 1840, and on the 8th December embarked on board the ship *George* under Captain Donaldson, and proceeded to the Cape, and thence to Algoa Bay.

CHAPTER IV.

On the way out to South Africa the vessel on which Livingstone travelled called at Rio de Janeiro, in Brazil. Here, for the first time, he gazed on the glories of tropical vegetation, and was deeply impressed by this aspect of nature. His senses were also somewhat captivated by the gorgeous ritual of the Roman Church, and in a letter to his friend, the Rev. G. D. Watt, he writes : " The Church Establishment there (at Rio) is beautiful ; they really do the thing in style. If ever I join an establishment, it won't be the poor degenerate ' sisters' at home, but the good mother herself in Brazil." On the voyage out his untiring industry led him to learn to take astronomical observations under the captain's instructions, and this new knowledge rendered him a real geographical explorer.[1]

In those days the voyage to Africa occupied three months instead of the three weeks now spent in travel-

---

[1] Livingstone was perhaps the most exact computer of astronomical observations who has yet appeared among African explorers. With reference to the instruction he had received from Captain Donaldson, he remarks in the above-quoted letter to Mr. Watt : " The captain of our vessel was very obliging to me, and gave me all the information respecting the use of the quadrant in his power, frequently sitting up till twelve at night for the purpose of taking lunar observations with me. The captain is of a most agreeable nature, a well-informed, shrewd Scotchman, but no Christian."

ling by the slowest of the steamers which ply between England and Cape Town, so that it was well on in the spring of 1841 before Livingstone had reached Algoa Bay, which he finally left on the 20th May to start for Kuruman, in Betshuanaland.   In the same interesting letter addressed to his friend, Mr. Watt, from which I have already quoted, he gives such a vivid picture of his first impressions of travel, his longings for exploration, and at the same time such a frank exposition of the character and condition of the missionary work then existing, that I cannot do better than produce considerable portions of it *in extenso :*—

"I was introduced by Dr. Philip to the Colonial Secretary, and the 'cases' were promptly ordered.   I found three of them, but most unfortunately an error in packing has caused the destruction of many of the glass vessels.   I hope, however, to have as many as may make one complete case ; and if so, I may say, from what I have seen of the animals of this country, that it won't be difficult to make a collection of some value to Mr. Owen.[1]   I saw many specimens of agatised wood.   The concentric rings were beautifully distinct, and the pith crystallised regularly, and as clear as a crystal ; but the edges of the crystals were mostly rubbed off by friction amongst other stones.   In a plain about fifty miles from the river I passed an entire tree completely agatised, yet retaining so much of the original appearance that I took it at first for real wood. It was broken into blocks of about a foot and a half in length. I took pieces of it ; but I must not begin to describe all or any of the wonders I have seen.   Any book of travels will supply you with wonders *ad infinitum.*

"The missionaries on this side the river are in a sad state. Every man's hand is against his neighbour.   Whatever may have been the original cause of dispute, the present state of feeling amongst our brethren is disgraceful. —— is not on

---

[1] Now Sir Richard Owen.

speaking terms with the Griqua Town missionaries, and takes
another route when visiting the colony to avoid seeing them.
They, in their turn, *hate* the brethren in the colony, and
amongst the whole there exists a pretty considerable amount
of floating scandal, one against the other ; all uniting on this
side to scandal (*sic*) Dr. ——, and on the other side generally
favourable to the Doctor and unfavourable to those on this side.
The devil is in it, but they cannot see him, or rather won't.   I
am determined to stand aloof from both parties.   I confess I
feel every difficulty on the subject of the Doctor's superin-
tendence now, but you must not imagine I am in the least
changed in my views respecting thorough-going independency.
The burden of Mr. and Mrs. ——'s song to me was always
derogatory to the character of Dr. and Mrs. ——.   This
filled me with prejudice against the latter.   A month's residence in their house, during which time I had sufficient op-
portunities of scrutinising their characters, has completely
dissolved the whole of it.   With respect to his superintend-
ence, he told me he never had considered himself as anything
more than the money agent of the Society.   With spiritual
affairs or modes of operation he had nothing to do, and never
wished to interfere in these matters ; but he had been frequently compelled, by the Society referring disputes to his
decision, to act a part he had no inclination to, for generally
one party was dissatisfied and became his calumniator.   He
may have domineered in some instances, but —— is, I understand, not the man who should cast the first stone.   The
Doctor is now in his dotage, and won't do any more harm ;
but were he in his vigour, I should greatly prefer the des-
potism of *one* to that of many.   The latter —— seems bent
on establishing, and my poor neighbour here seems delighted
with the idea of having a 'presbytery.'   I hope Griffith is a
staunch independent.   You see the part I must act.   The
present system is real liberty-committee-ocracy.   I feel I am
giving you a very partial view of the subject.   It would take
a day's talk to explain the whole subject.   I can't fully explain the Colonial feeling.   It is somewhat like caste in India.
Dr. Philip has been a staunch advocate of the coloured population.   There is a strong feeling amongst the Colonists against

E

him, and they (and, strange to say, most of the Doctor's
enemies) have imbibed it—I mean of the missionaries.   I
won't say all, but all I have seen certainly have.   They divide
into Radicals and Conservatives.   They have not these names,
but it is of that nature.   *You* would be a friend of the natives ;
you would plead their cause against the Boers.   I know you
would, for I know your feelings on that subject, and from this
I conclude you would take sides with the Doctor and his
friends.   I can't help feeling friendly to him when I think of
all he has done in the cause of liberty, and when he tells me
distinctly that he will not interfere at all in my operations,
that he wishes all the missionaries to follow their own plans,
for these are generally the most efficient that they as individuals can employ.   Every one has his own way of doing
things, and each can do more in his own way than he can by
adopting the plans or modes of operation of another. . . .

"I find that the fresh-water lake[1] of which Mokotere told
us is a pond about which there is an anxiety amongst all the
missionaries to do something.   Every one would like to be
the first to see it, for it is quite certain that one does actually
exist.   The distance is two months in bullock-waggon, and
the French missionaries have it in contemplation soon to
take a trip thither.   One of them of rather an enterprising
character was solicited to become a corresponding member of
the Geographical Society, but declined, as he meant to give
all his discoveries to his Missionary Society, and let them
make what use of them they choose.   His brother-in-law
sounded me as to my intentions, but got nothing out.   Mr.
Moffat has got £400 from some gentleman in England for
the purpose of fitting out an expedition to it.   This I heard
incidentally.   R—— blabbed it out in my presence to one of
Mr. M.'s chief friends at the Cape.   I am afraid this will
find its way to the ears of the French missionaries, who will
be sure to lose no time in setting out.   If they give your
humble servant a month so as to acquire the colloquial
language, they may spare themselves the pains of being first
'in at the death.'   I can acquire the language while travelling

---

[1] The first rumours of Lake Ngami.

without this ponderous vehicle, as well as by remaining at Kuruman : perhaps better, for I shall live as they do and mix constantly with them, and I can obtain information respecting the population, &c., at the same time. I wish you were here to give me some lessons in composition. I am a bad hand at that, never having studied it, and my poor friend R—— has such a precious idea of his extensive learning that I have not the heart to ask him. I dare say I would, after all, stoop from my pride were I not fully convinced by all I have seen of him that he knows very little about that or anything else. He and I are not on good terms because I speak out and pay no more regard to his opinions on the ground of his nine years' education (his wife's boast) than if he were my Hottentot boy and could not read. I could have made something by Dr. H——, but this man is mule-headed beyond calculation. His wife is sensible, but his wife, though married, will remain an old maid to the end of the chapter. As for 'olive plants round the table,' *cheu fugaces post*, &c. ! They are both adjuncts of or to Mr. M. Nothing is right but what he has said. Mrs. Sewell tells me in a letter I received at the same time with yours that she believes you are heartily sorry you had not a helpmate with you. I have told her I am sure you were not. I am conscious myself that I am better without ; and with respect to scandal arising amongst the natives, no fewer than five married missionaries have been charged with incontinency. The charge, however, in each case has been, I believe, quite groundless. I can be in no worse plight than they, should anything of that sort arise. . . . From these and other considerations which I need not mention, I conclude that marriage, like vaccination in small-pox, is not a specific preventive of scandal in Africa. (By the way, tell me if the matter which is called 'grease' in horses'-heels is used in India in the same manner that the *vaccine virus* is here and in Britain.) All the missionaries' wives I have seen denounce my single-blessedness in no measured terms. Some even insinuated that the reason why I am thus is, that I have been unable to get a spouse, but I put down that very speedily by assuming that it is a great deal easier for a missionary to get married

in England than to come out single, as in the latter case a
vigorous resistance must be made, but in the former only
yield up the affair into the hands of any friend and it is
managed for you in a twinkling; only hold the neck down
like one of our oxen and the yoke is fixed, and no mistake.

AN OLD BUSHMAN.

Of course I have abundance of instances at my finger-ends,
and don't fail to point to all the silly married people I can
remember as proof of how easy it is to get noosed. This is a
digression, but perhaps it will come in seasonably if Mr.

Kennedy's spouse is hard upon you. You can, however, defend yourself well enough. What do you say to my going up to Abyssinia? This is talked of by many of the missionaries as a desirable object, and some propose doing it. Would it not promote our cause by making known to the Churches the awfully degraded state of an immense population? Looking at the map published by the Society for the Diffusion of Useful Knowledge, you see far beyond us a 'very populous country,' &c. I think one may be quite safe if alone and without anything to excite the cupidity of the natives. I should cost the Society nothing during these years I should be away. It might be six or seven years before I should return, but if languages are dialects of the Bechuana, I could soon make known a little of the blessed plan of mercy to the different tribes on the way ; and if I should never return, perhaps my life will be as profitably spent as a forerunner as in any other way. I thank God I have no desire to accumulate money. Whatever way my life can be best spent to promote the glory of our gracious God, I feel desirous to do it."

CHAPTER V.

MARRIES, TEACHES, AND IS TROUBLED.

THE headquarters of the London Missionary Society in the interior of South Africa had been established in those days at Kuruman,[1] in about 27° 20′ S. lat. and 23° 20′ E. long., on the upper part of the Kuruman affluent of the Molopo River, and then in the debatable land between the country of the Betshuana and the Grikwa.[2] This district between the Orange River and the Molopo, which is now called British Betshuanaland, is a great plateau with an average altitude of about 4500 feet above the sea. Except in one or two favoured spots where there is running water, or where man has interfered with the natural conditions by artificial irrigation, the country presents a singularly dreary aspect of partial or complete desert. Even at the present day round Kimberley, beyond the web of gardens and parks which surround that flourishing city of corrugated iron,

---

[1] Now a flourishing township in British Betshuanaland.

[2] Grikwa (a Hottentot word : in the *singular*, Grip ; *plural*, Grikwa) is the name given to the considerable population of half-castes which sprang up on the northern and north-eastern border-lands of Cape Colony by the intercourse between the Dutch and the Hottentots. These hybrids held aloof from their Hottentot mothers' people, and were cast out by their white fathers, so they constituted in time a tribe of their own. I believe they are dying out, like their Hottentot relations, before the vigorous competition of the white man and the Bantu negro.

70

you see a dreary waste, sparsely dotted with low thorny acacias, whose scanty foliage scarcely veils their gaunt skeletons of white boughs and long thorns.   But at Kuruman, as elsewhere in Africa, the advent of the missionaries effected an immediate change for the better :—

"Kuruman has been made all that it is by the almost slave-drudgery of its missionaries.   They have had to dig its canals themselves, and from the nature of the country this was no small task.   All round is a dreary desert for a great part of the year ; enough, indeed, from its nakedness and sand to give its people most of that ophthalmia with which they are so often afflicted.   There is not a tree near the station which has not been planted by the missionaries.   Some stunted scraggy bushes, many of them armed with thorns villainously sharp and strong, are the chief objects which present themselves to the eye."

Without waiting at Kuruman longer than was necessary to recruit his oxen, which were pretty well tried by the long journey from Algoa Bay (Port Elizabeth), Livingstone made a rapid journey of about 300 miles northwards into Betshuanaland to visit an important chief called Setshele, who was then residing at Shokwane. Then, after returning to Kuruman from this reconnaissance, he once more started for Betshuanaland, intending to make a settlement at what is now called Molepolole, a place or district which was at that time called Kolobeñ or Litubaruba, where he spent six months isolated from all European society in order to gain an insight into the habits, ways of thought, laws, and language of that section of the Betshuana race called the Ba-kwena.[1]   From the Molepolole he extended his

[1] Ba-kwena (formerly and incorrectly spelt Bakwains) means literally the "Crocodile People."   *Kwena*, the word for crocodile in

journey even farther north till, without knowing it, he
came to within a short distance of Lake Ngami. Returning, however, to Kuruman in order to bring up his
luggage to the proposed settlement, he was followed by
the news that his friends the Ba-kwena had been
driven from their town by the Ba-roloñ, another section
of the Betshuana. He, therefore, decided to select
another locality for the establishment of his station, and
finally fixed on Mabotsa,[1] which was a little nearer to
Kuruman than Molepolole, and now lies within the
boundaries of the Transvaal Republic. Here it was
that the adventure with the lion befell him, which has
been so often quoted in works of natural history and
lives of Livingstone that I will only make this brief
allusion to it here. The Betshuana country, like most
other parts of South Africa in those days, was infested
by lions, though this beast is now nearly extinct in
British South Africa.[2] Livingstone had joined the
people of Mabotsa in a lion-hunt, and had wounded a
lion, which sprang at him and dragged him to the
ground, where it crunched the bone and bit the flesh
of his left shoulder. The effect of this mishap was
the partial disablement of his left arm for the rest of
his life.

It is rather amusing to notice how, in his private

Betshuana, is a very widespread Bantu root. The original form was
ñgwena, which becomes ñwena, ñwina, kwena, gwona, ñgone, ñwone,
&c., and this root extends in its range from the Cameroons to Zululand, though it is not present in every tongue.

[1] This word means "marriage feast."

[2] Formerly the lion ranged over all South Africa down to the sea-
coast. Now it is quite extinct everywhere within the boundaries of
Cape Colony, Natal, the Orange Free State, and the south-east and
west of the Transvaal. It has also disappeared from Southern Betshuanaland.

correspondence, Livingstone's views on marriage gradually changed during his first few years in the African
wilds. At first he was inclined to deprecate marriage
on the part of missionaries, and writing to his friend
Watt in 1843 he says: "I suppose from the tenor of
your last letter—it being in a kind of apologetic-for-
marriage strain—you are now nearly about to multiply,
increase, and replenish the earth. Hoot! man, there
are plenty at that work without you. But I hope you
will be happy, however it is. . . . Here, although I was
inclined at first to be foolish, there is nobody worth
taking off one's hat to. Daughters of missionaries have
miserably contracted minds. Colonial ladies are worse
and worse. There is no outlet for me when I think of
getting married than that of sending home an advertise-
ment for the *Evangelical Magazine*, and if I get old it
must be for some decent widow. In the meantime I am
too busy to think of anything of the kind."

Nevertheless, soon after writing this letter Livingstone
made the acquaintance of Miss Mary Moffat, at Kuruman (the daughter of the celebrated Dr. Moffat, the
greatest of South African missionaries), and was married
to her towards the end of 1844. His choice seems to
have been a thoroughly suitable one, for Mrs. Livingstone was just what a hard-working pioneer missionary's
wife should be : able to do, and to teach others to do, all
the work of a general servant; a good cook, a good
seamstress, a good housewife, and yet possessing the
instincts and tastes of a cultured woman. In a private
letter written soon after his marriage, Livingstone, in his
quaint, prosaic manner, describes his wife as being " not
romantic," but " a matter-of-fact lady, a little, thick,
black-haired girl, sturdy and all I want." In other and

succeeding letters he speaks with enthusiasm of the comforts and refinements of his home, which he owes to his wife's hard work and housewifely skill. The young couple settled down at Mabotsa, where Livingstone built with his own hands a large, strong house. He had a companion at his station, a Mr. Edwards, who was a carpenter and builder by profession; but between him and Livingstone there seems to have been considerable incompatibility of temper. Edwards rendered Livingstone practically no assistance in the building of his house, although that may be said to have come within his own special province. He showed ridiculous jealousy of Livingstone as an explorer, threatened to bring a series of charges before the committee at Kuruman; and though he afterwards withdrew these charges and wrote apologetically to Livingstone, he made himself so very disagreeable that, sooner than continue these acrimonious disputes, Livingstone and his wife quitted the station they had organised at such personal trouble and expense, and moved to a place called Tshonuane, about forty miles to the north, and the headquarters, at that time, of the well-known Setshele, the Betshuana chief. From Tshonuane he made a long journey eastwards to the Kashane Mountains or "Magaliesberg," through the heart of what is now known as the Transvaal State. While at Tshonuane his eldest son Robert[1] was born. At Tshonuane, however, they found that the

[1] Robert Livingstone, when a youth, rather impulsively went off to America and joined the Federal army. He was wounded in battle, and died in a hospital in North Carolina in 1865. He will be best remembered by having given his mother her African name. In Betshuanaland a mother is always called after the name of her first-born. Thus, Mrs. Livingstone's first-born being named Robert, she was always henceforth known to the natives as "Ma' Robert," *i.e.*, "Mother of Robert."

increasing drought which was afflicting the country rendered agriculture almost impossible. The Ba-kwena people under Setshele were already suffering grievously from lack of rain, and Livingstone relates with humour, and with a kindly tolerance rare in those days amongst the usually bigoted missionaries, the efforts of the native rain-doctors to break the spell of continuous drought, and the arguments by which they sought to adduce the efficacy of their "rain-medicines." All things considered, the heathen was not much more unreasonable in his theory of provoking supernatural interference with the weather than the Christian disputant. The latter says, "So you really believe that you can command the clouds? I think that can be done by God alone." And the rain-doctor replies, "We both believe the very same thing. It is God that makes the rain; but I pray to Him by means of these medicines, and, the rain coming, of course it is mine. It was I who made it for the Ba-kwena during many years, when they were at Shokwane; through my wisdom, too, their women became fat and shining. Ask them; they will tell you the same." To which Dr. Livingstone answers, "But we are distinctly told in the parting words of our Saviour that we can pray to God acceptably in His name alone, and not by means of medicines." "Truly!" replies the rain-maker; "but God told us differently. He made black men first, and did not love us, as He did the white men. He made you beautiful, and gave you clothing, and guns, and gun-powder, and horses, and waggons, and many other things about which we know nothing. But toward us He had no heart. He gave us nothing except the assegai, and cattle, and rain-making; and He did not give us hearts like yours. We never love each other.

Other tribes place medicines about our country to prevent
the rain, so that we may be dispersed by hunger, and
go to them and augment their power. We must dissolve
their charms by our medicines. God has given us the
knowledge of certain medicines by which we can make
rain. We don't despise those things which you possess,
though we are ignorant of them ; we don't understand
your book, yet we don't despise it. *You* ought not to
despise our little knowledge, though you are ignorant
of it."

Setshele's people at this time had recourse to driving
the wild animals of the district into the *hopo* trap for
the purpose of obtaining meat, as their cattle were dying
fast from the drought. This *hopo* consisted of two
hedges in the form of the letter V, which were very high
and thick near the angle. They did not, however,
actually join at this point, but were extended parallel in
a narrow lane, at the extremity of which a pit was
formed six or seven feet deep and about twelve or fifteen
in breadth and length. Trunks of trees were laid across
the margins of the excavation, and more especially over
the brink nearest to the end of the lane where the
animals were expected to leap in. Tree-trunks formed
an overlapping border, and rendered escape impossible.
The fragile surface was carefully strewn with short
green rushes and grass and twigs, so as to completely
conceal the pitfall. As the hedges were about a mile
long, and nearly that distance apart at their extremities,
a tribe making a circle three or four miles round the
country adjacent to the opening, and gradually closing
up, were almost sure to encircle a large body of game.
Driving the animals up with shouts to the narrow part
of the *hopo*, the men who were secreted there would

throw their assegais into the affrighted herds, while the poor beasts rushed on and into the opening presented at the converging hedges, and, unable to stop their impetus, would smash through the frail covering of boughs and grass and collapse into the pit, until that excavation was full to the brim with a fighting, struggling, suffocating mass of antelopes, buffaloes, and zebras. Then the natives would close in and spear the animals at their leisure. In this way between sixty and seventy head of large game were often killed at the different *hopos* in a single week.[1]

Finding it impossible to carry on any agriculture at Tshonuane from the want of water that prevailed (for the rain-maker's medicines were futile in their effect), Livingstone moved westward another forty miles to the River Kolobeñ,[2] practically to the same district wherein he had wished to settle years before at the time of his experimental incursion in the Ba-kwena country. He not only moved himself and his wife and family to the Kolobeñ, and commenced building his third experimental mission station there, but he also induced Setshele and all his people to come with him. He taught them here how to irrigate their gardens by runnels from the never-failing river, and a prosperous agricultural colony soon sprang up.

Setshele, the chief of the Ba-kwena, was a good fellow, and an excellent type of the frank, straightforward,

---

[1] This method of killing game is by no means peculiar to South Africa, though it is not met with elsewhere in quite such thorough-going, extensive fashion. Converging hedges and pitfalls are in use among the tribes of the Batanga country south of the Cameroons for the capture of elephants. *Vide*, for an illustration of this, my "History of a Slave."

[2] *Kolobeñ* means "pig-stye," from *kolobe*, "pig," in Setshuana.

manly savage. His great-grandfather, Motshoasele, had
been a great traveller, and was the first that had brought
to the Ba-kwena news of the existence of white men.
Setshele's father, also called Motshoasele, was murdered
by his own people for taking to himself the wives of
his rich under-chiefs. The children being spared, their

A MA-KOLOLO.

friends invited Sebituane, the chief of the Ma-kololo,
who was then in those parts, to reinstate them in the
chieftainship, and in this way Setshele was ultimately
installed as chief over the Ba-kwena. In consequence
of this, he ever afterwards felt under a sense of obliga-
tion to Sebituane, his Ma-kololo ally. This occurred a

few years before Livingstone entered the country and made his acquaintance. An immediate friendship sprang up between the kindly, patient missionary and the impulsive chief full of zeal for new knowledge. Setshele was so anxious to learn to read, and applied himself with such assiduity to this task, that the change from his former life of a hunter to the sedentary existence of a student made him quite corpulent. He learned the alphabet in one day, and acquired rapidly a knowledge of arithmetic from a few lessons given him by Mr. Oswell, the celebrated traveller and hunter, who at various periods stayed with Livingstone at his station. Setshele's religious convictions were far more reasonably and intelligently acquired, and more clearly connected with his mode of life, than are those of most aboriginal heathen. Once being convinced himself as to the merits of Christianity as a religion, he was immediately anxious his people should follow him into the fold; so he proposed to Livingstone that they should be coerced into Christianity by the use of rhinoceros-hide whips. He was surprised when the missionary expressed disapproval of this mode of forcible conversion, and it became a matter of deep regret to him that persuasion, entreaty, and example failed to induce the bulk of his people to follow him into an acceptance of the new religion. "In former times," he said to Livingstone, "when a chief was fond of hunting, all his people got dogs and became fond of hunting too. If he loved dancing or music, all showed a preference for these amusements. If the chief drank beer, his people all rejoiced in strong drink. But in this case it is different. I love the Word of God, and not one of my people will join me." Setshele found out that, in order to be a consistent Christian according to the method of Christianity as taught by missionaries in the middle of the nineteenth century, a man must be the husband of one wife only;[1] and although he was far from being an uxorious man, his pity for the superfluous wives, who would be dishonoured in local opinion, through no fault of their own, by being dismissed, prevented him from immediately presenting himself for baptism. Nor did Livingstone hurry him towards this outward profession of conversion, because in his wise tolerance he sympathised with Setshele's position, and the unmerited wrong it would inflict on his wives. However, at last an arrangement was come to by which the supernumerary spouses were handsomely pensioned off and sent back to their families, the principal wife alone being retained. " She," says Livingstone, " was about the most unlikely subject in the tribe ever to become anything else than an out-and-out greasy disciple of the old school. Again and again have I seen Setshele send her out of church to put her gown on, and away she would go with her lip shot out, the very picture of unutterable disgust at his new-fangled notions." On the day when Setshele and his children were baptized, great numbers of Bakwena came to see the ceremony. During the service several of the old men were actually in tears, and gave as the cause of their weeping their belief that their father, Setshele, was henceforth " left to himself ; " that he had become, as it were, one set apart from the rest of the tribe and dissociated from them in the tenor of his life and the direction of his thoughts. There sprang up soon afterwards a considerable reaction against Chris-

[1] This was evidently the main reason of his sensual-minded subjects holding back from the white man's faith.

tianity on the part of the Ba-kwena, which was instigated by the friends of the divorced wives.

In this case there is little doubt that, had the missionary permitted, or, as it were, condoned the existence of polygamy for a while, the whole tribe of the Ba-kwena would have followed their chief's example and become Christians. You cannot hope so suddenly to change the habits and customs of a people. Suppress an institution in one form and it springs up in another. Setshele, it is possible, may have remained faithful to the one wife, but I think it not unlikely on his part that there were occasional lapses into incontinence. I know of an old chief in the Oil Rivers who became a Christian many years ago at the expense of dismissing all his legitimate wives but one. He was, and is, a really good man according to his lights, and he took back many of the discarded spouses as "concubines;" a practice which was not condemned by the local missionaries because they found a sanction for it in the lives of the Old Testament worthies.

Setshele is described by Livingstone as tall, rather corpulent, and typically negro in feature, with fine, large eyes, but a very dark skin. On account of his swarthiness he was called by his people "Black Setshele." He soon acquired great skill in reading, and was a fluent and effective orator. He taught his people zealously, and introduced something like good government among them, especially after a visit he paid to Cape Colony. Seeing convicts at work in the British possessions, he conceived the idea of turning his own criminals to useful account, and he introduced successfully into Betshuanaland the system of forced labour as a punishment in place of more barbarous penalties. Despite his original

F

belief at the time when Livingstone first visited him, that the Kalahari Desert was impassable on account of the drought, his faith in his missionary friend became so firm, that, when Livingstone made his first journey to the Zambezi, Setshele and large numbers of his people accompanied him thither. Setshele's increasing prosperity, and, above all, his friendship for the English, soon attracted the greed and aroused the enmity of the Transvaal Boers, to whose actions at this period in Betshuanaland I shall refer later on ; but, as far as Setshele was concerned, it may be well to give some idea of how this man was punished by the Dutch brigands for his encouragement of English missionaries and sportsmen.

They first of all demanded that he should place his territory under their rule, and that he should refuse a passage northwards through his country to the English and the Grikwa.[1]   Then, when he refused to comply with these orders, he was suddenly and unprovokedly attacked by four hundred Boers, who were despatched on this errand by the late Mr. Pretorius. The Dutchmen fired on the scarcely resisting people, of whom they killed sixty in their first encounter. They burnt the town down, plundered Livingstone's house, carried off all his stores, and those belonging to Gordon Cumming and other English hunters which had been safely deposited hitherto in the natives' keeping, and enslaved a number of men, women, and children, among whom where two of Setshele's own. Fortunately, the Boers did not get off quite scot-free, for the Bakwena collected themselves after their first dispersal, and managed to kill twenty-eight of the marauding

---

[1] Half-castes between the Boers and the Hottentots.

farmers. The only excuse offered by the Boer newspapers for this unprovoked attack on the Ba-kwena
was, that "Setshele was getting too saucy." As Livingstone says, his real faults in their eyes were "his
independence and love of the English."

Setshele was so hurt in his sense of justice at this
Boer raid, which, he felt, had been completely unprovoked, that he resolved to appeal to the Queen of
England for justice. He, therefore, scraped together
all the means at his command, and managed to get as
far on his way as Cape Town; but the coldness and
discouragement which he met with from the Colonial
authorities (who were at that time entirely indifferent
to what occurred in Betshuanaland, and by no means
sensitive to the rights of the natives), and the expenditure of his funds, prevented him from crossing the sea
to lay his griefs before the throne of the "Great White
Mother." He, therefore, wisely returned to his kingdom
and set to work to repair his losses. While he had been
absent a party of his young men had managed to seize
some of the Boer waggons and four Boers. This unexpected "turning of the worm" so completely took the
Boers aback that they sent to make proposals of peace,
and finally agreed to return Setshele's two sons, who
had been made the domestic slaves of a certain Scholz.
When one of these was returned it was noticed that his
body was a mass of burns.

With quiet, peaceful organisation, Setshele's power
greatly increased, and he reigned as king over his
district of Southern Betshuanaland until, long years
afterwards, his rule became merged into that of the
British Government. Setshele is living still, though a
very old man.

CHAPTER VI.

THE BOERS, "GOD'S CHOSEN PEOPLE."

REFERENCE having already been made to the interference of the Boers with the affairs of Betshuanaland, it may be well, before proceeding further with the account of how they came into conflict with Livingstone and with his *protégés*, to explain how they came to be in this country at all.

The first British occupation of Cape Colony (which was then limited to a small portion of the western half of Southern Africa, bounded on the east by the Great Fish River, and on the north by the Zeekoe [1] River) caused a change in the policy hitherto pursued by the whites towards the native races, besides breaking up a number of exclusive trading privileges and monopolies attached to the old rule of the Dutch East India Company. These changes, and the national spirit of the Dutch settlers, who naturally viewed with disfavour the British occupation of a Dutch colony, combined from the first to make the Boers averse to British rule, and disposed them to migrate farther and farther towards the north and east in order to escape from its unwelcome philanthropy. This feeling was intensified by the measures taken for the mitigation or suppression of slavery, which strongly incensed the patriarchal Boers,

---

[1] *Zeekoe* = sea-cow = hippopotamus.

who, during the " 'thirties" trekked away from Cape Colony to the number of nearly 10,000, as far as can be computed. They directed their exodus towards what are now the states of Natal, Orange River, and Transvaal. Their entry into Natal provoked a war between them and the treacherous and savage Zulus, which ended in a final victory for the Dutch. The Boer emigrants would probably have brought the whole of Natal under their domination in time, had it not been for the intervention of the British Government, who, after some vicissitudes, succeeded in inducing the Dutch to submit to British rule, and Natal was soon afterwards proclaimed to be a British colony. Others of the Boers, however, had occupied the Transvaal and Orange River territories, where they were practically allowed a free hand by the British Government at the Cape; in fact, so free a hand that, according to Livingstone, they were told by Sir George Cathcart, the Governor of Cape Colony, "that they might do as they pleased with the missionaries." The independence of the Boers across the Orange River and the Vaal having been recognised, a treaty was entered into with them by which the free passage of Englishmen to the interior across the Boer territories was conceded, and slavery disallowed in the Boer states.

Nevertheless it was by no means the intention of the Boers, under Pretorius, Potgeiter, and Kruger, to permit, if they could prevent it, any further advance of British influence towards the interior. By creating a continuous band of Boer rule from the Transvaal to Damaraland they hoped to effectually obstruct the extension northwards of British domination and British ideas, and beyond this boundary-line across South Africa they intended to reconstitute the goodly patriarchal life which they had hitherto enjoyed, and which is (alas! for it is so pleasant) quite in dissonance with nineteenth-century civilisation. Here they could continue to farm in their lazy, easy-going way, and live in rude comfort on the labour of the enslaved Kaffirs, Betshuana, and Bushmen. The Boer rule over the territory between the Limpopo and the Vaal had been recognised in a loose sort of way by the British Government; and nothing in the terms of this recognition debarred the Boers from further extending their rule westwards over Betshuanaland: indeed, I believe that, had it not been for the reckless, indiscreet way in which the Dutch farmers endeavoured at various times to assert their authority over the natives, Betshuanaland would have become a Boer state and a strong barrier in the way of a British movement towards the Zambezi.[1]

In their first invasion of the Transvaal, the Boers actually did good, by routing and dispersing the ravaging hordes of Mosilikatse, the father of Lobengula and the chief of the Matabele or Amandebele Zulus; and for a while the Betshuana country had cause to thank the Dutch for the check given to this Zulu conqueror; but they afterwards had occasion to complain that "Mosilikatse was cruel to his enemies and kind to those he conquered, but the Boers destroyed their enemies and made slaves of their friends." Those Betshuana tribes who were found by the Boers in what is now called

---

[1] So resolved were the Boers to prevent English access to Betshuanaland and the regions beyond, and to hinder the country from becoming known, that, besides waylaying, robbing, and expelling such English travellers and traders as found their way thither, they further seized one Maccabe, who had dared to write a letter to the Cape papers on the routes to Lake Ngami, fined him $500 for publishing this information, and kept him in prison until the fine was paid.

the Transvaal Territory were forced to perform all the labour of the fields, such as manuring the land, weeding, reaping, building, making drains and canals, and at the same time to support themselves at their own expense. Livingstone himself was an eye-witness of Boers coming to a village and, according to their usual custom, demanding twenty or thirty women to weed their gardens; and had seen these women proceed to the scene of unrequited toil carrying their own food on their heads, their children on their backs, and instruments of labour on their shoulders. When Livingstone taxed them with the meanness of thus employing unpaid labour, the Boers lauded their own humanity and justice in laying down such an equitable regulation. "We make the people work for us," they said, "in consideration of allowing them to live in our country." This species of *corvée* only being sufficient to meet the field-labour problem, they were obliged to have recourse to organised slave-raids for obtaining domestic servants. Knowing well the intractability of adult negroes, the Boers preferred as a rule to seize little children, whom they captured as young as possible, so that they might forget their parents and their native language. "It is difficult," writes Livingstone, "for a person in a civilised country to conceive that any body of men possessing the common attributes of humanity (and these Boers are by no means destitute of the better feelings of our nature) should with one accord set out, after loading their own wives and children with caresses, and proceed to shoot down in cold blood men and women, of a different colour, it is true, but possessed with domestic feelings and affections equal to their own. . . . It was long before I could quite give credit to the tales of bloodshed told by native witnesses, and had I

received no other testimony but theirs, I should probably
have remained sceptical to this day as to the truth of
the accounts; but when I found the Boers themselves,
some bewailing and denouncing, others glorying in the
bloody scenes in which they had been themselves the
actors, I was compelled to admit the validity of the
testimony, and try to account for the cruel anomaly.
They are all traditionally religious, tracing their descent
from some of the best men (Huguenots and Dutch) the
world ever saw.   Hence they claim to themselves the
title of 'Christians,' and all the coloured race are
'black property' or 'creatures.'   They being the
chosen people of God, the heathen are given to them
for an inheritance, and they are the rod of Divine
vengeance on the heathen, as were the Jews of old."

One of the cruellest, most unprovoked raids of the
Boers ordered by Pretorius was publicly justified in a
general sense by the instructions given to the Jewish
warrior in Deuteronomy xx. 10–14 : " When thou comest
nigh unto a city to fight against it, then proclaim peace
unto it.   And it shall be, if it make thee answer of
peace, and open unto thee, then it shall be, that all the
people that is found therein shall be tributaries unto
thee, and they shall serve thee.   And if it will make no
peace with thee, but will make war against thee, then
thou shalt besiege it : and when the Lord thy God hath
delivered it into thine hands, thou shalt smite every
male thereof with the edge of the sword.   But the women,
and the little ones, and the cattle, and all that is in the
city, even all the spoil thereof, shalt thou take unto
thyself ; and thou shalt eat the spoil of thine enemies,
which the Lord thy God hath given thee."   So easily,
in fact, did the Boers succeed in convincing themselves

that in slave-raiding and cattle-lifting they were obeying
the behest of Almighty God, that when Pretorius, the
arch-robber, died, it was said of him in his obituary
notice, "Blessed are the dead who die in the Lord."

After relating a number of atrocities committed by
the Boers in Betshuanaland, Livingstone supposes that
his readers will ask him how it is that, in view of this
treatment, the natives do not rise and annihilate the
Boers, whom they far exceed in numbers. He replies
to this imaginary question by pointing out that the
people attacked are Betshuana, not Kaffirs, and that the
former people, even if they possessed firearms, which
were then very rare, were singularly averse to attacking
white men, with whom they never engaged in war, unless
for the sheer defence of their lives. He goes on to say :
"We have a very different tale to tell of the Kaffirs,
and the difference has always been so evident to these
border Boers, that, ever since those ' magnificent savages '
obtained possession of firearms, not one Boer has ever
attempted to settle in Kaffirland, or even to face them
as an enemy in the field. The Boers have generally
manifested a marked antipathy to anything but ' long-
shot' warfare, and sidling away in their emigrations
towards the more effeminate Betshuauas, have left their
quarrels with the Kaffirs to be settled by the English,
and their wars to be paid for by English gold."

The Boers had already enslaved most of the eastern
tribes of Betshuanaland when they turned their attention to the Ba-kwena, who had removed to Koloben,
under their chief, Setshele, at Livingstone's advice. The
revived prosperity of this little tribe excited their greed
and apprehension, and they came to look upon Livingstone's presence there as a menace to themselves, inas-

much as they believed him to be supplying the Betshuana with guns and ammunition and instruction in warfare. An iron pot which he had given to Setshele was transformed by rumour into a cannon. As a matter of fact, at the time of Livingstone's residence at Koloben, the Ba-kwena had obtained five guns which they bought from English traders, from whom it is possible they also procured a little powder.[1]   However that may be, the Boers repeatedly declared that Livingstone and all other British missionaries must leave that part of the country, because they were making the natives "too saucy." At length, taking advantage of Livingstone's absence in Cape Town in 1852, they made, without warning and un-provoked, the raid on Koloben which has been already alluded to in connection with Setshele.   On this occasion they plundered Livingstone's house of everything it contained, they smashed his stock of medicines, sold all his furniture and clothing at public auction, and not caring for the trouble of transporting his books, they tore out handfuls of the leaves and scattered what had once been a good library all over the place.   They also seized and carried off all the stores and eighty head of cattle deposited there by English travellers and sports-

---

[1] The Colonial authorities of this period (1850 and subsequent years), oddly enough, placed no restrictions on the sale of arms and ammunition to the Boers and the Kaffirs, both of whom were then almost avowedly our enemies, but stringently forbade all trade in guns and powder with the Betshuana and Grikwa, then and always the friends of the British.   So ready, in fact, were the Colonial authorities of Cape Town to believe the Boer allegations as to Livingstone supplying his people with the means to defend themselves, that he was not permitted by the Magistrates of Cape Town to take with him on his great journey to the Zambezi more than 10 lbs. of gunpowder, lest by design or chance it should fall into the hands of the Betshuana, who at that time were actually holding open for the British the route to the Zambezi.

men. No reparation for these robberies was ever obtained.

However, the Boers did not succeed in permanently conquering West Betshuanaland; for the natives, under Setshele, plucked up spirit and made a resistance sufficiently serious to prevent the Boers from incorporating their territory with the Transvaal State. The struggle languished during nearly three decades, but revived again after the Transvaal surrender of 1881, when the Boers, flushed with their easy victory over the English, made a determined attempt to annex Betshuanaland. Under the *contre coup* of our abnegatory policy in the Transvaal, this was more than the now better-instructed British public could stand, and public opinion insisted that Betshuanaland should be placed under British control and protection. This step was brought about from first to last solely by the insistence of the missionaries, to whom alone we owe that condition of affairs which prevented our giving up the route to the Zambezi to those recalcitrant white men who have ever been so hostile to the spread of British civilisation. "The Boers resolved to shut up the interior," writes Livingstone, "and I determined to open the country; we shall see who have been the most successful in resolution, they or I."

CHAPTER VII.

MISSION-WORK; ITS FAILURES AND SUCCESSES.

LIVINGSTONE's thoughts while at Kolobeñ were continually directed towards the unknown interior. Underlying the many excellent reasons he gives himself and then the public to justify his adoption of the life of a travelling pioneer of Christianity rather than that of a settled teacher with a fixed abode and a limited influence, we can see that he possessed (at first unconsciously) the real fever of geographical discovery which forces so many of our countrymen to explore strange countries under the guise of missionaries, naturalists, sportsmen, soldiers, and traders. But he gives several valid reasons why he should become a missionary-explorer. He reckons the whole population of Southern Betshuanaland at no more (then) than 12,000; and he justly asks if these 12,000 scattered people should occupy the whole attention of the London Missionary Society. He points out, moreover, that it would be highly desirable that the missions should attempt to reach those populous tribes of the unknown interior beyond the Kalahari Desert while they remained in their virgin savagery, unprejudiced against white men by the lawless deeds of the South African colonists and the Boers, and innocent as yet of the brutalisation caused by the introduction of European vices, diseases, and intenser forms of alcohol. That part of Betshuanaland in which the Mission had its chief establishment appeared to be afflicted by increasing desiccation. Everywhere the springs and rivers were drying up or diminishing in volume. "Would it not be better," argued Livingstone, "that we should endeavour to find a land with an abundance of water, where the people settled round our missions could devote themselves with some success to agriculture?"

Livingstone's views on missionaries and mission-work were at all times thoroughly sound, and free from anything like hypocrisy, or the deliberate over-colouring and falsification of reports which is so striking a blemish in the publications of most Christian missionary societies even at the present day. The opinions which he held, and which he set forth clearly in his first book, and in his letters to his friend, Mr. Watt, may be summed up by the phrase, "You can't expect wolves to be turned into sheep-dogs in one generation." Livingstone saw plainly that it takes several generations to implant real, sound civilisation and Christianity in the negro race. He admitted that many of the native Christians around him were but weak-kneed brethren in their effective observance of religious principles. They would lie, steal, drink, and fornicate in spite of their conversion. He saw the hollowness of their glib professions of faith, of their lusty psalm-and-hymn-singing; but he distinguishes these cardinal facts : that the worst of negro Christians is more amenable to civilisation than the best of heathens, and that even among these faulty disciples of a new faith there are here and there "shining lights"—real, honest, faithful, sober, chaste Christians, as earnest in their religion, and as desirous of acting up to its precepts, as any white Christian in our own country.

He prophesies, moreover, that the next generation will be better than the first, and that though the seed scattered by the missionaries is often generations in germinating, yet, after long delay and in unexpected places, it will produce a sudden harvest. And his conjecture has proved a true one, for Christianity is almost universally professed by the natives of Betshuanaland at the present day, and in their mode of life they show the marked improvement which the practice of this religion almost always brings about. The Christianity of the Betshuana may be of a lower and more concrete kind than the faith held by the majority of English people. For instance, the observance of the Sabbath has become elevated into a disagreeable dogma, which surpasses in importance any other detail of religion.[1] But this is counterbalanced by the more organised industry which is displayed on the six working-days of the week, and by the contrast which the harmless, decent excesses in singing, praying, and preaching of their emotional Christianity offer to the beastly, degrading orgies of drunkenness and debauchery which formerly accompanied such feeble worship of ghosts and demons, such superstitious "rain-making" and "witch-finding," as they practised in their old heathen days. When Livingstone first came among them, the Betshuana endeavoured to make rain by administering an infusion of poisonous roots to a sheep, which in a few minutes caused it to expire, while parts of the same roots were burnt and their smoke ascended to the sky as the sheep gasped in its death-agony. Now they put up prayers

---

[1] The Sabbath as an institution has met with peculiar favour among the negroes as a special sanctification of inactivity. They are also a naturally devotional race, and enjoy nothing more than meeting together to perform noisy religious rites.

for rain, just like the Archbishop of Canterbury. So little of a humbug was Livingstone, however, that in dissuading the poor people in time of drought from "making rain" after their old fashion, he did not teach them to rely solely on beseeching by their prayers a Providence too often deaf to man's piteous entreaty, but taught them to act on the sound principle that "the gods help those who help themselves." As I have before related, he showed the Betshuana how, in the absence of rain, they might keep their crops and cattle alive by a system of irrigation.

Livingstone strongly advocated that principle of making black Christianity self-supporting by the raising up of a native pastorate which is nowadays much favoured by the Universities' Mission and the Church Missionary Society. While he considered that for some time to come the supreme directorate of the black churches should be placed in the hands of Europeans, he argued that white teachers, being so much more ex-- pensive to maintain than black men, should not be lavished in numbers on small areas, but should be scattered far and wide to form the centres of great *radii* of evangelising influences, and that native Christians should be trained up to do all the lesser work of teaching and preaching among the people of their own colour. In spite of much discouragement and disappointment caused at times by individual cases where the black pastor has not always maintained the high level of precept and example expected of him, I think Livingstone was right, and that our great missionary societies may hold this as a sound principle, that, while for some time maintaining the supreme control over the black churches in Tropical Africa in the hands of the white men, they should gradually train up the negro Christians to be self-sufficing and self-supporting.

The London Missionary Society's work in Livingstone's day, and up to the present time (as far as I can understand), was and is conducted on Democratic principles. That is to say, all its white *employés* are equals, no one occupying especially a headship over the others, and the affairs of each separate mission—such as that of South Africa, Tanganyika, or Madagascar—are managed by the majority of the agents being formed into a committee. This system is a weak one. In every organisation which wishes to be successful there must be a head, a leader who can combine the divergent, conflicting wills of many into one clear, determined intention. " I only wish we had a bishop over us," said one day to me one of the most capable of the London Missionary Society's agents on Lake Tanganyika, when he was complaining of the delays and vacillation caused by the difficulty of getting his local committee to decide on any line of action. Livingstone uses almost the same words in his private letters, wherein he describes the disputes and sometimes acrimonious differences which attended the attempt on the part of the committee of which he was a member to make up their minds as to the policy they should pursue on matters great and small. But if there had been a bishop appointed in those days to control the actions of the London Missionary Society's agents in South Africa, it is probable that Livingstone would have lived and died comparatively unknown beyond the narrow circle of his fellow-evangelists, for his career as an explorer would almost certainly have been discouraged and compressed. His brother-missionaries at that time, and the directorate of the Society at home, did not always

view with satisfaction the roving life to which he became addicted after a while. Though it is possible that,
in spite of all difficulties, he might have become an
explorer even at the cost of abruptly abandoning the
Mission, yet I think that he was too much attached to
spreading the Gospel as the first chief object of his life to
forswear himself in outward appearance, and to bring
scandal on the faith by his falling away. Besides,
although he was far from being a mercenary man, the
meagre pittance of £100 a year which was allowed him
by the Missionary Society was all he had to look to for
the maintenance of himself and his family, and he would
not have been able to throw that up suddenly without
the prospect of other and certain emoluments to live on,
and this he could hardly have obtained before he had
made a great name as an explorer. Consequently, we
owe it to the somewhat free and independent organisation which prevailed in the London Missionary Society
that Livingstone gradually glided insensibly from the
missionary into the explorer without offence, naturally,
and himself scarcely conscious at the time of the change
taking place in his career.

CHAPTER VIII.

MISSIONARY BECOMES EXPLORER.

On the 1st of June 1849 Livingstone started from Kolobeñ with two English sportsmen (Messrs. Oswell and Murray)[1] to search for the rumoured lake in the interior to which the name of Ngami, Ñami, Ñhabe, or Ñǁabe has been varyingly given.[2] This lake was evidently far larger than it is at the present time, when it appears a mere insignificant pool compared to the great inland seas with which Africa abounds. It is fed by the Okavango River (called in its lower course the Teoge

---

[1] There is a flippant little passage in Sir Samuel Baker's otherwise admirable book, "Wild Beasts and their Ways" (vol. i. pp. 108-9), in which he says, "Oswell and Murray took Livingstone with them when they discovered the Lake Ngami." This is a totally incorrect statement, and I have Mr. Oswell's direct authority for saying so. Livingstone (as one may see by perusing his letters and published works) had contemplated searching for Lake Ngami ever since he landed in Cape Colony, and his preparations for this journey extended over many years. When at last able to start, he invited his friends, Messrs. Oswell and Murray, to go with him. They willingly accepted the proposition, and bore their due share of the expenditure.

[2] The name of this lake is said to be derived from a Bushman word, Ñǁabe, which means "giraffe," the shape of the long, sloping lake resembling in a fantastic way the contour of that animal. As, however, the commonly accepted form of the word is *Ngami*, I shall spell the name of the lake in that way throughout this book, especially as the Bushman word Ñ͂ǁabe is almost unpronounceable by those not to the manner born or trained. The Setshuana name for Ngami is *Tutla* or *Tletle*, also meaning "giraffe."

or Tonke), coming from the well-watered country to the south of Angola,[1] and several intermittent streams which drain the highlands of Damaraland. Out of the eastern end of Ngami flows the Zuga River[2] in an easterly direction, ending in a lot of salt swamps and lakes on the western borders of Matabeleland.

Lake Ngami, with its neighbouring pools and salt lakes and swamps and salt-pans, and its network of dry or intermittent watercourses, is a curious hydrographical region, which has given rise to many speculations. Livingstone, I believe, is responsible for the rather ingenious suggestion that, before the Zambezi forced its way through a fault in the basaltic rock into its present channel towards the Indian Ocean, it flowed southwards, and ended in a great lake, of which Ngami and its attendant lakelets are the half-dried-up relics. If there ever was any outlet of the Ngami watershed, it would appear to have been towards the Limpopo River.

The subsequent discoveries of Tanganyika, Victoria Nyanza, Nyasa, Bangweolo, Moero, and the other great lakes of Africa put the nose of Ngami out of joint, so that until this narrow lakelet quite recently acquired an adventitious political interest, it had for a while been almost forgotten. In the earlier days of African exploration, however, it was the constant objective of adventurous journeys from the south and west. Mr. Francis

[1] In the upper portion of its course, the Okavango is a simply-flowing river with an undivided course, but south of Ndala its flow separates into numerous branches, which form a large "sponge." Lake Ngami only begins to rise after this sponge has become saturated, and hence the apparent anomaly of this rise taking place at a time when the river is at its lowest.

[2] During the dry season, when the waters of Ngami shrink, the Zuga flows into the lake; and when Ngami rises above a certain level its waters flow out by the Zuga.

Galton attempted to reach this lake in 1851 by an interesting but very difficult journey from Walfish Bay, but he did not succeed in getting nearer to Ngami than the banks of a dried-up watercourse called the Omaramba. Andersson, however, in 1855, left Walfish Bay, and travelling through Obampoland, managed to arrive at the shores of Ngami. Green explored the lower course of the Okabango-Teoge in 1856, and in later years Baines added to the foregoing examination into the geography of the Lake and its surroundings. All these journeys have enabled us to fix the position of Ngami with tolerable certainty. It is *not* likely to be found "a degree out in longitude," as was currently reported at the time of the Anglo-German negotiations.

The route followed by Livingstone northwards skirted the eastern limits of the Kalarahi Desert until he came to the vicinity of Shoshoñ. Then he turned off to the north-west, and boldly struck across a corner of the desert, wherein he had to go three or four days without water. This portion of the journey is even more difficult since Livingstone's day, for the desiccation of the country has increased, and some of the pools at which he drank have since dried up. In the centre of what is now called Khama's country, viz., that of the Batletle, they came upon a number of shining salt-pans covered with a white efflorescence which Livingstone thought might prove to be nitrate of soda. When the sinking sun cast a beautiful blue haze over the incrustations, it made the surface of these pans look exactly like a lake, and Livingstone and his companions were deceived by the appearance, and believed they had arrived at the long-looked-for Ngami, the more so as the River Zuga, which was close by, was called by the natives by the same name as

Ngami, viz., " Water of the Tletle."[1] Livingstone
found the Zuga to be a running river as late as the
4th July, which is almost the height of the dry season.
I believe this stream, too, has begun to dry up since

LAKE NGAMI.

Livingstone's first visit, and that travellers have found

[1] It is a very common thing in Africa for the natives to be unable to
discriminate between lake and river, especially if the river is at all a
broad one. The River Shire, for example, is called by the natives on
its banks "Nyanja " or " Nyasa," which is the same term as that
applied to the lake from which it flows. The root Tletle has already
been referred to as the Setshuana equivalent to Ngami—i.e.,
"giraffe."

less and less water in it—so much so, that in some of the
later German maps of this country the Zuga is represented as a dry watercourse. However, on the occasion of Livingstone's visit there was so much water in
the Zuga that the party left their oxen and all their
waggons except one at a place called Ngabisane, and
entered the canoes of the Bakoba. They passed the
mouth of the Tamunakle or Tamalakane (a river flowing
from a big marsh in the north, and almost seeming to
have had some ancient connection with the Tshobe or
Kwando, an affluent of the Zambezi), and passed on to
the north-east end of Lake Ngami, which they reached
on the 1st August 1849. So large did the lake appear
at this time, that from this point Livingstone could see
no horizon when he looked to the south-south-east. He
guessed its size from the reports of the inhabitants at
about seventy miles in circumference. The water of
Ngami he describes as perfectly fresh when the lake was
full and flowed out into the Zuga, but brackish when
the level of Ngami was low and the water stagnant.
The altitude of the lake above sea-level is variously
stated to be 2100 feet (Livingstone), 2260 (Chapman),
and 2664 (Dr. Holden). There is a great divergence
among the results of these calculations, and it would
be interesting to have the question of Ngami's altitude
set at rest by a series of exact calculations, as it is a
point which has a decisive bearing on the former connection of the Ngami basin with the Zambezi.[1] However, now that this interesting hydrographical region
has more or less come within the sphere of action of the
British South African Company, we may hope soon to

---

[1] The height of the Zambezi above the Victoria Falls is 2608 feet
above sea-level.

obtain a more precise knowledge of its physical geography.[1]

[1] The following particulars about Lake Ngami given by Livingstone may be of interest : "Lake Ngami is the southern and lowest part of the great river system beyond, in which large tracts of country are inundated annually by tropical rains. . . . A little of that water, which in the countries farther north produces inundation, comes as far south as 20° 20′, the latitude of the upper end of the lake, and, instead of flooding the country, falls into the lake as into a reservoir. It begins to flow down the Mbara, which divides into the rivers Tsö and Teoge. The Tsö divides into the Tamunakle and Mababe ; the Tamunakle discharges itself into the Zuga, and the Teoge into the lake. The flow begins either in March or April, and the descending waters find the channels of all these rivers dried up, except in certain pools in their beds, which have long dry spaces between them. The lake itself is very low. The Zuga is but a prolongation of the Tamunakle, and an arm of the lake reaches up to the point where the one ends and the other begins. This last is narrow and shallow, while the Zuga is broad and deep. The narrow arm of the lake, which on the map looks like a continuation of the Zuga, has never been observed to flow either way. It is as stagnant as the lake itself.

"The Teoge and Tamunakle, being essentially the same river, and receiving their supplies from the same source (the Mbara or Vara), can never outrun each other. If either could, or if the Teoge could fill the lake—a thing which has never happened in modern times—then this little arm would prove a convenient escapement to prevent inundation. If the lake ever becomes lower than the bed of the Zuga, a little of the water of the Tamunakle might flow into it instead of down the Zuga ; we should then have the phenomenon of a river flowing in two ways ; but this has never been observed to take place here [It has, however, by other travellers.—H. H. J.], and it is doubtful if it ever can occur in this locality. The Zuga is broad and deep when it leaves the Tamunakle, but becomes gradually narrower as you descend about 200 miles ; there it flows into Kumadau, a small lake about three or four miles broad and twelve long. The water, which higher up begins to flow in April, does not make much progress in filling this lake till the end of June. In September the river ceases to flow. When the supply has been more than usually abundant, a little water flows beyond Kumadau, in the bed first seen by us on the 4th July ; if the quantity were larger, it might go farther in the dry rocky bed of the Zuga, since seen still farther in the east. The water-supply of this part of the river system . . . takes place in channels prepared for a much more copious flow. It resembles a deserted Eastern

Livingstone, Oswell, and Murray returned to Kolobeñ, and remained there until 1850, and then left again for the north in company with his wife, his three children, and the chief Sctshele, with the intention of proceeding up the northern bank of the Zuga till he reached the Tamunakle, and then ascending that river to visit the great Betshuana chief, Sebituane, in the north, of whose greatness he had heard rumours on his previous visit to Ngami. On this first journey he had also learned that in following up the Tamunakle one came to a region full of big rivers and tall trees—a land of forest, in fact; and this, as he says, was the first assurance he had that the interior of Africa was not the sterile, sandy waste it had been imagined by the geographers of the first half of the nineteenth century.

At the confluence of the Tamunakle with the Zuga he first heard of the existence of the tsetse-fly.[1] This new and unexpected danger to travelling with oxen and waggons obliged Livingstone to give up proceeding very

garden, where all the embankments and canals for irrigation can be traced, but where, the main dam and sluices having been allowed to get out of repair, only a small portion can be laid under water. In the case of the Zuga the channel is perfect, but water enough to fill the whole channel never comes down ; and before it finds its way much beyond Kumadau, the upper supply ceases to run, and the rest becomes evaporated. The higher parts of its bed even are much broader and more capacious than the lower towards Kumadau. The water is not absorbed so much as lost in filling up an empty channel, from which it is to be removed by the air and sun. There is, I am convinced, no such thing in the country as a river running into sand and becoming lost. This phenomenon, so convenient for geographers, haunted my fancy for years ; but I have failed in discovering any-thing except a most insignificant approach to it."—*Missionary Travels and Researches*, page 66 *et seq.*

[1] The tsetse-fly was first brought to the notice of scientific men by Major Vardon in 1848, who found it on the banks of the Limpopo (*vide* Chapter X.).

far on his way up the Tamunakle with his wife and
family. He therefore went once more to Lake Ngami,
where he arrived in time to find that a party of Englishmen had recently reached the shores of Ngami in search
of ivory, but were all down with fever. One of them,
indeed, named Alfred Rider, an accomplished artist,
had died a few days before Livingstone's arrival. The

W. OSWELL.
(*From a Photograph by Percy S. Lankester.*)

others were very tenderly nursed by Mrs. Livingstone,
and recovered.

Still desirous of visiting Sebituane, but not liking
to take his wife and family on such a risky journey,
Livingstone arranged to leave them in charge of a
friendly chief on the shores of Lake Ngami whilst he

rode northwards on a riding-ox; but his children and servants becoming prostrated with fever, he was unable to carry out his intention, and returned once more to Koloben. Hence, after a brief visit to Kuruman, he started again for Sebituane's country, on the banks of the Tshobe, little thinking that he was on his way to the discovery of the Zambezi. On this third journey across the Kalahari he was again accompanied by his wife and family, and by Mr. Oswell. As this latter gentleman figures so much in these early explorations of Livingstone's, and proved such a true and good friend to the great traveller, it may be of interest if I give some particulars about him. He was one of the greatest among those British Nimrods of that earlier day who did so much to increase our knowledge of the African *fauna*. He made three important journeys with Living-stone: two to Lake Ngami and one to the Zambezi, and he had previously travelled in other parts of South Africa with Major Vardon. Livingstone says of him that he was declared by the natives to be the greatest hunter that had ever come into the country. He had been known to kill four large, old male elephants a day, and as he hunted without dogs, which materially in-creased the difficulty and risk (for a few yelping curs are of great assistance to the elephant-hunter, as they serve to distract the attention of the wounded beast from the sportsman), Mr. Oswell was consequently looked upon by the Betshuana as an exceptionally courageous man, and when they wished to flatter Livingstone they would say, "If you were not a missionary you would be just like Oswell; you too would hunt without dogs." Oswell contributed liberally to the expense of Livingstone's preliminary journeys; and when, in 1852,

Livingstone returned from his first expedition to the Zambezi, and proceeded with his wife and family to Cape Town, Oswell provided an outfit for Livingstone's wife and children (who were returning to England) which cost over £200, performing also many other acts of kindness which Livingstone warmly acknowledges in his private letters.   Mr. Oswell's hunting adventures in South Africa were but an interlude in an Indian career. In India he distinguished himself as a sportsman to an exceptional degree, and later on performed some very remarkable journeys in South America.   He eventually returned to England, and settled down in his beautiful home on the border-line between Kent and Sussex, where he lives surrounded by one of the finest collections of African trophies that any one man possesses.   Some idea may be obtained of the wearing-out of Livingstone's life when one reflects that he died in 1873 a prematurely old man, while his erst companion, Mr. Oswell, not very much younger than Livingstone, is still, in 1890, a hale and hearty, bright-eyed man, who drives, rides, shoots, and walks with scarcely diminished vigour.

At the end of June 1851 Livingstone and Oswell first sighted the Zambezi at a place called Sesheke, having travelled thither by a more eastern route than their previous journeys, and having crossed on the way the network of rivers, streams, and marshes called the Tshobe.   Before they reached the Zambezi, however, Livingstone and Oswell had stayed for a little while at Linyanti, the residence of the great Ma-kololo chief, Sebituane, who had so long desired to meet with white men, and who had facilitated Livingstone's journey by the orders he had sent to his subsidiary chiefs, Letshula-tebe of Ngami, Sekomi of the Bamangwato, and Setshele,

chief of the Ba-kwena, to do their utmost to assist the
white travellers on their way with guides and provisions.
Unfortunately, soon after Livingstone had arrived, poor
Sebituane, who had greeted his coming with such joyful
hospitality, fell sick of inflammation of the lungs, and
died. The last words he uttered were directions to one
of his servants to take little Robert Livingstone away
to one of his wives, who would give him milk.

Sebituane's career had been a remarkable one. He
originally came from the East Betshuana or Basuto
stock, and was born near the sources of the Vaal River
in the eastern part of the Transvaal State. Various
inter-tribal conflicts drove him, with a number of his
companions and relations, to the west, where they were
mixed up in an indiscriminate horde of Betshuana, who
attempted to settle down in the Kuruman Valley, in
which one of the earliest mission stations had been established. They were driven away from Kuruman, however, by the Grikwas; and Sebituane, with a small following of braves and a few cattle, fled northwards across
the eastern fringe of the Kalahari Desert. At a place
called Melita they were met by a coalition of the Ba-
waketse, Ba-kwena, Ba-katla, and Ba-hurutse; but
Sebituane, with desperate courage and clever strategy,
completely routed these forces, and took possession of
the Ba-ñwaketse country. Here he was several times
attacked by the Matabele-Zulus, but although he held
his own against these raiders, he moved on again northwards to find a securer, better-watered country. In this
pursuit he arrived at Lake Kumadau, a widening of the
Zuga River, in the country of the Batletle. Starting
again from here, he conquered all the Ngami country
right away to the borders of Damaraland, and struck

still farther north with his ever-swelling tribe of warriors, who had come to be called the Ma-kololo or Ba-
kololo.[1] At length he settled himself firmly in the angle
of country between the Liambai or Upper Zambezi and
the Tshobe. His successful raids over the Zambezi
countries attracted the attention of Umsilikazi or Mosilikatse,[2] chief of the Matabele, and drew down on him an
attack which caused him considerable loss ; but he soon
rallied his forces and defeated the Matabele on several
occasions, and finally drove them away. He then over-
ran the whole country as far as the River Kafue, and
eventually conquered the Barotse Valley of the Upper
Zambezi. His raids into the Ngami district had brought
to his knowledge the existence of white men on the west
coast, and he became filled with a desire to open up trade
with the Europeans. His conquest of the Barotse country brought him in contact with black and half-caste
Portuguese slave-traders, locally known as "Mambari,"
and these people opened up a trade between Sebituane
and the country of Bihe, which lay at the back of the
Portuguese colony of Benguela. His fame as a conqueror also attracted to his court some Zanzibar Arabs,
who came there to purchase slaves.

    Sebituane created a great kingdom in the Barotse
Valley, and his introduction of the sturdy Basuto-Ma-
kololo into the countries of the Upper Zambezi was an
interesting event in the history of Central Africa. They
formed a useful counterpoise to the devastating work of
the Matabele-Zulus. By their conquest of the Barotse
Valley they facilitated Livingstone's exploration of the

---

[1] These were nearly all of Basuto origin.
[2] The former is the Zulu, the latter the Betshuana, rendering of the
same name.

Upper Zambezi, and the subsequent settlement of a few members of their tribe on the Shire River became the nucleus of a resistance to the encroachments of Portuguese rule, which finally ended in the establishment of a British protectorate over Nyasaland.

Finding that the unhealthiness of these swampy countries between the Tshobe and the Zambezi would preclude his wife and family from making any long stay in this region, Livingstone returned with them once more to Kolobeñ, resolving to leave them there whilst he proceeded again to the Zambezi Valley, to thoroughly explore the course of that river and seek out an easy means of communication with the west coast.

On the way back across the desert another child was born to him, whom he christened "Oswell," after his friend the sportsman.

But on arriving at Kolobeñ they found that all further mission-work at that place was rendered futile by the threats and raids of the Boers, so Livingstone decided to despatch his wife and family to England, especially as he reflected that in the roving life they were leading at present the children were growing up without education. Accordingly he journeyed with them from Kolobeñ to Cape Town, and, with the generous help of Mr. Oswell, provided them with a good equipment and took their passages to England. When they had left Cape Town, and Livingstone was free and unencumbered, he took advantage of his stay in the capital of South Africa to place himself under the tuition of Sir Thomas Maclear, the Astronomer-Royal. Under this gentleman's instructions he perfected himself in astronomical observations, and acquired in this respect a skill and accuracy which few subsequent travellers have possessed to a like

degree. In Sir Thomas Maclear he found one of the
best friends and helpers he ever possessed, and his lasting
gratitude towards him is manifested by frequent reference to him in his books and journals down to the last
year of his life. He named after him the most striking
promontory on Lake Nyasa—Cape Maclear—a point at
which I have often called, and which is destined perhaps
to be the great English capital on Nyasa.

Having fitted himself out with such stores as he was able
to procure, and obtained what little quantity of caps and
gunpowder a grudging and suspicious Colonial Government would allow him to purchase (though they freely
permitted their sale to hostile Boers and Kaffirs), he once
more turned his face northwards, in June 1852, and
after staying a few days at Kolobeñ to counsel the
recently raided Ba-kwena and bemoan the loss of his
library, which had been destroyed by the Boers, he journeyed on northwards with little incident of note till he
reached Linyanti, the capital town of the Ma-kololo amid
the Tshobe marshes. Here he was received with surprise
and delight by the Ma-kololo. Desirous of opening up
commerce among these people and teaching them something better than the slave-trade, Livingstone had persuaded one of the leading merchants of Cape Town to
send with him on this journey to the Zambezi a negro
trading-agent, named George Fleming, in order that he
might settle down there and open a trading-store. They
found, on their arrival at Linyanti, that Sebituane had
been succeeded by his son, Sekeletu. Here during a
month Livingstone prepared for his exploring journey
northwards along the course of the Upper Zambezi,
while at the same time he assisted Fleming to establish
himself as a trader.

Before relating Livingstone's further explorations, I
will briefly pass in review the natural features, animals,
and human inhabitants of that large district of Central
South Africa which may be called Betshuanaland, wherein
Livingstone had spent the first eleven years of his life as
a missionary; for, although in some senses he remained
a missionary of Christianity to the end of his days, his
purely missionary work may be said to have ceased when
he arrived at the Zambezi for the second time and became
an explorer, first and foremost, in his resolve to trace the
course of that river from its source to the sea.

CHAPTER IX.

BETSHUANALAND.

It is a curious fact that in the northern and southern hemispheres the regions of tropical heat and moisture are separated from the temperate zone by areas of nearly rainless desert. Although these bands of arid country are in some parts broken in their continuity by the special atmospheric conditions brought about by high ranges of mountains, or diverted by the same cause to the northwards into the temperate zone or southwards to the vicinity of the equator, they may still be regarded as forming a more or less regular band of desert country separating the region of equatorial rains from the land-surface of the temperate zone wherein rain also falls with certainty and regularity. North of the equator we have the Deserts of the Sahara, of Arabia, Persia, Northern India, Tartary, and Mongolia. South of the equator there are the Atacama and Chaco Deserts of South America, the Kalahari Desert of South Africa, and the almost rainless districts of Central Australia. In Southern Africa the desert region does not uniformly extend across the continent. On the west coast it begins in about 14° south latitude and spreads out south-wards almost as far as the 32nd parallel, but the con-tinuous extent of this arid country over South Africa

from sea to sea is interrupted by a narrow strip of
elevated land, with a fairly regular rainfall, stretching
from the Mashona Territory to the Transvaal State.
Eastwards, again, of this, the country resumes, in Gaza-
land, much of its dried-up, waterless character. Still,
the eastern half of South Africa may be said, as a general
rule, to be far better supplied with rain than the western
half. When the term "desert" is used to indicate
regions like these, and like the Sahara in Northern
Africa, it means a country in which rain falls to the
extent of only three or four showers every year, and the
surface of which is largely covered by loose sand. This
sand is produced by the friable rocks being disintegrated
by the extremes of temperature which prevail in these
rainless lands where radiation of heat is very rapid. The
temperature of over 110° Fahr., which may be reached
at noonday under a usually cloudless sky, rapidly dimin-
ishes after sunset; and before the dawn there may be
two or three degrees of frost on the ground. This varia-
tion of temperature causes a constant contraction and
expansion of the rocks, which in this way split up and
crumble, and are triturated into finer and finer sand by
the action of the wind. But alternating with hopeless
tracts of nothing but sand are regions in which a little
scanty vegetation grows, and even certain trees specially
adapted to a desert life, such as acacias and tamarisks.
There are yet other portions of the so-called desert
which, but for their nearly rainless character, scarcely
differ from the better-watered regions beyond in the
extent of their vegetation; but this is generally owing
to the presence of underground springs. Indeed there
is a curious and fortunate compensation in all these
African deserts for the absence of rain, in that water

is almost always to be obtained—and sometimes not many feet from the surface—by sinking wells.

Such are the atmospheric conditions of Betshuanaland north of the Orange River, west of the Transvaal and the Matabele country, south of the Zambezi, and east of Damara-Namakwa-land. In these last-named countries lying to the west of Betshuanaland, the conditions of rainlessness are really the same save in one or two specially favoured patches, or in valleys among the high mountains. In fact, Betshuanaland and the Kalahari Desert are almost convertible terms. Over all this country, as over the Sahara Desert, a process of desiccation has evidently been going on. The Sahara in the time when the Romans ruled in North Africa had a greater rain-supply, and consequently was more covered with vegetation than it is at the present day, and was therefore far easier for man to traverse. This is shown by the fact that a constant trading communication was kept up between the Mediterranean Littoral and the Land of the Blacks, southward of the Sahara, by means of journeys on foot and in bullock-waggons. The rock-drawings discovered by Richardson and others in Fezzan show that oxen were used as beasts of draught and burden in the Sahara Desert, where they took the place of the camel, which was not introduced into use in the Sahara Desert until the great Arab invasions of the twelfth century. At the present time it would be impossible for oxen to cross the Sahara, as there would not be sufficient verdure for them to feed on, and the distance between the watering-places would be too great. Then, again, there are many vestiges in North African and Egyptian deserts of the former existence of extensive forests, now represented only by semi-fossil fragments

of the trunks of trees. The dried-up watercourses which
traverse the Sahara in all directions, and some of which
are nearly a thousand miles in length, and in beds of
which water is often to be found at a depth of from eight
to ten feet from the surface, testify to the former existence of mighty rivers. Lake Tshad is but a shrunken
nucleus of what was once a mighty inland sea.

This condition of affairs is very similar to the past
history of Betshuanaland, as far as that history can be
deciphered by the evidence left in the dry river-beds,
the evaporated lakes which are reduced to salt-pans, the
traces of a once luxuriant vegetation, the traditions of the
natives, and even the first period of eleven years' observations during which Livingstone recorded his proofs
of the increasing desiccation. However, the Kalahari
Desert, though it no longer possesses running water, can
hardly be called a wholly rainless region even at the
present day, when the rain-supply is even less than it
was forty years ago, at the time of Livingstone's travels.
There are occasional heavy showers in the months of
March and April; and as the sun-baked alluvial soil in
the beds of the dried-up rivers is of a more or less im-
permeable character, water often lies in scattered pools
in the desert for several months after the close of the
rainy season before it is finally evaporated by the sun.

From the Orange River northwards to the 22nd degree
of latitude, Betshuanaland is mainly a broken plateau of
4000 feet to 5000 feet in height above the sea, dry and
devoid of perennial streams, swept with scorching winds
at certain seasons of the year, exceedingly hot in the
day-time, and with the thermometer frequently below
freezing-point at night; yet amazingly healthy, one of
the healthiest parts of the world, and singularly effica-

cious in its climate for the curing of lung diseases. Beyond the 22nd parallel, however, the plateau slopes gradually down to the basin of Lake Ngami, which is little more than 2000 feet above the sea. In this lower region one enters " Unhealthy Africa."

The general aspect of Betshuanaland to a superficial observer would be that of a desert, a blank, hopeless wilderness of rocks and sand, and grey, lifeless scrub. As a matter of fact, it consists, generally speaking, of a sun-baked tableland, from which rise flat-topped hill-ranges with steep, crumbling sides, like cake roughly cut with a knife. These latter are really the remains of a still higher plateau that has been eaten away, carved, and crumbled by water, wind, sun, and frost, till there are but the harder, less friable portions remaining in these low ranges of table-mountains, or in the isolated stools or hillocks which the Dutch call *kopjes*.[1] Dry watercourses, broad enough to be the beds of first-class rivers, wind and wiggle-waggle between the fragments of the broken tableland, which they, when they were strong streams of water in the distant past, cut up and parcelled out into isolated blocks. Here and there in these old river-beds are spots of greenery, which mark the presence of water near the surface of the white sand, in a hollow among grey boulders, perhaps. Round these moister places grow tall acacias, with grey-green trunks and a thin but vivid green crown of foliage, among which glitter the spiteful thorns set at all angles on the twigs among the tiny little pinnate leaves. At some seasons of the year these acacias make an act of grace for their churlish thorns and their mean, shade-less foliage. They break out on the under side of the

[1] Pronounced "koppies" = "little heads."

boughs into a yellow dust of small blossoms, which are all stamens and without a petal, but which emit a scent that is thick with almost palpable sweetness, and can be smelt far and wide over the desert. Also round the hidden water other acacias grow which form low scrub, with villainous "wait-a-bit" thorns, curved and sheathed like a cat's claw, with leaves few and far between, and with small white tufts of flowers; and yet another species of acacia which has mauve blossoms, sensitive leaves, and thorns, of course, and which creeps along the ground. *Cyperus* grasses, with their stiff mop-head crowns of leaf-blades, and their long, continuous stems; tiny lawn-grasses, forming a tender green turf, sweet for the antelopes to browse on; rambling cucurbits with coarse yellow flowers and scarlet cucumber-like fruit; aloes with fleshy purple-blotched leaves and spikes of waxy-red or waxy-yellow tube-flowers; sky-blue blossoms of the creeping *Commelyna ;* a few yellow and purple and pink bean-flowers—these are the chief concomitants of the rare presence of water near the surface in these dried-up Betshuanaland river-beds.

On the high banks of the vanished stream an occasional glaucous-green Borassus fan-palm grows, sombre-looking with its sage-coloured spiky fronds, but graceful and correct in its sad symmetry. Or there is a weird Candelabra Euphorbia, like a bunch of scorpions with their tails in the air; or a huge, gouty baobab-tree, with its enormous trunk and its spindly branches, bare of leaves save for two months in the year, and hung for the rest of the time with large, grey-brown calabashes. The baobab looks like a leprous vegetable, a tree in the last stages of *Elephantiasis*. Its swollen body, of disproportionate girth, simulates, with its longitudinal clefts and

its dimples, two huge thighs and legs fused together—
here parting somewhat, there uniting, but both grossly
swollen, as it were, with this hideous disease; and presents a further resemblance to leprous limbs and trunks
in the pinkish-grey, shiny, glabrous bark with which it
is covered.

For a few weeks in the year, about April, at the end
of the rainy season, these dry river-beds become rushing
torrents of turbid water. The few heavy showers which
cause this renewal of the streams suddenly bring to life
a varied vegetation on the sandy flats. The straggling
gourds revive, put out green leaves, flower, and rapidly
fruit. Myriads of juicy water-melons are soon strewing
the desert. The forgotten bulbs of lilies send up single
blossoms of immaculate white, or vigorous crowns of
many flowers which are pink or blue, or pink and white,
or green and white, according to the species. The dry
bushes of papilionaceous shrubs put forth green leaves
and violet blossoms in place of the old brown foliage
and the empty seed-pods still hanging on the branches.
The Mopane trees, with their bifid leaves, have become in
the long drought a sickly yellow; they too, when the
air is suddenly moistened by the showers, develop new
leaf-shoots, which begin by being a tender pinkish-blue,
and pass on, as they expand, to blue-green and the
yellow-green of maturity. Still, this revival of verdure
is evanescent, and the ever-blazing sun soon withers up
the flowers, grass, and bushes into rattling seed-pods,
blackened tufts, and grey skeletons. The perennial
greenery round those weak spots in the sandy hollows
of the river-bed, where the cool water is percolating
through the sand not far from the surface, still remains,
but is a tiny, unimportant patch compared to the vast

shadeless solitudes of grey rocks and yellow sand ; and if
you passed over the land in a balloon, and could take it in
at a glance, you would sum it up with the words which
began this sketch, " Desert . . . blank, hopeless desert ! "

Yet, if you soared thus over the length and breadth
of Betshuanaland, the monotony of the desert would be
sometimes broken by the gleam of lakes : not all of
which, however, are of water. Some are evaporated to
great salt-pans, which are a whitish-grey in colour seen
close at hand, but a delicious, pale, sparkling azure
when viewed from a height or from a distance, and
when the sun is shining on them. In the midday heats
the cruel mirage plays about the saline, concave bed of
the evaporated lake, and brings back the ghost of the
vanished water, making it ripple and sparkle in the
hazy sunshine, and break, seemingly, into wavelets on
the marge, while stately non-existent trees and bosky
islands of equal unsubstantiality dot the shimmering
expanse, and repeat themselves in reflections down the
streaky mirror of the unreal water.

Yet, in spite of their aspect of desolation and their
starved and scanty *flora*, these vast deserts of Betshuanaland are full of animal life. The hot sand and the
barren, crumbling rocks are the haunts of fierce scorpions,
centipedes, and busy hunting-spiders. In the "veldt,"
with its thin grass and low shrubs, there are innumerable wasps, hornets, bees, grasshoppers, locusts, crickets,
ants, ant-lions, and flies ; a variety of butterflies and a
few monstrous moths, whose huge caterpillars are fat
and good to eat, with the taste and colour of pistachio-
nuts. In the few rivers which retain pools of water
throughout the year, and in the Lake Ngami, there are
said to be found more than ten kinds of fish—mostly

siluroids, eels, barbel, African mullet, and the interesting "mudfish" (*Protopterus*), which latter habituates
itself to living half the year or more without water by
burying its body in the mud of the drying pools, where
it lies dormant till the reviving floods return.

Toads and frogs are here, more than one would think
a desert might harbour. One or more of the larger
frogs are good to eat, and are reckoned a dainty item in
their diet by the Bushmen and Betshuana. Crocodiles
in numbers frequent such lakes and pools as are peopled
with fish. *Varanus* or *Monitor* lizards are likewise met
with, and the abundance of insect life affords sustenance
to numerous geckoes, skinks, agamas, zonures, and
other lizards which are mainly protectively coloured and
mottled brown-grey, like the sandy soil.

Large and small land-tortoises browse on the scanty
vegetation, and themselves are eaten by the omnivorous
Bushmen.

Snakes are almost more abundant in Africa south of
the Zambezi than to the north of that river. Except
one or two species which are peculiar in their distribution to the West African sub-region, South Africa
possesses all the serpents of wide African range, and a
few more which are specially its own. Its poisonous
snakes [1] are more abundant both in the species and in

[1] The chief poisonous snakes of Betshuanaland are the puff-adder
(*Vipera arietans*), the horned viper (*V. cornuta*), the Cape adder
(*V. atropos*), the African cobra (*Naja haje*), the ring-hals (*Sepedon
hœmachatis*), the Cape viper (*Causus rhombatus*), and the Tree-cobras
(*Dendraspis angusticeps* and *D. Jamesoni*) generally known as the
black and green "mamba." The "Mamba," which in three or four
species is found all over Tropical Africa, and which is peculiar to
that continent, belongs to the Cobra family—the Colubrine group of
poisonous snakes. From its fierceness and the rapidly fatal character
of its venom, it is justly dreaded.

the individual, more prominent in the fatal results from their bites than those in Central, Eastern, or Western Africa, where as a rule one very rarely hears of death from snake-bite among the natives.

The ostrich of the common or North African species (*Struthio camelus*) is found all over Betshuanaland, right up to the Zambezi, but not beyond that river. It feeds on grasshoppers and other insects, pods, seeds, bulbs, water-melons, grass, and leaves. The Bushmen, as is well known, stalk the ostrich, and approach near enough to kill it, by disguising the upper part of their bodies with the cleverly stuffed skin of a cock-ostrich. This disguise attracts both the males and females among the inquisitive birds to a close inspection of the hunter, who, however, occasionally finds himself thwarted by his own cleverness, for he imitates so closely the appearance, gait, and voice of a cock-ostrich, that before he has time to shoot his poisoned arrow, some furiously jealous male among the real ostriches rushes up and strikes his supposed rival to the earth with a stunning blow from his powerful two-toed foot.

Others among the commonest or most characteristic birds of Trans-Zambezian Africa are bustards, cranes, plovers, "thick-knees," guinea-fowl, sand-grouse, turtle-doves, and tiny little pigeons; grey desert larks, grey touracoes, brown cuckoos, small grey-yellow-and-blue parrots, wee finches the size of large beetles, grey and red, grey and blue in colour; black and white shrikes and wagtails, metallic-tinted sunbirds; glossy starlings and black and white crows. Kites and hawks in numbers soar over the hot plains and build among the precipices of the older tableland. Vultures swarm, as they do in most desert countries, because there are few trees and brushwood to obstruct their vision. The long-legged secretary-bird, half-way in structure between vulture and bustard, stalks through the scrub and grass of the less arid portions of the land searching for the snakes which it kills and eats. And the handsome bateleur eagle, with short tail, rich black and chestnut-brown plumage, scarlet cheeks and feet, and full-feathered thighs, perches on the topmost boughs of the emaciated acacias and looks out with his large, keen eyes for his prey, the jerboas, the antelope-fawns, and the desert hares.

In the marshes of the Botletle River and round about the grassy flats which border Lake Ngami the elephant still lingers; the hippopotamus frolics in these waters and delights to smash and upset the frail canoes of the native fishermen. The white rhinoceros—the climax and crown of the *Rhinocerotidæ*, with its huge pinkish, yellowish-grey body, and its long head with the two long, flattened, attenuated horns, is, alas, extinct! He seemed to be a beast peculiar to Southern Africa, and has never been met with to the north of the Zambezi. But the other and smaller rhinoceros, the black one, still abounds in Betshuanaland. The giraffe still scuds over the dreary plains in little herds of ten to twenty, and browses on the tops of the low acacias. The eland, the kudu, the hartebeest, the blessbok, the gemsbok, the sable antelope, the equine antelope, the pallah, and the gnu still range in numbers over the desert and round the salt-pans and through the thorn thickets, careless how long they go without water. The springbok, that beautiful species of gazelle peculiar to South Africa, still appears occasionally in enormous flocks that number thousands of individuals, moving compactly forwards, and heeding but little the lions and cheetahs and servals and hunting-dogs who prowl wonderingly and longingly round the outskirts of the closely serried flock, able only to attack those who get separated from the mass of their fellows. The buffalo still frequents the deep kloofs of the dried-up river-valleys, the grassy tablelands, and the reed marshes of the salt-lakes. The zebra (*Equus Bur-chellii*—not the true zebra or the quagga ;[1] they, alas ! having already been almost stamped out by man) still frisks and gambles and trots and gallops through Betshuanaland ; but not, I fear, for long. Not for much longer, unless measures are taken for their protection, will these interesting or pretty beasts frequent the plateaux of Africa south of the Zambezi. The main object of all the lusty young Englishmen to whom Africa is now becoming fashionable, and who pour into the country to join pioneer forces or expeditions, is to slaughter the game recklessly, right and left, uselessly, heedlessly. A few years more and Betshuanaland will be able to boast of no mammals but the little conies (*Hyrax capensis*) which lurk among the rocks, the desert hares, and jerboas ; tiny, lovely little foxes (*Canis caama*), the earth-pig or *Orycteropus* (an ant-eating edentate) ; wart-hogs, hyænas, jackals, hunting-dogs, mice, porcupines, and shrews, which find a scanty living in the

---

[1] The quagga is an interesting half-way stage between the fully-striped zebra and the dun-coloured asses of North-Eastern Africa, which are only striped on the shoulder and occasionally on the legs. I believe, however, it is not a case of spots and stripes being developed, but rather that the genus was both spotted (in the horses) and striped (in the asses) in its earlier types, and that the wild asses of North-East Africa and Central Asia, and the modern horse, which also came from Asia, have gradually assumed a dun-colour or bay tint all over for protective purposes or from various other causes, just as the originally spotted lion and puma have gradually become uni-coloured cats.

desert or on the desert fringe, and which are too insignificant to merit extinction at the hands of British sportsmen and colonists, who do more damage to the larger mammalia than a geological epoch.

The great man-like Tshakma baboons still haunt the vicinity of the watercourses and of human settlements in Betshuanaland, and a few species of small *Cercopithecus* monkeys linger in the patches of forest along the banks of the Zuga, but these animals too are tending to disappearance; they are being driven away or exterminated by the increasing drought and the intolerance of their successful cousin, man, who grudges them such subsistence as they are able to pilfer from his gardens.

The human inhabitants of Betshuanaland are of the highest and lowest varieties of mankind. There is, for instance, the little Bushman, who will linger long in this country, because he is more adapted to the exigencies of a difficult existence in the desert than the baboon. The Bushman rarely exceeds five feet in stature where he is unmixed with other races. He has scattered clumps of wool on his head, a yellow skin, small slanting eyes, no bridge to his nose—only raised nostrils—high cheek-bones, a retreating chin, small hands and feet, and spindle-legs. He speaks a language full of inarticulate clicks, which recall not wholly fancifully the spluttering, clucking, squeaking chatter of a monkey. He lives in little holes dug in the ground or in caves, like the prehistoric savages of Europe; and, like those prehistoric savages, he is a great hand at drawing. Pictorial representation, indeed, seems to be one of the lowest and first of the arts evolved by man. The Bushman draws—or used to draw, before he was

worried into becoming civilised—frescoes in various tints
on the flat surfaces of rocks, which represent mainly antelopes, ostriches, and men. The Hottentot, distant cousin
to the Bushman, but higher in the scale of humanity,
can scarcely be said to inhabit Betshuanaland at the
present day, unless it be in the extreme south-west. He
is fast becoming exterminated by his vices, and before
long the only trace of his race that will remain will be
the half-breeds which are freely produced between him
and the Europeans.

Then come the darker-coloured Betshuana, who have
given their name to this district. They are a section
of the great Bantu group which extends from the
Cameroons and the Victoria Nyanza to Zululand. The
Betshuana people, among whom may be included the
Basuto and all the negro tribes of the western part of
the Transvaal State and the whole of Betshuanaland up
to the Tshobe affluent of the Zambezi, were the *avant-
couriers* in this region of the invading Bantu; and as
they were the first to tackle the Hottentots and Bushmen brought to bay in the south-west angle of the continent, they absorbed a good deal of Bushman and some
of the Hottentot blood. They are consequently more
yellow in complexion than the usual type of Bantu
negro, who is of a dark chocolate or even a bluish-
black. The Betshuana are a smart, intelligent people,
who have begun to adapt themselves very remarkably to
the requirements of civilisation. The majority of them
now are Christians, and they live in a more civilised
fashion than the more recalcitrant Kaffirs and Zulus.
Khama, the great Betshuana prince under whose en-
lightened rule the bulk of this nation is gathered, is a
Christian and a gentleman, and a standing beacon of

hope to those who believe in the civilisation of the
negro. There are probably, however, at the present
time no more than fifty thousand Betshuana ranging
over the whole country between the Tshobe on the
north and Cape Colony on the south, Matabeleland
and the Transvaal on the east, and Damaraland on the
west.

The white settlement of Betshuanaland has confined
itself mainly, up to the present time, to the more fertile,
better-watered, south-eastern border-land of that vast
district; though there are signs of approaching colonisation in the vicinity of Lake Ngami. Betshuanaland, up
to the 22nd degree of south latitude, is remarkably, exceptionally healthy—one of the most healthy climates in the
whole world; but beyond the 22nd parallel, northwards,
you enter the fever district, and also come within the
range of the tsetse-fly; and both these plagues will prove
for some little while a hindrance to the occupation of
the country by Europeans. But for a long time to come
this occupation will not be hindered, as it is in other
parts of South-East Africa, by a numerous and com-
peting population of blacks; for, as I have already
pointed out, this district, larger than England, Scotland,
and Ireland put together, has, at most, a native population—Bushmen and Hottentots included—of scarcely
more than fifty thousand.

CHAPTER X.

FEVER, TSETSE-FLY, AND HORSE-SICKNESS.

LIVINGSTONE's plans for the establishment of white missionaries on the Upper Zambezi and in Central Africa were doomed to be frustrated for a while by three obstacles which he had not altogether anticipated : African fever, the tsetse-fly, and horse-sickness. The first-named seemed to render impossible the prolonged residence of white men within the limits of tropical Africa. The second and third attacked the cattle and horses, and thereby destroyed the white man's chief means of transport.

African fever is no doubt to some extent the same disease as the ordinary intermittent and remittent fever which prevails in most hot parts of the world, but yet it has peculiarities of its own. It offers two distinct types of malady. One, and the less dangerous form of the two, resembles an aguish influenza of a more or less intermittent type ; the other is a severe bilious remittent, usually accompanied by hæmaturic symptoms, which appears to be a kind of malignant jaundice, and to resemble in many points the yellow fever of tropical America, differing from it, however, in not being infectious.[1] It

[1] It is a remarkable fact that the yellow fever of tropical America originated among African slaves who, in their horrible confinement in the slave-ships, developed this awful disease, which, without much

is very hard to decide what is the cause of the ordinary intermittent aguish fever which is so prevalent all over Africa. It is no doubt allied to the various kinds of ague which prevail in most marshy localities, even in the temperate zone; for instance, in our own Fens, and in part of Kent, in Finland, and in temperate North America. Intermittent fever is usually attributed to "malaria," whatever that vague term may mean; and the scientific explanation of this theory is, that ague is usually prevalent in marshy localities because the air which comes off the swamps carries with it a quantity of germs, which, being absorbed into the human system, rapidly multiply in the blood and produce fever. Quinine and certain other bitters are credited with being a poison to these germs. These drugs, by killing the microbes, stop the attacks of fever, which otherwise continue with a regular periodicity until at last the patient's system becomes so weakened and deteriorated that he dies, not so apparently from the ague as from some subsidiary disease which it has provoked. The germ theory is usually accounted as the only way of explaining fever, and marshy localities have been universally considered as unhealthy. Nevertheless, authorities like Sir William Moore, who have studied tropical diseases on the spot, are beginning to be convinced that the main and direct cause of ordinary fever is catching cold. The fact is, that most people suffer more or less from feverish attacks in hot countries, because they lead a kind of Turkish-bath existence (owing to the excessive heat), and any imprudent exposure of their perspiring bodies to a cold

stretch of imagination, may be represented as the punishment following on the crime. Yellow fever in its present acute form, and as a contagious disease, was not known in America till the slave-ships introduced it.

I

breeze causes the same dangerous chill which would result from one's walking out in *pyjamas* from the hot room of a Turkish-bath into the cool outside air without the preparatory cold douche which closes the pores of the skin. There is, however, little doubt that the germ theory must find a place somewhere. It is especially noticeable in all parts of the world, but markedly in the tropics, that people who turn up the virgin soil which has hitherto not been disturbed, and inhale the odour of the freshly-exposed mould, are singularly liable to attacks of fever, as though they had in this way absorbed some distinct poison. I think the true explanation of the problem is this, that in marshy localities and in tropical climates, especially in those parts of the world which possess an exuberant vegetation, the human system becomes more than usually liable to these attacks of fever-producing *bacteria ;* and that these little germs, ordinarily kept under control in a healthy state of the body, and prevented from increasing to the degree which causes fever, take advantage of that lowering of the system caused by a chill (which produces a special condition of the blood favourable to the rapid increase of the germs), and by multiplying beyond bounds, provoke by their ferment an increase in the temperature of the blood, which is, in other words, fever.

Catching cold is the most common provocative of fever in Africa ; over-exposure to the sun, indulgence in alcohol, nervous shocks, severe wounds, and mental worry—anything, in fact, which lowers the vitality—are other predisposing causes. One of the greatest malefactors, in the present writer's opinion, is the sea-breeze. The wind coming off the land is usually blamed for bringing sickness in its train, but it is the sea-breeze, misnamed "the doctor," which is the real culprit. It blows up wet and chilly from the sea in the hottest time of the day, and strikes you, all bathed in a refreshing perspiration, with a sudden chill, if you are foolish enough to expose yourself to its deceitful caresses. Much fever is also caught by imprudently leaving the body uncovered at night when the sudden drop in the temperature occurs between midnight and 3 A.M.[1]

The cause of the dangerous bilious remittent fever which afflicts most parts of tropical Africa, but more especially the equatorial zone, is even less clearly determined than that of the ordinary intermittent ague. In its worst form, this *febra perniciosa*, as the Portuguese call it, is a rapid and deadly malady. The patient, who has possibly felt well and strong in the morning, is taken with vomiting and pains of the back and cold shivers at midday. Hæmaturia soon makes its appearance, and the discharge from the kidneys is of a deep "porter" or claret colour, owing to the effusion of blood. The next morning the skin and whites of

[1] People go to bed with a temperature possibly of 80° or 85°, and impatiently push all coverings from them, sleeping almost naked. Then after midnight the temperature rapidly falls ten or more degrees, and the perspiring sleeper is struck with a sudden chill, which abruptly checks the perspiration and inflames the kidneys and other organs. If ever anything occurs in a hot climate to check perspiration suddenly, the person affected should immediately take measures for causing a reopening of the pores and that healthy action of the skin which enables the human body to remain cool within by the evaporation which goes on without. A familiar example of this action is seen in the porous water-coolers used in hot climates. These are generally vessels of clay or stone which permit of the gradual exudation of the water with which they are filled. The moisture which percolates to the outside of the water-cooler evaporates, and causes a cooling of the contents within. Consequently a stoppage of perspiration in the human body causes an increase of interior temperature, and therefore fever.

the eyes are orange in colour, owing to the enormous
quantities of bile which have been developed, and which
have permeated the whole body to the surface of the
skin. There is generally a high temperature, strong
fever, and delirium, though in some cases these symptoms
are not so marked. Incessant vomiting and great loss
of blood from the kidneys are the chief causes of the
patient's rapid exhaustion. The disease in its worst
form may terminate fatally in thirty hours to two days,
but in milder cases it lasts much longer. About sixty
per cent. of those attacked with *febra perniciosa* recover.[1]
The convalescence which ensues is long and tedious, and
for some time afterwards the patient's constitution is
greatly debilitated. The nerves of the eye are apt to
become affected in those who suffer from this bilious
fever, and temporary or even intermittent blindness is
a not infrequent result. This severe form of fever is the

---

[1] Bilious fever (which is known by various names in Africa, such
as malignant jaundice, hæmaturic fever, *febra perniciosa*, bilious remittent and "black water" fever) is liable to occur, sometimes in
epidemics, without a clearly traceable cause, among Europeans on the
Zambezi, in Nyasaland, at Zanzibar, in the Congo Basin (especially),
on the Lower Niger, and on the west coast of Africa. It is, however,
more especially frequent in Western Africa, and, on the other hand,
seems to be entirely absent from those parts of the Dark Continent
which are of a semi-desert character. I am, therefore, disposed to
think that it must be to a great extent associated with regions of
exuberant vegetation, and no doubt is caused by the prevalence of a
special organism. It can no doubt be induced or aggravated by chills,
or by imprudent excess in eating and alcohol; but yet, as I have already
pointed out, it often occurs without any direct cause, and in people
who have lived with the utmost prudence. If attended to immediately by a qualified doctor, there is a considerable hope of the patient
pulling through. The most effective remedies are quinine administered
in very large doses; ice (if obtainable) to allay the vomiting, or a few
drops of creosote on sugar; diaphoretics such as opium, which provoke perspiration and thus relieve the kidneys; and dry cupping over
the small of the back.

of African fever. Most doctors is in all conscience bad enough, but medical men know frequently it is not fever but jolly well kills — Bravely, blackwater and idleness are more than the climate. When once fairly established and reputed safe, there will be no lack of religious teachers — and it will then escape the heavy burden of being a scene of martyrdom.

FACSIMILE PORTION OF LETTER FROM DAVID LIVINGSTONE.
(By permission of Mrs. A. Livingstone Bruce.)

only really dangerous disease in Africa which cannot be directly traced to the sufferer's own imprudence. Dysentery is not nearly so common in Africa as it is in other parts of the tropics, and where it occurs is always traceable to a definite and preventable cause, such as extremely bad water, getting wet through and not changing one's clothes, or putting one's self in contact with infection.

Ordinary fever is so much the result of discomfort, worry, unhappiness of mind, bad food, and bad conditions of life, that I really believe, with the introduction of perfect civilisation in Africa, we shall get rid of it as much as we have done in India.

But in Livingstone's day, and indeed to a lesser extent at the present time, the permanent settlement of Europeans in the neighbourhood of the Zambezi was and has been found well-nigh impossible owing to the prevalence of both the forms of fever I have mentioned. Consequently, his "call" to the Upper Zambezi, which was answered by the London Missionary Society after a short delay, ended disastrously in the death of most of the missionaries sent to Linyanti. A French Protestant Mission has since been established there, but has suffered greatly and has lost several of its agents.

When Livingstone first reached the southern slope of the Zambezi Basin, which marks the end of the Betshu-analand deserts and the beginning of the zone of abundant vegetation (which, however attenuated in parts, is still continuous between the Limpopo River and the Zambezi Valley), he came into contact with the tsetse-fly.[1] The existence of that insect had been previously made known by Major Vardon and other English sports-

---

[1] *Glossina morsitans.*

men who had visited the Limpopo Valley, but Livingstone was the first to give any popular account of the insect and its ravages. The tsetse has an insignificant appearance, and is scarcely larger than a common housefly. It is chiefly remarkable by a rather lengthy, rigid proboscis, which apparently cannot be coiled up close to the head, like that of the common fly. The tsetse is brown in colour, but with three or four yellow bars across the hind-part of the body, and yellow streaks on the shields covering the upper part of the thorax. The wings, when closed, project considerably beyond the end of the fly's body. At the base of the proboscis there is a curious bulb-shaped thickening which is said to be the gland containing the poison. The tsetse presumably injects its venom into the blood for the same purpose of thinning or diluting it as is attributed to the mosquito, the flea, and other poisonous or irritating insects. The tsetse has a peculiar singing buzz, which immediately attracts the attention of those who have once heard it, and who have reason to fear for their cattle or horses.

It is a remarkable fact that the bite of this insect should be harmless to mankind and to all wild animals, and even to the calves of domestic cattle or foals of horses while the latter are very young and chiefly nourished on milk.[1] When a man is bitten by the tsetse, he simply feels the slight itching which follows on the bite of a mosquito, and no further symptoms follow. But in the case of domestic cattle, horses, and dogs, the bite of the tsetse brings on a disease which proves fatal either in a few days or in a few months. No other animals than those mentioned are so seriously

[1] This exception, however, does not apply to young dogs, who, even while being fed on milk, are liable to die from tsetse-poison.

susceptible to the poison of the tsetse. The mule, ass, goat, and sheep enjoy nearly the same immunity from its bites as men, apes, cats, pigs, zebras, buffaloes, and antelopes.

In the case of some flies, sores are produced in man and other mammals by the fly lodging its ova beneath the skin of its victims by means of the sharp proboscis or the ovipostor. The grub then hatches in the flesh and eats away round its environment until it sets up an inflammation and an abscess which eventually expel it from the body. But in the case of the tsetse the mischief is brought about by the injection of venom through the middle prong of the proboscis from the bulb at its base.

"When the tsetse is allowed to feed freely on the hand," writes Livingstone, "it is seen to insert the middle prong of the three portions into which the proboscis is divided somewhat deeply into the true skin; it then draws it out a little way, and it assumes a crimson colour as the mandibles come into brisk operation. The previously shrunken belly swells out, and if left undisturbed the fly quietly departs when it is full. . . . In the ox this same bite produces no more immediate effects than in man. It does not startle him as the gad-fly does; but a few days afterwards the following symptoms supervene: the eye and nose begin to run, the coat stares as if the animal were cold, a swelling appears under the jaw, and sometimes at the navel; and, though the animal continues to graze, emaciation commences, accompanied with a peculiar flaccidity of the muscles, and this proceeds unchecked until, perhaps months afterwards, purging comes on, and the animal, no longer able to graze, dies in a state of extreme exhaustion. Those which are in good condition often perish soon after the bite is inflicted with staggering and blindness, as if the brain were affected by it. Sudden changes of temperature produced by falls of rain seem to hasten the progress of the complaint; but in general the emaciation goes on uninterruptedly for months, and, do what we will, the poor animals perish miserably.

"When opened, the cellular tissue on the surface of the body beneath the skin is seen to be injected with air, as if a quantity of soap-bubbles were scattered over it, or a dishonest, awkward butcher had been trying to make it look fat. The fat is of a greenish-yellow colour, and of an oily consistence. All the muscles are flabby, and the heart often so soft that the fingers may be made to meet through it. The lungs and liver partake of the disease. The stomach and bowels are pale and empty, and the gall-bladder is distended with bile.

"These symptoms seem to indicate what is probably the case, a poison in the blood, the germ of which enters when the proboscis is inserted to draw blood. The poison-germ, contained in a bulb at the root of the proboscis, seems capable, although very minute in quantity, of reproducing itself, for the blood after death by the tsetse is very small in quantity, and scarcely stains the hands in dissection."

It is curious that the tsetse shows a marked dislike to animal excreta, and when a village is planted in the middle of its *habitat*, and becomes in time surrounded by the *exuviæ* of its inhabitants, the tsetse abandons the locality in disgust. This fact, according to Livingstone, has been turned to account by some of the native doctors, who mix the droppings of animals, milk, and various medicines together, and smear with it the cattle that are about to pass through a tsetse-infested district; but this, though it proves a preventive at the time, is not a permanent deterrent unless frequently renewed. Once the disease has manifested itself from the tsetse-bites, there is as yet no known cure, but it is possible that some great doctor like Pasteur or Koch might excogitate a successful process of inoculation if he gave his mind to it. At present the inoculation caused by one or two bites of the fly which have not proved sufficient to kill the animal constitute no immunity from further attacks, for the same animal bitten more frequently subsequently may die from the greater amount of poison injected into its system. The tsetse not often having horses and cattle and dogs placed at its disposal for its sustenance, feeds mainly on the wild animals, especially on the antelopes and buffaloes. As this big game, however, is gradually reduced or exterminated or driven away, so the tsetse disappears, either because it follows the game in its migrations, or because with its extermination it has no sufficient source of nourishment left. But nothing seems to more effectually scare it away than the presence of man, especially of native man, with the attendant concomitants of uncivilised settlements, which are delicately described in medical reports as " lack of all sanitary precautions." As Central Africa becomes opened up and continuously peopled, the tsetse-fly will disappear and the keeping of cattle and horses become possible.

This noxious insect is distributed over Africa, as far as we can learn, in a very patchy manner. It is particularly faithful to the valley of the Zambezi, though even here it is by no means universally present, being sometimes a positive pest on the south bank, while it is totally absent from the opposite district on the north. Still, its partiality for the Zambezi Valley is so marked that its *habitat* runs northwards in little tongues along the course of the Zambezi affluents. Thus, the tsetse is found everywhere along the banks of the Loangwa River right up to the edge of the Nyasa-Tanganyika plateau, where that stream takes its rise ; but the insect is absent from the watershed of the Tshambezi River, which rises not far from the Loangwa (and which is a tributary belonging to the Congo System), and from much of the northern and western shores of Lake Nyasa. Along the course of the Shire River the tsetse is found in patches, sometimes not more than a few miles in area. It is absent from the elevated part of the Shire high- lands. It is passing away from much of the littoral of Eastern and Western Africa, and is seldom met with in the north-central or north-eastern portions of the con- tinent. In many parts of West Africa horses and cattle die rapidly, especially in newly cleared districts of the forest regions ; but this is owing much less to the attacks of the tsetse-fly (for this insect is not common in the dense forests) than, in the case of the horse, to a kind of pneumonia which I shall further allude to as " horse- sickness," and amongst the cattle to poisonous herbs and grasses which their instinct has not yet taught them to avoid.

The " horse-sickness," which Livingstone distinguishes as *peripneumonia*, is a disease particularly affecting the equine genus throughout a considerable portion of tropi- cal Africa, but more especially in that part of the conti- nent which lies to the south of the equator. It is pre- valent in Southern Africa between the Zambezi and a line drawn across the continent at about 27° S. latitude. It reappears in parts of South-West Africa, less upon the sea-board, however, than in the interior; is prevalent in such parts of the Congo Basin as those in which horses or asses have yet been tried; it is met with in districts of Nyasaland and on the shores of Tanganyika; and on some parts of the west coast of Africa, such as Sierra Leone. But, like the range of the tsetse-fly, the areas in which "horse-sickness" prevails are often disconnected and alternate with regions in which a horse may be kept without any difficulty and even to advantage. For instance, whereas at Sierra Leone it is almost impossible to keep horses for any length of time, they flourish on the Gambia. Lagos is well suited to them, and yet parts of the Oil Rivers, with an absolutely similar climate, conditions of soil, and vegetation, are actually deadly to the horse. In one district of the Gold Coast they can be kept, and in another part it is impossible to maintain them long alive. On the east coast, it may be observed that they flourish at Zanzibar, and yet do not succeed at Mombasa, or have not done so hitherto. They prosper at the north end of Nyasa, and they die on the south coast of that lake. In Angola, horses thrive to such an extent in the vicinity of Loanda that there is, or was at the time of my last visit there, a regular horse-breeding establishment on the north side of the city, near the River Bengo, while on the neighbouring River Kwanza horses rapidly pined away with "horse-sickness." At Mossamedes, lower down on the coast, they succeed remarkably well, and continue to find the country suitable for a distance of a hundred miles inland; but no sooner are they taken up the Shela Mountains to the Mpata and Wila plateaux beyond than they sooner or later succumb to this strange malady.

This disease appears to be coincident in the commencement of its attacks with the beginning of the rainy season, and seems, as far as the horse is concerned, to be in some way connected with the unusual moisture of the atmosphere which prevails at this period, and at the same time to be caused or aggravated by the eating of excessive quantities of green food. Although it generally attacks the horse and, to a lesser extent, those wild species of horse which we call zebras, cattle, sheep, and antelopes are also liable to its attacks, but with those ruminants it does not appear to have such a fatal or widespread effect as on the horse tribe, and especially on the domestic horse. All horses, however, who are attacked with it do not die; some recover, and those who have passed through the ordeal successfully are termed "salted" horses, and are no longer liable to the attacks of the disease. This is the reason a salted horse is so much more costly in South Africa than a horse who has not had the "sickness" and lived through it. I believe that it is generally considered that by breeding from a "salted" stud you gradually obtain a race of horses less and less subject to this disease. The symptoms of the malady appear to vary somewhat according to the district, but they generally include a gradual emaciation of the animal and, as he grows weaker, less and less disposition to work or eat ; *hæmaturia ;* and, in the latter stages, foaming at the mouth and at the nostrils. If by any chance the flesh of cattle, sheep, antelopes, or horses which have died from this disease is eaten by man, it is liable to cause a malignant carbuncle in those who have partaken of it, which is frequently fatal.   Livingstone states that the *virus* in the flesh of the diseased animal is not destroyed either by boiling or roasting.

These were the chief obstacles to a colonisation of Central Africa by white men in the days when Livingstone first beckoned to the lands beyond the Zambezi—fever, tsetse-fly, and "horse-sickness." Surely we may hope that no one of these obstacles is permanently insurmountable! The dangers of fever begin to diminish—as they have diminished in India—with comfortable houses, good food, hard work, and pleasant society. The tsetse-fly disappears before the settlements of man and the diminution or suppression of large herds of wild beasts; "horse-sickness" is gradually wearing itself out as salted horses increase in number and perpetuate their greater powers of resistance to the disease. Other difficulties may arise to prevent the white settlement of South-Central Africa, but I do not think they will be any of these three in persistence which hampered the immediate fulfilment of Livingstone's aspirations.

CHAPTER XI.

ARRIVED for the second time at Linyanti, Livingstone found that Sekeletu, the son of Sebituane, had been elected king in his father's stead.

Sebituane himself before his death had appointed his daughter Mamotshisane to be his successor in the chieftainship; but she, having no taste for rule, transferred her powers to her brother Sekeletu, who at that time was a young man of eighteen years of age. But another and an elder brother, Mpepe, claimed the throne, and got up a revolution just about the time of Livingstone's arrival, in which he invoked the assistance of the "Mambari" (the half-caste Portuguese slave-traders) who had arrived from the west coast. The Mambari espoused Mpepe's cause, on the consideration that, if the weight of their intervention turned the scale in his favour and enabled him to depose Sekeletu, he was to reward them with a large number of slaves. However, Mpepe's rising was put down almost without a struggle. He asked for a conference with Sekeletu, intending to suddenly assassinate him as they sat together, and then his followers, who had brought their weapons with them into the hut where the meeting took place, were to rise at this signal and murder all Sekeletu's followers; but Mpepe's plans were frustrated, half accidentally and half intentionally,

144

by Livingstone, who came to the conference and placed himself between Mpepe and Sekeletu. Consequently, Mpepe, fearing to injure the white man, abstained from carrying out his intention, and did not attack Sekeletu; but the plot being revealed to the king that night, he sent one of his captains to take his half-brother by surprise and kill him. The brother, who seems to have been a very unsuspicious personage himself, considering the tenuity of his relations with Sekeletu, received the messenger unarmed, and was suddenly overpowered, bound, led out into the wilderness, and killed. This nipped the revolution in the bud, and Sekeletu reigned afterwards as undisputed king over the Barotse until his death in 1864; after which the usual anarchy ensued which supervenes in all African empires after every two or three reigns, and which in this case resulted in the break-up of the Makololo power, the return of many of the Makololo to Lake Ngami, and the revival of the indigenous Barotse as a ruling race.[1] But on the

---

[1] As far as one can piece it together from the scattered and often contradictory statements of travellers, this has been the history of the Barotse country during the present century. The valley of the Upper Zambezi ninety years ago was in the possession of the Barotse people, who formerly called themselves Balui or Baloi, and also Baloiana, which is the diminutive form of the original name Balui, and expresses the meaning that that portion of them which afterwards occupied the valley of the Upper Zambezi was a minor tribe of the Balui race, which still inhabits the region bordering on the Lunda country, in the land which is the watershed of the Zambezi and the Congo. The Balui were closely related to the tribes of the south-western part of the Congo Basin. They had gradually descended the Upper Zambezi until they approached its confluence with the Tshobe, and thus came into contact with the Ba-toka, who in language belong more to what may be called the Zulu-Kaffir stock. The Baloi having fallen out among themselves, a part of them called in the intervention of Sebituane, the powerful Makololo chieftain who had emigrated from the Basuto country and had established himself near the Zam-

K

occasion of Livingstone's second visit to the Zambezi there was no sign of the approaching breaking-up of this Makololo empire, the influence of which extended northwards to near the sources of the Zambezi.

Livingstone's first ostensible object was to ascend the Liambai until he could get out of the swampy district and find some spot favourable for the settlement of an European missionary. He accordingly journeyed with Sekeletu and about a hundred and sixty attendants up the Zambezi (or the "Liambai," as the river is usually called in that district) as far as the confluence of the Kabompo and the Liba.[1] But in all this journey he found the tsetse-fly prevailing in the districts along

bezi. Sebituane came and conquered the Baloiana or Little Baloi, and established the Makololo along the valley of the Upper Zambezi. For some reason or other, the Makololo called the Baloi the "Barotse," which name has stuck to them ever since. The few hundred Makololo, who were, of course, simply Basuto from Basutoland, had such a powerful influence over the Baloi that they gradually imposed on them the So-suto language, which is a dialect of the Se-tshuana group, and this tongue still maintains its sway among the Barotse, although the political influence of the Makololo has passed away. After the death of Sekeletu, the last of the Makololo kings, in 1864, a period of internecine war ensued, and resulted in the rising of the Barotse and the downfall of the Makololo power. Nearly all the Makololo men were massacred, but the women were spared and mated with the victorious Barotse. The Barotse chiefs, however, quarrelled a good deal among themselves after reconquering their country from the Makololo. The Barotse had next to deal with the Ba-toka of the Central Zambezi, and then with the Ba-shukulumbwe, both of which tribes they reduced to a kind of vassalage, and thus created the powerful and extensive Barotse empire of to-day, which occupies nearly all the country between the Upper and Central Zambezi and the Iramba and Mushinga Mountains. There were many quarrels, however, among the Barotse chieftains, and eventually the throne was seized, and has since been held by the present king, Liwanika, who originally came from the country near the junction of the Kabompo and the Liba. The present Barotse capital and royal residence is Lialui.

[1] Liba is the name given to the extreme Upper Zambezi.

the banks of the river, and from the apparent unhealthiness of the country, he concluded that it was not yet
suitable for the establishment of colonies of Makololo on
the upper banks of the Zambezi which would serve as
the bases for the foundation of European missionary
settlements. So, wanting an excuse for the exploring
mania which was in him, and which he was not able to
admit to himself—and indeed did not consciously recog-
nise as the true motive for his divagations—he recurred
to his alternative plan of opening up communications
with the west coast of Africa, so that there might be a
nearer way to the sea over Northern Betshuanaland
than—what was in those days—the long, weary journey
over the Kalahari Desert to Cape Town or Algoa Bay. As
the natives reported the prevalence of the tsetse to the
westwards of Linyanti, he resolved not to attempt a
direct overland journey thence to the west coast, at
Benguela or Mossamedes, but, instead, to reascend the
Liambai to where it was formed by the junction of
two streams, the Kabompo and the Liba.[1] The Liba,
according to native accounts, came from the north-west,
and Livingstone hoped to follow it for a very considerable distance, until he should come within a hundred and
odd miles to the River Kwanza, which he proposed to
descend until he emerged at the coast near São Paulo de
Loanda, the capital of the Portuguese province of Angola.
He accordingly applied to Sekeletu for help in the way
of canoes and men, and held out as the chief inducement

---

[1] It is somewhat difficult to decide which of these two rivers can be
considered as the main Zambezi. Livingstone opined that it was the
Kabompo, which to him appeared broader by a hundred yards than
the Liba, but subsequent travellers have decided in favour of the
Liba, as being the stream with a longer course and greater volume
than the Kabompo.

for this journey the opening up of the country for trade between the Makololo and the Portuguese colonies. A "Pitso"[1] was held to consider the question of agreement with Livingstone's views. The general voice of this assembly was in his favour, and so a band of twenty-seven men was appointed to accompany him to the west, their services being given to Livingstone for nothing. Only two of them were real Makololo, that is to say, of actual Basuto origin; the rest consisted of Barotse, Ba-toka, Bashubia, and Ambonda.

Having committed his waggon and his remaining goods to the care of Sekeletu, Livingstone started on his journey to the west coast with an outfit which was indeed modest compared to that with which most modern African expeditions are provided.[2]   But, as Livingstone

---

[1] A council of deliberation.

[2] The following is the outfit with which Livingstone started from Linyanti to go to Loanda on the 11th November 1853 :—

"I had three muskets for my people, a rifle and double-barrelled smooth-bore for myself ; and, having seen such great abundance of game in my visit to the Liba, I imagined that I could easily supply the wants of my party. Wishing also to avoid the discouragement which would naturally be felt on meeting any obstacles if my companions were obliged to carry heavy loads, I took only a few biscuits, a few pounds of tea and sugar, and about twenty of coffee, which, as the Arabs find, though used without either milk or sugar, is a most refreshing beverage after fatigue or exposure to the sun. We carried one small tin canister, about fifteen inches square, filled with spare shirting, trousers, and shoes, to be used when we reached civilised life, and others in a bag, which were expected to wear out on the way ; another of the same size for medicines ; and a third for books, my stock being a nautical almanac, Thomson's Logarithm Tables, and a Bible. A fourth box contained a magic-lantern, which we found of much use. The sextant and artificial horizon thermometer and compasses were carried apart. My ammunition was distributed in portions through the whole luggage, so that, if an accident should befall one part, we could still have others to fall back upon. Our chief hopes for food were upon that, but in case of failure I took about 20 lbs. of beads, worth forty shillings, which still remained of the stock I brought

remarks and leads us to infer in various passages of his writings, the simplicity of his outfit was not by any means an unmixed good. He points out that, had he been more comfortable on this and other journeys, he would not have suffered so much in health. Indeed, it is no exaggeration to say that, had he from first to last travelled with that reasonable amount of comfort which would provide a bed to sleep on and a rain-tight tent to sleep within, good clothes, good books, a sufficiency of medicines, a little good wine, small luxuries in the way of preserved provisions, and various other items which are now thought necessary in a traveller's equipment, he would have completed his great scheme of geographical discovery, and have been alive now in the enjoyment of honours and competence, as are several of his old companions.[1]

Livingstone left Linyanti for his west coast journey

from Cape Town ; a small gipsy tent, just sufficient to sleep in ; a sheepskin mantle as a blanket, and a horse-rug as a bed. . . . The instruments I carried, though few, were the best of their kind : a sextant, by the famed makers, Troughton & Sims, of Fleet Street ; a chronometer watch, with a stop to the seconds'-hand—an admirable contrivance for enabling a person to take the exact time of observations. . . . Besides these, I had a thermometer by Dollond ; a compass from the Cape Observatory, and a small pocket one in addition ; a good small telescope with a stand capable of being screwed into a tree."—*Missionary Travels and Researches*, pp. 230, 231.

[1] Although Livingstone, from want of means, hurry, and latterly a somewhat listless inattention, did not travel provided with a good many articles of comfort which would have materially aided him in maintaining his health, he was very far from recommending a shabby and careless method of equipment and personal appearance. He always endeavoured to be both neat and clean, and to maintain a distinctly European mode of life. He says, with reference to a slipshod, dirty appearance which travellers of common mind and vulgar dispositions are liable to descend to, that "it is questionable if this descent to barbarous ways does not lower the man in the eyes of the savages."

on the 11th November 1853. He first descended the
Tshobe, and then turned round and ascended the Liambai
or main Zambezi. He travelled, of course, in canoes,
and suffered terribly from fever on this journey. Indeed,
the whole Barotse Valley of the Upper Zambezi seems
to be a peculiarly unhealthy district, judging from the
accounts of Livingstone, Arnot, and Coillard. The River
Zambezi, between the confluence of the Tshobe and the
junction of the Kabompo and Liba, that portion of the
river, in fact, which goes by the name of Liambai, is
not continuously navigable, even for canoes, between the
Tshobe and Kabompo. The rapids of Katema-Mololo,
of Bombwe, of Kale, and of the Falls of Gonye, are all of
them quite impassable in the dry season, and the canoes
have to be taken out of the water and carried overland
round these cataracts; but it would seem as though,
when the river rises in the rainy season, all these rapids
could be passed in canoes, with the exception of the Falls
of Gonye, which are at least thirty feet in their descent.
In the narrow gorge below Gonye the river rises sixty
feet above the low-water level when in flood.

Without incident of note, save the charming observations on natural history with which Livingstone's
narrative of this journey is sprinkled, and which will
be noticed in my general review of the Upper Zambezi
region, Livingstone's party reached Libonta, the last
town of the Makololo kingdom going towards the north
(which was situated a short distance beyond the present
capital—Lialui). Here they had to remain collecting
fat and butter, to be afterwards given as presents to the
Ba-londa chiefs of the country beyond. While waiting
at Libonta he writes in his Journal a little description
of the manner in which his camp is organised while

travelling; and as this was the mode he frequently followed in nearly all his journeys, and, with certain extensions and amplifications, is almost exactly the method which most well-advised African travellers adopt when circumstances permit, it merits being described at length in Livingstone's own words :—" As soon as we land, some of the men cut a little grass for my bed, while Mashauana plants the poles of the little tent. These are used by day for carrying burdens, for the Barotse fashion is exactly like that of the natives of India, only the burden is fastened near the ends of the pole, and not suspended by long cords. The bed is made, and boxes ranged on each side of it, and then the tent pitched over all. Four or five feet in front of my tent is placed the principal or 'kotla' fire, the wood for which must be collected by the man who occupies the post of herald, and takes as his perquisite the heads of all the oxen slaughtered, and of all the game too. Each person knows the station he is to occupy, in reference to the post of honour at the fire in front of the door of the tent. The two Makololo occupy my right and left, both in eating and sleeping, as long as the journey lasts. But Mashauana, my head boatman, makes his bed at the door of the tent as soon as I retire. The rest, divided into small companies according to their tribes, make sheds all round the fire, leaving a horseshoe-shaped space in front, sufficient for the cattle to stand in. The fire gives confidence to the oxen, so the men are always careful to keep them in sight of it. The sheds are formed by planting two stout forked poles in an inclined direction, and placing another over these in a horizontal position. A number of branches are then stuck in the ground in the direction to which the poles are inclined,

the twigs drawn down to the horizontal pole and tied
with strips of bark. Long grass is then laid over the
branches in sufficient quantity to draw off the rain, and
we have sheds open to the fire in front, but secure from
beasts behind. In less than an hour we were usually all
under cover."

From Libonta they journeyed on to the confluence of
the Liba and the Kabompo, through a country that was
radiant with the advent of spring, and swarming with
game to a degree never before witnessed by Livingstone,
who writes in ecstasy of the enormous numbers of mammals and birds which he saw on this part of his journey.
He ascended the Liba for some distance, meeting with
no natural hindrance to its navigation; but in passing
through the Lunda country he had some difficulty in
averting a hostile reception, because the Makololo had
recently been raiding in those countries, and naturally,
therefore, the Ba-lunda people were not disposed to receive Livingstone's canoe-men as friends. Nevertheless,
with his usual tact and patience he explained away all
their apprehensions and won their friendship. Most
of the chiefs he found to be chieftainesses, for in
this country women are held in higher estimation
than is usual in Africa, and frequently ruled as queens
or great ladies. A prominent personage in this land
was the queen Nyamoana, who dwelt at about the
limit of navigation on the Liba. This lady took a
great interest in Livingstone's journey, and in his desire
to open up a direct trade between the west coast and
the Barotse country. She objected, however, to his
continuing his water-journey up the Liba any farther,
on the plea that there were impassable cataracts farther
on, and that the Ba-luvale tribe of the Lunda people who

dwelt by the banks of the Upper Liba would certainly kill his Makololo boatmen, unless an explanation of his coming had been made to the supreme chief of the country, whose name appears to have been either Kabompo or Shinte, but who was usually called by the latter appellation. Accordingly, Queen Nyamoana despatched Livingstone on the back of a riding-ox overland to Shinte's capital, and sent her daughter Manenko with him as guide and protectress. Manenko was a fine, Amazon type of woman, quite a princess-royal, with a commanding manner, and a very subservient husband whom she treated quite as her chattel. She started on the march with her husband, her drummer, and a suite of ladies and gentlemen, and walked at the head of the caravan herself, in the slightest possible clothing, and at such a pace that few of the men could keep up with her.

On the road to Shinte's town, Livingstone for the first time entered the true tropical forest which is so characteristic of the greater part of the Congo Basin and of Western Equatorial Africa, and which, from Livingstone's account, would appear to extend over a portion of the extreme Upper Zambezi Valley. He found considerable pleasure, in spite of incessantly rainy weather, in this new scenery. The deep gloom of the dense forest contrasted strongly with his remembrance of the shadeless glare of Betshuanaland. Though drenched day by day—for he was travelling during the rainy season—it was long before he could bring himself to complain of the profusion of water which created such a splendid *flora*.

He arrived at the town of Shinte[1] on the 16th January 1854, and found himself emphatically in West

---

[1] Latitude 12° 37′ 35″ S., longitude 22° 47′ E.

Central Africa, for the town was embowered in magnificent banana groves, shaded with huge trees, with straight
streets and rectangular houses.[1] Two mulatto Portuguese traders were here, together with a large number
of Mambari (as the natives of Bihe and the interior
of West Africa call the black Portuguesised natives of
Angola). The Portuguese, of course, had come here to
buy slaves, and as it was the first time Livingstone's
Makololo had seen a slave-gang in chains, they affected
to be very shocked at such treatment.

Shinte gave Livingstone a magnificent reception in
the true West African style. The place of audience was
about a hundred yards square, and was shaded by two
enormous trees, under one of which sat the chief, Shinte,
on a sort of throne covered with a leopard-skin. He
had on a checked jacket and a kilt of scarlet baize edged
with green ; many strings of large beads hung from his
neck, and his limbs were covered with iron and copper
armlets and bracelets ; on his head he wore a helmet
made of beads woven neatly together, and crowned with
a great bunch of feathers from a spur-winged goose.
After the various companies of soldiers had performed
war-dances, and had saluted their chief by companies,
the spokesman of Livingstone's party recited in a loud
voice the objects of the expedition. Behind Shinte sat
about a hundred of his wives, clothed in a profusion of
red cloth (his chief wife, Odena, was a Matabele-Zulu).
During the intervals between the speeches these ladies
broke forth into a sort of plaintive ditty in praise of the
orator, of Shinte, and of themselves. The clamour was

---

[1] The native house along the Zambezi, in all South-West, South, and
East Africa, besides North-Central Africa and much of the west coast,
is round. The style of hut which prevails in the Congo Basin and
West Equatorial Africa is usually rectangular and oblong.

increased by a party of musicians who went round the square drumming on the typical West African drum,[1] or else playing on another West African instrument, the " marimba." [2] Altogether about 1300 people were present, including 300 soldiers ; and nine orators spoke before the chief.

Shinte was apparently a man of fifty-five years of age, of frank and open countenance, and about the middle height. Curiously enough, like the greater part of the Congo Basin, which his country (though on the Zambezi watershed) so closely resembles, the land of Lobale or Luvale, in which Shinte dwelt, possessed apparently no domestic cattle, and the chief consequently asked Livingstone for an ox. The traveller somewhat re-luctantly presented one to him, suggesting at the same time that he might open a trade in cows with the Makololo.[3] This gift of Livingstone's, however, very

[1] These drums are made of the hollowed trunk of a tree, and are four to six feet in length. The ends are covered with tightly-stretched skin, which is either the skin of an antelope, a goat, or a serpent (in the more cannibal countries it is not infrequently man's skin). There is a small hole in the side which Livingstone speaks of as being covered by spider's web, but 1 have not noticed this kind of covering myself. The instrument is usually beaten with the hands, but some-times a drumstick is used.

[2] " The ' marimba' consists of two bars of wood placed side by side, here quite straight, but farther north, bent round so as to resemble half the tire of a carriage-wheel ; across these are placed about fifteen wooden keys, each of which is two or three inches broad, and fifteen or eighteen inches long ; their thickness is regulated according to the deepness of the note required : each of the keys has a calabash beneath it ; from the upper part of each a portion is cut off to enable them to embrace the bars, and from hollow sounding-boards to the keys, which also are of different sizes, according to the note required ; and little drumsticks elicit the music. Rapidity of execution seems much admired among them, and the music is pleasant to the ear."
—LIVINGSTONE.

[3] Which hint was afterwards taken.

much angered the Lady Manenko (who, it appeared, was
Shinte's niece). She complained "that the white man
belonged to her; she had brought him here, and therefore the ox was hers, not Shinte's." She therefore
ordered her men to take it away from Shinte, got it
slaughtered, and presented her uncle with one leg only.
He did not, however, seem at all annoyed at her impetuous behaviour.

Livingstone had brought with him a magic-lantern
which exhibited Scriptural slides, and the exhibition of
these pictures was received by the Ba-lunda with the
utmost delight and astonishment. The use of the magic-
lantern, in fact, is one of the most potent aids to friendship with savages that I know of. There are very few
missionary stations in Africa which are without it.

This part of the Lunda [1] country was found by Livingstone to be much given up to drunkenness, and its
inebriety was produced solely by enormous quantities of
what Livingstone calls "mead," and which *may* have
been made from honey (which is very abundant in that
land), but which I should myself think was the fermented sap of palms, as that is the usual native in-
toxicating drink over all West Central Africa. [2]

[1] Livingstone writes this word sometimes *Londa* and sometimes
Lunda. The latter I believe to be the most usual pronunciation.
There is the same hesitancy between *Luvale* and *Lobale*, the fact being
that native pronunciation often fails to discriminate distinctly between
o and *u* and *b* and *v*.

[2] The drunkenness in Shinte's territory, where, at the time of
Livingstone's visit, people had nothing to get drunk on but the
intoxicants which they themselves made out of the products of their
country, may be compared with the remarkable inebriety which
prevails in parts of Nyasaland, where the people are equally confined
to the use of such fermented liquors as they can make for themselves,
and are not "corrupted" by the introduction of European forms of
alcohol.

The heavy rains and the drunkenness of the people
delayed Livingstone for ten days in Shinte's town, but
on the 26th January he got away, and travelled in a
northerly direction more or less parallel with the course
of the Liba, the main stream of which he crossed near
its confluence with the Lukalueje affluent, which, together
with a number of little tributary streams, flows through
the great Luvale flat, and renders it a vast sodden marsh
for more than half the year.   In the middle of this
swampy prairie is the little Lake Dilolo, about twenty-
eight miles in extent in the rainy season.   It was at
one time thought that this lake gave rise, not only to
the affluents of the Zambezi, but also to streamlets
flowing north into the Congo Basin ; this has since been
shown to be incorrect.   These vast marshy plains of
Luvale apparently have a tilt both to the north and
south, and therefore feed both the Zambezi and the
Congo systems.   In spite of this, the Luvale flats seem
to be a great sponge from which the water is never
properly drained, but merely sinks a little below the
surface, and there keeps the earth perpetually sour.
For this reason but little forest grows thereon, though
here and there a few trees are seen surrounded by
hillocks of elevated soil which dot the surface of the
marsh.

Near the shores of Lake Dilolo was the straggling
village of Katema,[1] who was then the great chief of the
Luvale country.   Here Livingstone had to stay for a
few days.   He was well treated, but found that Katema
paid but little heed to religious instruction, distinctly
showing his boredom when attempts were made to
describe Christianity.   He was, however, very suscep-

[1] His town has since been moved to the north side of the lake:

tible to compliments, and was much pleased at being congratulated on possessing a herd of thirty cattle. Domestic oxen were apparently very rare in these countries, and the people were quite unused to utilising them for milk or for labour. Katema's cattle, in fact, were so wild that when he wished to kill one he had to shoot it as though it were a buffalo. Katema was evidently an immigrant from the north, and not a native of the Luvale country.

Obtaining guides from this man, Livingstone pursued his course north-westwards across the Kifumaji and Dilolo flats to the banks of the Kasai or Kasabi, one of the great affluents of the Congo. He discovered, somewhat to his surprise, that this almost level swampy plain which he had crossed over was the watershed between the Congo and the Zambezi, and having reached its northern limits, he found that the wet tableland in its descent towards the Kasai was scored with deep valleys, strangely contrasting with the monotonous levels of the elevated plain above. In all directions, as he descended from this raised-up marsh, which had a mean level of nearly 5000 feet, he saw water oozing or spurting out from the stream-furrowed soil.

On arriving at the banks of the Kasai, Livingstone describes this stream as being a most beautiful river, and therefore, like a Scotchman, at once compared it with the Clyde. Where he struck it (about 220 miles from its source) it had a width of over a hundred yards, and was winding slowly from side to side in a beautiful green glen, flowing towards the north-east. The slopes of its valley were finely wooded, but in some places they receded to a little distance from the banks, and the river flowed through rich grassy meadows. The inhabitants dwelling along the Kasai told Livingstone that one might sail down this stream for months and yet turn back without seeing the end of it—a perfectly truthful piece of information when one looks at the since-discovered course of the Kasai as represented on the latest maps. This river is to the main Congo on the south what the great Mubangi-Welle is on the north.

The subjects of the chief Kagenke, who ruled on this portion of the Kasai, were fairly friendly, but exceedingly mean about selling food; and Katenke, another chief, was not much more hospitable. Still, no serious obstacles were put in the way of Livingstone's party. They crossed the Kasai, and directing their course due west, entered the extensive country of Kioko.[1] On the borders of this land a little incident occurred in the crossing of a flooded stream which well illustrates the affectionate relations which had sprung up between Livingstone and his Makololo. Livingstone attempted to cross the river by swimming his ox over and laying held of its tail, but the ox had already dashed into the deepest part of the stream before he could dismount. He was therefore obliged to throw himself off the creature's back and swim over to the opposite bank by himself. His Makololo were dreadfully alarmed when they saw him parted from the ox, and about twenty of them made a simultaneous rush into the water to his rescue, and helped him out of his difficulty very speedily. Great was the pleasure they expressed when they found he could swim like themselves, without being obliged to hold on to the

---

[1] The original name of this land seems to have been Kiboko or Kibokwe. Livingstone calls it Tshibokwe. On the other hand, Cameron and many of the Portuguese write the word Kioko (Quioco), which seems to be the more widespread and more modern form of the name.

tail of the ox. After this they all laughed at the idea of being frightened by rivers, and said, "We can all swim ; who carried the white man across the river but himself ?"

The country of Kioko seemed to Livingstone and his men so perfectly adapted for the breeding of cattle, and yet so devoid of the domestic ox in any numbers (though such herds as were possessed by the big chiefs were in a flourishing condition), that he formed the belief that the general scarcity of oxen throughout these lands which lie along the southern basin of the Congo arose from the former prevalence of the tsetse-fly, but that since the inhabitants had received guns and powder from the Portuguese they had resolutely set to work to slaughter and exterminate the big game, and that with the disappearance of the large wild herbivora the tsetse-fly had died out, leaving the land open to the introduction of cattle.

The Va-kioko or Va-tshibokwe were a somewhat turbulent, ill-conditioned people, who endeavoured to put many obstacles in Livingstone's way, and seized every pretext for robbing him, fining him, or opposing his progress through their country. By dint of much patience and a few judicious payments, and a quiet, unaggressive obstinacy in pushing on, Livingstone passed through their country without any breach of the peace. During this part of the journey he suffered incessantly from attacks of fever, but really one cannot wonder at his ill-health when it is considered what very little care he took of himself along this portion of his route. He had to cross streams or rivers daily, and on these occasions was always wetted up to his thighs, if not up to his neck. It never seems to have occurred to him to change and dry his clothes; he either attempted to dry himself by walking on through the blazing sun, or he did not even make that attempt, but sat down or remained stationary in his wet clothes whenever he had occasion to wait for his men or to stop for any purpose on the line of march. Is it surprising under these conditions that he was attacked with fever? Is it not rather surprising that he lived through such experiences at all?

The difficulties of the Kioko country began to have a bad effect on the *morale* of Livingstone's expedition, and but a few days after the loving devotion evinced by his men in rushing into the river to save him from the least chance of being drowned, some of these same people began to grumble at the small amount of beads distributed for the purchase of food; and although he explained this away and remonstrated with the grumblers, their demeanour waxed in noisiness and impudence, until it amounted to open disregard of his orders, which · was the more serious because he was very ill with fever. Finding that kind words and patient arguments were of no use, he resolved to try sterner measures, which he describes in the following language: "Knowing that discipline would be at an end if this mutiny were not quelled, and that our lives depended on vigorously upholding authority, I seized a double-barrelled pistol and darted forth from the domicile, looking, I suppose, so savage as to put them to a precipitate flight. As some remained within hearing, I told them that I must maintain discipline, though at the expense of some of their limbs; so long as we travelled together they must remember that I was master, and not they. There being but little room to doubt my determination, they

L

immediately became very obedient, and never afterwards
gave me any trouble, or imagined that they had any
right to my property."

I mention this little incident to show that—collo-
quially speaking—Livingstone was no fool. No one had
a greater sympathy or a more indulgent regard for the
black people than he, and even he knew that they are
only grown-up children, that they must be made to submit to a certain amount of direction for their ultimate
good and for the eventual benefit of their country ; and
when this direction is not accepted by them after verbal
arguments, as a last resort force must be used to compel
them to do as they are told. Livingstone never forgot
that we stand to the negro *in loco parentis*. A wise
father endeavours to persuade his son to follow in that
line of conduct which, in the opinion of the father and
according to the father's lights, is the best calculated to
cause his son to succeed in the world; but when verbal
persuasion is of no use and the naughty child absolutely
refuses to obey, then even the kindest of fathers is compelled to resort to a gentle smacking as a final argument.
Later on we shall see that in his last journeys many of
Livingstone's disasters came from his want of firmness
with his men ; but in his first great expeditions in Africa
he just hit upon the happy medium of conduct towards
his black followers. He was kind, considerate, and even
affectionate towards them, but he never allowed them to
forget that he was the master, and that his will must be
implicitly obeyed, and the result was the quite extraordinary success of his journey across Africa from the
Zambezi to Loanda, and from Loanda to Quilimane.

On leaving the country of the Kioko and entering the
valley of the Kwango, Livingstone quitted the region

of the great Congo forest through which he had been travelling, and re-entered that typical African park-land so characteristic of the greater portion of the continent within the tropics. Before he reached the banks of the Kwango, which was in those days and is still—practically —the eastern boundary of Portuguese West Africa, he suffered much from the hostility of the Ba-shinje people, who very nearly provoked his party to a breach of the peace. However, in spite of the orders of the Ba-shinje to return, Livingstone steadily kept on his way; and being aided by a continuous downpour of rain, which damped the fighting spirit of his persecutors, he managed to reach the banks of the Kwango without being attacked. Where he crossed it, the Kwango was a fine river of 150 yards in width and very deep. It was impossible to traverse it without canoes, and here another difficulty arose, because the natives refused to ferry him over to the western bank unless he gave one of his followers as a slave. Just when he was almost in a state of despair with worry and fever, a young half-caste Portuguese sergeant of militia, named Cypriano de Abreu, made his appearance, and advised Livingstone and his people to move down to the shore of the river, so as to be more out of the reach of attacks from the disagreeable natives. This advice they took, and only just in time, because as soon as they moved away the natives opened fire on them with their guns, hoping by this display of force to cause a rout of the expedition; but, as Livingstone and his party walked on quietly without hurry, the firing ceased, and, through the persuasion of Cypriano, the natives in charge of the ferry were induced to transport the whole party across to the Portuguese bank, which was reached without further difficulty.

On the other side they found a little garrison of
Portuguese militia (mulattoes), who received Livingstone
with kindness and respect. As to their commander,
Cypriano, he seems to have been a friend in need,
and to have exhibited that extraordinarily kind-hearted
hospitality which is a marked characteristic of the
Portuguese.

For the first time after leaving Koloben, Livingstone
experienced something like civilisation at this little
Portuguese settlement on the left bank of the River
Kwango. The good food, comfort, and well-ordered,
decent behaviour of the settlement did much to restore
him to health. He found that all the members of this
little garrison could read and write with ease, and that
they possessed in their little library Encyclopædias, medical works, dictionaries, and religious books. This is not
a bad certificate for the state of Portuguese rule in West
Central Africa in the year 1854.

Four or five days' journey beyond the Kwango brought
Livingstone to the important trading settlement at Kasanji, which was then a regular Portuguese town, but
which has since had many fluctuations of prosperity.[1]
At Kasanji the kindness and hospitality he received
from the Portuguese was such as to move him to expressions of the deepest gratitude.[2] "May God remember
them," he writes, " in their day of need ! "

[1] At the time of my own journeys in Angola, in 1882, Kasanji had
been abandoned by the Portuguese garrison, and the farthest inland
station occupied by the Portuguese in this direction was Malanje. I
believe, however, that Kasanji has now been reoccupied.

[2] In another part of his Journal he says : " The universal hospitality
of the Portuguese was most gratifying, as it was most unexpected.
And even now, as I copy my Journal, I remember it all with a glow
of gratitude."

Under the guidance of a black Portuguese soldier, and with much general assistance rendered by the Portuguese authorities at Kasanji and by others on the way, he reached the River Kwango, and thence passed on to Ambaka and Golungo Alto, traversing some of the most beautiful scenery in Africa and a thickly-populated, well-cultivated country. He received everywhere an unvarying kindness and hospitality from the Portuguese, but was in a frightfully debilitated state from the constant attacks of fever, which were the results of his past hardships. However, a few days' rest with Lieutenant Antonio Canto e Castro,[1] the commandant of Golungo Alto, and the careful treatment he received from his kind host, enabled him to regain much of his strength. He could look with pleasure on the luxuriant scenery around him. "We were quite shut in among green hills, many of which were cultivated up to their tops with manioc, coffee, cotton, ground-nuts, bananas, pine-apples, guavas, papaus, custard-apples, pitangas, and jambos, fruits brought from South America by the former missionaries. The high hills all round, with oil-palms on many points, made this spot appear more like the Bay of Rio de Janeiro in miniature than any scene I ever saw; and all who have seen that confess it to be unequalled in the world beside. The fertility evident in every spot of this district is quite wonderful to behold."

Several times, on passing through Angola, the teasing natives had frightened Livingstone's Makololo by telling them that their leader was only taking them to the coast to fatten them and sell them to the white men to be

---

[1] "A young gentleman whose subsequent conduct will make me remember him with affection."—LIVINGSTONE.

eaten. The silly fellows, in spite of their filial attachment to Livingstone and their occasional bursts of passionate affection for him, actually attached credence to
these jesting remarks, and on one or two occasions were
very nearly deserting. Such are the fluctuations of the
negro's childish disposition. One must always guard
oneself from disappointment in expecting too much
consistency from these poor savages. They will live
with a good master for two or three years, and become
apparently so much attached to him that he vaguely
pictures to himself their remaining with him till a good
old age and being pensioned off, when one day, on the
slightest pretext, or no pretext whatever, they will leave
him for good and for all, and show no sign afterwards
of regret or gratitude. However, Livingstone's patience
and tact allayed their suspicions, and although they
approached the coast with much doubting and dread,
they followed their leader without serious demur.
When, after leaving Golungo Alto, they came to the
verge of the elevated plains behind Loanda and first
beheld the sea, they looked upon the boundless ocean
with awe. Afterwards, on describing their feelings,
they remarked that "we marched along with our
Father, believing that what the ancients had always
told us was true, that the world has no end, but all at
once the world said to us, 'I am finished; there is no
more of me.' "

As Livingstone himself came within sight of Loanda
he was depressed in spirits, and filled with apprehension
lest his welcome to civilisation should be a cold one. He
had understood that in a population of 12,000 souls
there was but one English gentleman. He felt anxious
to know whether this British representative was of a

kindly nature or not, as it was a matter of the greatest importance to him that he should meet with a kindly, helpful reception in his worn-out, destitute condition.

Livingstone reached São Paulo de Loanda, the capital of the Portuguese possessions in West Africa, on the last day of May 1854. All doubts as to the manner in which he would be received by the one Englishman residing in that place (who was Mr. Gabriel, H.M. Commissioner for the Suppression of the Slave-Trade, and Consul for Angola) were soon set at rest. "When I entered his porch," he writes, "I was delighted to see a number of flowers cultivated carefully, and inferred from this circumstance that he was—what I soon discovered him to be—a real, whole-hearted Englishman. Seeing me ill, he benevolently offered me his bed. Never again shall I forget the luxuriant pleasure I enjoyed in feeling myself again on a good English couch, after six months' sleeping on the ground. I was soon asleep; and Mr. Gabriel, coming in almost immediately, rejoiced at the soundness of my repose."

CHAPTER XII.

FROM LOANDA TO QUILIMANE—ACROSS AFRICA.

Soon after Livingstone arrived at Loanda he was the recipient of marked courtesies from the leading Portuguese of that place, and especially from the Bishop of Angola,[1] who was at the time the acting Governor-General. Some of our ships of war, notably the *Pluto* and the *Philomel*, called at Loanda during Livingstone's stay, and their commanders offered him a passage to St. Helena, whence he could return easily to England; but, tempting as the offer was, he would not accept it, because, in the first place, he felt bound to escort his Makololo back to their country; and, second, finding the impracticability of the existing route between the

---

[1] Livingstone says of this prelate: "His whole conversation and conduct showed him to be a n an of great benevolence and kindness of heart. Alluding to my being a Protestant, he stated that he was a Catholic from conviction; and though sorry to see others, like myself, following another path, he entertained no uncharitable feelings, nor would he ever sanction persecuting measures. He compared the various sects of Christians, on their way to heaven, to a number of individuals choosing to pass down the different streets of Loanda to one of the churches—all would arrive at the same point at last. His great influence both in the city and the country is universally acknowledged: he was promoting the establishment of schools, which, though formed more on the monastic principles than Protestants might approve, will no doubt be a blessing. He was likewise successfully attempting to abolish the non-marriage custom of the country; and several marriages had taken place in Loanda among those who, but for his teaching, would have been content with concubinage."

Zambezi and the west coast as an outlet for the Makololo country, he had determined to follow the Zambezi down to the sea in order to ascertain if an easier road to the sea-coast lay in that direction. Accordingly he remained, staying on at Loanda till the 20th September (he had reached that place about the 1st June), as his departure for the interior was repeatedly delayed by attacks of dysentery, which reduced him to a state of prostration. During his stay in this place, however, his Makololo became profitably acquainted with the outer world and the manners, customs, and dignities of the white men. They were shown over our ships-of-war and allowed to fire cannons, they were taken to see the services in the Cathedral,[1] they were employed at unloading ships and in cutting firewood, and these latter occupations brought them in respectable earnings, which they invested in articles of trade to take back to their own country.

When Livingstone finally quitted Loanda to return to the Zambezi, the acting Governor-General (the Bishop of Angola already referred to) directed that he should be furnished with a handsome present for Sekeletu, and he was also provided by the Portuguese authorities with letters of recommendation to the Portuguese officials in Eastern Africa. The same Government further supplied him with carriers, and sent forward orders to all the com-

---

[1] "The gorgeous ritual of the Roman Church did not arouse in them very reverent feelings. The frequent genuflections, changing of positions, burning of incense with the priests' backs to the people, the laughing, talking, and manifest irreverence of the singers, &c.," says Livingstone, "did not convey to the minds of my men the idea of adoration. I overheard them, in talking to each other, remark that they had seen the white men charm their demons; a phrase identical with one they had used on seeing the Ba-londa beat drums before their idols."

mandants of the district through which he was to pass
to render him every assistance in their power. His
friends on board H.M. ship *Philomel* had made him a
good new tent, and he had supplied himself with a large
stock of trade goods, the money of the interior. To
each of his men also was given a new musket and
ammunition. He was accompanied on his way as far
as the River Bengo by his excellent host, Mr. Edmund
Gabriel, H.M. Commissioner and Consul, whose geniality
and goodness to Livingstone and his men created a
lasting impression on their memories.

In connection with the River Bengo, Livingstone
notes an interesting fact which accords with my own
experiences to some extent; namely, that mosquitoes
abound much more in the vicinity of muddy rivers than
by those which have clear water.

From the Bengo, Livingstone struck across to the
Kwanza to visit the important town of Massango.
From there he returned to Golungo Alto. Arrived once
more in this beautiful part of Angola, he visited the
remains of the old Jesuit settlements. Of the work of
the Jesuits in Angola [1] he always speaks with intelligent
approbation.

After leaving Golungo Alto, Livingstone proceeded to
the remarkable district of Pungo Andongo, where he
took up his abode for nearly three months with a Portuguese officer, Colonel Manoel Antonio Pires.

---

[1] The Jesuits did more than any one else to create the strong
Portuguese influence which has spread over Western Africa south of
the Congo. They laid the foundation of much of the civilisation
which still prevails in those regions. In course of time, however, by
a decree of the Marquez de Pombal, they were expelled (in 1760, or
thereabouts) from Angola, as from all the Portuguese possessions
(*vide* Chap. II.).

Pungo Andongo is celebrated for its extraordinary columns of rock, which, in their disposition, may be said to resemble a gigantic Stonehenge.   Each isolated mass of rock is upwards of 300 feet in height from the soil at

PUNGO ANDONGO.

its base, and is composed of a conglomerate of gneiss, clay, shell, mica, sandstone-schists, trap-rock, and porphyry embedded in a matrix of dark red sandstone. These rocks rest on a thick stratum of this same sand-

stone. Livingstone attributes their formation to a current of the sea having flowed through this country, and
believes that the rocks of Pungo Andongo are the fragments of an old sea-coast; but this theory is scarcely
tenable with our larger knowledge of the geology of this
district. The Pungo Andongo rocks, and many similar
fragments of sandstone which we meet with in this part
of Africa reduced to little isolated fingers and columns,
are probably the result of the heavy tropical rains wash-
ing away the softer parts of an old tableland, and leaving
these columns of rock as vestiges of the old plateau,
which, from their harder nature, have not yet been
washed away.

Soon after arriving at the well-ordered establishment
of Colonel Pires, Livingstone received the news of the
total loss, off Madeira, of the mail-steamer *Forerunner*,[1]
in which he had sent home all his despatches and maps
describing his journey from the Zambezi to Loanda. He
therefore set to work with dogged perseverance to write
out the whole thing again from memory as far as possible, aided no doubt by the note-books in his possession.

Leaving Pungo Andongo on the 1st January 1855,
he passed on rapidly westwards through the district of
Malange and over the heights of Tala Mungongo, and
reached once more the town of Kasanji in about seven-
teen days from the time of leaving Pungo Andongo, with

[1] The *Forerunner* was the first steamer which the African
Steamship Company despatched to the west coast of Africa. She
was wrecked off the coast of Madeira. Her loss, however, did not dis-
courage her owners from this enterprise, and the African Steamship
Company, in conjunction with its closely affiliated Association, the
British and African Steamship Company, carries our mails at the present day to all the ports on the west coast of Africa from the Gambia
to Loanda.

no more unpleasant incidents on the way than one or
two attacks from the brownish-red soldier-ants which
are so characteristic of Central Africa. The description
which Livingstone gives of these pests is so truthful,
and these ants form such a feature in the experience of
African explorers, that I venture to append his account
of them in a footnote.[1]

[1] "These ants are frequently met with in numbers like a small army.
At a little distance they appear as a brownish-red band, two or three
inches wide, stretched across the path, all eagerly pressing on in one
direction. If a person happens to tread upon them, they rush up his
legs and bite with surprising vigour. The first time I encountered
this by no means contemptible enemy was near Cassange. My attention being taken up in viewing the distant landscape, I accidentally
stepped upon one of their nests. Not an instant seemed to elapse
before a simultaneous attack was made on various unprotected parts,
up the trousers from below, and on my neck and breast above. The
bites of these furies were like sparks of fire, and there was no retreat.
I jumped about for a second or two, then in desperation tore off all
my clothing, and rubbed and picked them off *seriatim* as quickly as
possible. Ugh! they would make the most lethargic mortal look
alive. Fortunately no one observed this *rencontre*, or word might
have been taken back to the village that I was mad. I was once
assaulted in a similar way when sound asleep at night in my tent, and
it was only by holding my blanket over the fire that I could get rid of
them. It is really astonishing how such small bodies can contain so
large an amount of ill-nature. They not only bite, but twist themselves
round after the mandibles are inserted, to produce laceration and
pain more than would be effected by the single wound. Frequently,
while sitting on my riding-ox, as he happened to tread near a band,
they would rush up his legs to the rider, and soon let him know that
he had disturbed their march. They possess no fear, attacking with
equal ferocity the largest as well as the smallest animals. When
any person has leaped over the band, numbers of them leave the ranks
and rush along the path, seemingly anxious for a fight. They are
very useful in ridding the country of dead animal matter, and when
they visit a human habitation, clear it entirely of the white-ants and
other vermin. They destroy many noxious insects and reptiles. The
severity of their attack is greatly increased by their vast numbers,
and rats, mice, lizards, and even the *Python natalensis*, when in a
state of surfeit from recent feeding, fall victims to their fierce on-
slaught. These ants never make hills like the white-ant. Their nests

While at Kasanji, Livingstone received a packet of newspapers, with news of the Crimean war up to the charge of the Light Brigade. He well describes the tantalising effect of the news breaking off at this juncture, and the thought that he would get no more until he reached the eastern side of the continent.

From Kasanji he was strongly inclined to start for the capital of Mwata Yanvo's country in company with a Portuguese mission which was just starting to visit that important chief, but his Makololo followers did not approve of the idea, and he was not willing to exercise any pressure on them in the matter. Accordingly, he merely journeyed on in company with the Portuguese to the River Kwango, and crossing that stream, passed on without any difficulty through the country of the Bashinje people, who had formerly tried to quarrel with him. But, just as he was about to enter the land of Kioko, the heavy rains which he had to endure daily, and the soddened condition of the soil at the camping-places, brought on a severe attack of rheumatic fever. With this he became so ill during eight days, that he was indifferent to all that was going on around him, and would probably have ended his experience of Africa then and there had it not been for the nursing of Senhor Antonio Narcisso Pascoal, a half-caste Portuguese, who arrived at Livingstone's camp just when he was at his worst, and relieved his acute pain in a very practical manner by utilising the leeches which swarmed in the neighbouring rivulets, and applying them to Livingstone's

are but a short distance beneath the soil, which has the soft appearance of the abodes of ants in England. Occasionally they construct galleries over their path to the cells of the white-ant, in order to secure themselves from the heat of the sun during their marauding expeditions."—*Missionary Travels and Researches.*

neck and loins. After seeing his patient take a turn for the better, Senhor Pascoal had to move on to another village in advance, in order to procure food for his large party. Meanwhile Livingstone lingered in a dreary convalescence at the miserable little village where he had been taken ill. Just as he was about to start to join Pascoal, the Pombeiro,[1] a disagreeable incident occurred, which, however, brought out well the firmness of Livingstone's character in dealing with the natives. The head-man of the village wherein he had been lying sick had begun quarrelling in his camp about a piece of meat, and one of Livingstone's men, losing patience, had struck him on the mouth. Willing to give redress for this hasty act, Livingstone paid five pieces of cloth and a gun to the head-man as compensation for the slap; but no sooner had he done this than the wretched little chieftain became outrageous in his demands, and attempted to raise all the country-side to assist him in attacking and plundering Livingstone's party. Seeing that it was useless to argue any further with this cantankerous personage, Livingstone left the village with his men to join Senhor Pascoal, but soon after he had started he was attacked from behind by a large body of natives, who fired off their guns and knocked the burdens off some of his men's shoulders. Livingstone promptly got off his riding-ox, and in spite of his weak state of health, rushed up to the chief who was the cause of all this trouble, and presented a six-barrelled revolver at his stomach. This demonstration had an immediately pacifying effect, and the chief declared he had only come to speak to Livingstone, and his men protested their amic-

---

[1] Pombeiro is the name applied to the half-caste Portuguese traders who range over the West of Africa.

able intentions, and finally retreated without attempting to renew the attack.

Livingstone soon afterwards joined Senhor Pascoal, and travelled with him through the gloomy forests of Kioko and Southern Lunda as far as the town of Kabango, where he parted company with him, having decided to abandon the idea of proceeding to Mwata Yanvo's capital, and to return as quickly as might be to the Zambezi, in order to resume his direct journey to the east coast. Had he decided otherwise, and accompanied the Pombeiros to Mwata Yanvo's court, the results of Livingstone's explorations might have been altogether different. He would probably have followed the Kasai down to its junction with the Congo, and to a great extent have anticipated Stanley's discoveries. As it was, he collected a considerable amount of information about the Kasai and the rivers which join it, which, in the light and fuller knowledge of to-day, is shown to be singularly correct. Numerous southern affluents of the Congo and some of the big lakes of Central Africa, besides important African tribes whose real existence has only been quite recently ascertained, are mentioned by Livingstone in his *résumé* of the information acquired by him from the Portuguese and Arabs of the geography of the Congo Basin.

Livingstone and his Makololo were received with hospitality and rejoicing by their old friend Katema, near Lake Dilolo, and by Shinte, farther south. Unfortunately, on returning to the Zambezi Valley, although they found themselves once more among friends, they also had re-entered the home of the tsetse fly, and Livingstone's riding-ox, "Sinbad," who had carried him all the way from the Barotse country to Angola and back again, was so bitten by these pests that it fell sick, and eventually died. Everywhere, however, they were greeted with such affection by the Ba-lunda people of the Upper Liba, that it was almost like returning home again. This friendliness, however, had a somewhat demoralising effect over his men, one of whom deserted him in order to settle down under a chief called Masiko.

When the party reached the town of Libonta, and were back again in the Makololo empire, they were received with extravagant demonstrations of joy. The women came forth to meet them, making curious dancing gestures and singing loud " lulliloos." Some carried a mat and stick, in imitation of a spear and shield. Others rushed forward and kissed the hands and cheeks of the different persons of their acquaintance among the party of returned travellers, raising such a dust that it was quite a relief to get away from them to the staider men assembled in decorous council in the "kotla." Livingstone and his men were looked upon as persons risen from the dead, for the most skilful of their diviners had pronounced the whole party to have perished long ago. "The following day," he writes, "we observed as our thanksgiving to God for His goodness in bringing us all back in safety to our friends. My men decked themselves out in their best, and I found that, although their goods were finished, they had managed to save suits of European clothing, which, being white, with their red caps, gave them rather a dashing appearance. They tried to walk like the soldiers they had seen in Loanda, and called themselves my ' braves ' (batlabani). During the service they all sat with their guns over their shoulders, and excited the unbounded admiration of the women and children. I addressed them all on the goodness of God

M

in preserving us from all the dangers of strange tribes and diseases. We had a similar service in the afternoon." The men of Libonta gave Livingstone two fine oxen for slaughter, and the women supplied the expedition abundantly with milk, meal, and butter. These presents were made without thought of any return, as the white men and his followers had expended all their means and demonstrated their inability to make return of presents.

Their continued progress down the Barotse Valley was like a triumph. Every village gave them an ox, and sometimes two. The people felt that, in opening up a possible trade-route with the west coast, Livingstone had worked well in the interests of the Makololo, and they were unstinting in their favours. The very face of the country, too, seemed to rejoice at the wanderers' home-coming. The land, which had hitherto been exhibiting all the signs of the African winter,[1] was just beginning to show the first promise of spring in the new leaf-shoots.

Livingstone remarks with accuracy on the beautiful and strange tints assumed by the young expanding leaves in an African forest. The present writer has generally observed in tropical Africa that much of the very young foliage is red, a kind of brownish-crimson.

---

[1] The winter, or period of rest, is coincident with the dry season, and is much more apparent in those parts of Africa where the year is divided sharply into two seasons, wet and dry. In the basin of the Congo and in Western Equatorial Africa this winter is much less noticeable than in the regions north and south and east, owing to the frequency with which rain falls throughout the year in the first-named districts. Livingstone noticed, when he passed from the densely-forested Lunda country into the watershed of the Zambezi, how markedly wintry was the aspect of the trees, which in those countries where there was a clearly-defined dry season shed their leaves just as do the deciduate trees of the temperate zone.

This tint, as the leaf expands, changes to a most delicate mauve, and from that into a bluish-green, and so
on to the grass-green or olive-green which it will
eventually remain when mature.   But this progress of
colouring is not always the same in all trees and shrubs.
In some of them, as Livingstone observes, the early tints
of the leaves are yellow, purple, copper, liver-colour, and
even inky-black.

Without incident of importance in their descent of
the Liambai, save the upsetting of their canoe by an ill-
tempered female hippopotamus, they reached Sesheke,
where Livingstone found that a number of packages had
been sent to him from Mr. Moffat by means of Matabele
carriers.   On opening his letters and papers he discovered that Sir Roderick Murchison (the President of
the Royal Geographical Society) had already formulated
the same theory about the dish-like contour of the
African continent as Livingstone had arrived at independently through his own observations.[1]   Sir Roderick's
theory was mainly based on a geological map of South
Africa prepared by Mr. Bain, and Livingstone appears
to have shown some regret at being forestalled in the
promulgation of this Central-African basin theory.   " I
had cherished," he writes, "the pleasing delusion that I
should be the first to suggest the idea, that the interior
of Africa was a watery plateau of less elevation than
the flanking hilly ranges."

[1] The theory of the dish-shaped structure of the southern half of
Africa, or even, as it was thought, of the whole of the continent,
never seemed to the present writer a very exact or brilliant hypothesis,
or one which is borne out to any extent by what we now know of its
actual surface-contours.   Like most sweeping and would-be brilliant
generalisations, it becomes minimised and split up and modified by a
more careful examination in detail.

From Sesheke, Livingstone and his party rode to Linyanti, and found the waggon and all the stores which they had left there nearly two years before perfectly safe. A grand meeting of all the Makololo people was called to receive his report and the presents which had been brought from Loanda. Such an excellent impression was produced by the descriptions of their experiences given by the Makololo who accompanied Livingstone that he soon received offers of service from other Makololo, who volunteered to go with him to the east coast. The men who had been with Livingstone to Loanda were to remain behind at Linyanti and rest themselves, and afterwards proceed on another trading adventure to the west coast. Meanwhile Livingstone rested too, and quickly recovered the health and strength he had lost in the feverish regions of the Barotse and Ba-lunda. During his stay at Linyanti he conversed with Ben Habib, an Arab who had arrived there from Zanzibar, and whose description of the relatively easy route he had followed from the Zanzibar coast across the lands of Ugogo and Wunyamwezi, the Nyasa-Tanganyika plateau, and the country of the Kazembe seemed to promise an easy and peaceful route to the east coast. But Livingstone, after weighing the matter carefully, decided to keep to his original intention of following the course of the Zambezi, so that he might discover what value that river had as a direct waterway into the interior.

Whilst waiting at Linyanti for the commencement of the rains, so that the ground might be cooled before they set out on their journey to the east, Livingstone spent his time in imparting religious instruction to the people, in inquiring into their needs and wants, and suggesting many practical methods of bettering their existence and creating profitable trade products. He also noticed with surprise that the two horses he had left behind him at Linyanti had not suffered from the tsetse-fly, which was a very remarkable fact, because that insect existed in numbers in the vicinity of Linyanti. Indeed, these two horses of Livingstone's seem to have been the forerunners of the establishment of a regular breed in the Barotse country. Livingstone had also brought with him one horse and several donkeys from Loanda. The donkeys and one or more of the horses he took with him on his journey to the east coast. It is interesting to remark that on all his earlier journeys Livingstone scarcely ever walked if he could help it. He either travelled on ox-back, or horse-back, or donkey-back, or in canoes ; or, in later times, in his second Zambezi expedition, in boats and steamers. When, in his third and last expedition, he was compelled to walk over great distances, the exertion seems to have told on his health more than any other fatigue of travel.

He left Linyanti on the 3rd November 1855, and was accompanied by Sekeletu and about two hundred Makololo as far as Sesheke. Sekeletu supplied him with twelve oxen, a number of hoes and other trade goods, and abundance of good fresh butter and honey ; in fact, as he remarks, he was indebted to the bounty of the Makololo for his means of reaching the east coast.

In following the course of the Zambezi he discovered the celebrated Victoria Falls, which are one of the wonders of the world. The Makololo had called these mighty cataracts " Mosioatunya " (" smoke or vapour sounds there ") ; but Livingstone, finding no generally accepted native name for this African Niagara, called the cataracts in the English tongue "The Victoria Falls."[1] As I shall deal in detail with this remarkable feature of the Zambezi River in an ensuing chapter, I shall not delay the reader with any description of it here.

Before leaving the Victoria Falls, Livingstone planted in one of the islands ever watered by the fine, diffused spray of the cataract a hundred peach and apricot stones[2] and a quantity of coffee-seeds, and he also, for the first and only time in his travels, had the pardonable vanity of cutting his name on a tree overlooking the Falls.

Having accompanied Livingstone as far as the Victoria Falls, Sekeletu bade good-bye to him there, and furnished him with a company of one hundred and fourteen men, and with these he passed along through the country of the quarrelsome Batoka.   Livingstone's observations on natural history on this part of his journey are incessant and deeply interesting to read.   He makes a useful contribution to our knowledge of the part played by the termites (the so-called white-ants) in the creation of the soil, a part somewhat analogous to the *rôle* filled

---

[1] Possibly no monarch that ever lived had his or her name so widely spread about the surface of the globe as is that of our good Queen. In Africa she has the finest of lakes, the grandest of falls, a branch of the Nile, the highest peak of the Cameroons Mountains, and a town at its base called after her.   In tropical America the most gigantic water-lily in the world bears her name.   In our little Chinese colony, Hong-Kong, the capital is "Victoria."   One of the highest points of New Guinea is the "Victoria Peak" of the Owen Stanley Mountain. The most flourishing colony of Australia, the capital of Vancouver Island in North-West America, and many little-known rivers, islands, mountains, lakes, towns, birds, beasts, butterflies, and plants, have been christened with the same justly honoured name.

[2] These seeds germinated, but the young saplings were devoured by the hippopotamuses.

by the earth-worm in more temperate regions, though the action of the white-ant is vaster and speedier in its effects. In his short essay on this subject (pp. 539, 540 of his " Missionary Travels in South Africa ") Livingstone forestalls Professor Henry Drummond, whose pleasantly-written essay on the white-ant is no doubt founded to a great extent on Livingstone's opinions as well as on his own observations.

Passing along through the Batoka country and the southern borders of the land inhabited by the Bashuku-lombwe, and managing, with his usual tact, to appease the suspicions of these people, who had never seen a white man before, and only associated the idea of our race with slave-raiding,[1] Livingstone crossed the Kafue and the Loangwa, affluents of the Zambezi, and arrived at Zumbo, where he first came in touch with Portuguese influence on the Zambezi. Zumbo at the date of his arrival (the 15th January 1856) was entirely abandoned by the Portuguese, who had withdrawn from this advanced post of their East African dominions in the early part of the nineteenth century. They were not apparently forced to leave by the natives, but their garrison had taken alarm at the approach of a plundering army, led by three chiefs, named Tshangamera, Ngaba, and Mpakane, and had retreated to Tete. This took place at the time of a general shrinkage of the Portuguese power in East Africa, which was to a great extent brought about by the damage and disorganisation of the Portuguese kingdom caused by the Napoleonic

---

[1] Their only idea of white men being obtained from the descriptions which had reached them of the half-caste Portuguese, who at that time, as still more at the present day, were known far and wide as merciless slave-raiders.

invasion.   Zumbo has since (1879) been reoccupied by
the Portuguese, but the following was the condition in
which Dr. Livingstone found it in 1856 :—

"I walked about some ruins I discovered built of
stone, and found the remains of a church, and on one
side lay a broken bell with the letters I. H. S., and a
cross, but no date. . . . We found seven mango-trees
and several tamarinds, and were informed that the chief,
Mburuma, sends men annually to gather the fruit, but,
like many Africans whom I have known, has not had
patience to propagate more trees. . . .

"Next morning we passed along the bottom of the
range, called Mazanzwe, and found the ruins of eight or
ten stone houses.   They all faced the river, and were
high enough up the flanks of the hill Mazanzwe to command a pleasant view of the broad Zambezi.   These
establishments had all been built on one plan—a house
on one side of a large court, surrounded by a wall; both
houses and walls had been built of soft grey sandstone,
cemented together with mud.   The work had been performed by slaves ignorant of building, for the stones
were not often placed so as to cover the seams below.
Hence you frequently find the joinings forming one
seam from the top to the bottom.   Much mortar or
clay had been used to cover defects, and now trees of
the fig family grow upon the walls, and clasp them with
their roots.   When the clay is moistened, masses of the
walls come down by wholesale.   Some of the rafters and
beams had fallen in, but were entire, and there were
some trees in the middle of the houses as large as a
man's body.   On the opposite or south bank of the
Zambezi, we saw the remains of a wall on a height
which was probably a fort, and the church stood at

a central point, formed by the right bank of the
Loangwa and the left of the Zambezi.

" The situation of Zumbo was admirably well chosen
as a site for commerce. Looking backwards we see a
mass of high, dark mountains, covered with trees ;
behind us rises the fine high hill Mazanzwe, which
stretches away northwards along the left bank of the
Loangwa ; to the S.E. lies an open country with a small,
round hill in the distance called Tofulo. The merchants,
as they sat beneath the verandahs in front of their
houses, had a magnificent view of the two rivers at
their confluence, of their church at the angle, and of
all the gardens which they had on both sides of the
rivers.   In these they cultivated wheat without irrigation, and, as the Portuguese assert, of a grain twice the
size of that at Tete."

Two days after leaving Zumbo, Livingstone met a
man coming from one of the islands of the Zambezi with
a jacket and hat on. He was quite black, but was a
Portuguese subject of Tete.   He informed the explorer
that that Portuguese settlement was at war with the
people of the chief Mpende, and advised Livingstone to
cross over to the south side of the Zambezi in order to
avoid the chief, who ruled on the north bank, and was
resolved to prevent the passage of white men through
his territories. However, when Livingstone proposed to
carry out this Portuguese negro's advice by borrowing
his canoes to cross the river in, he declined to lend
them; consequently, in spite of his warnings, Livingstone
was obliged to continue his journey through Mpende's
country.   Arrived at the village where this chief resided, their reception was a suspicious one ; but, as
usual, hostilities were avoided by patience and tact on

the part of this great explorer, who probably possessed the instinctive knowledge of how best to deal with savages better than any Briton who has yet travelled in Africa. Nevertheless, their reception from Mpende and his people was both absurd and full of provocation. Soon after Livingstone's arrival a party of Mpende's people came close to his encampment, uttering strange cries and waving some bright red substance. They then lighted a fire with charms in it, and departed uttering the same hideous screams as before. This was intended to render the strangers' witchcraft powerless, and also to scare them. When Livingstone's men went into the village to endeavour to buy food, a man walked round them making a noise like a lion. They were then called upon to do homage to the chief, and when they complied he presented them with some chaff, in mockery, as if it were a gift of food. Livingstone, fearing that a fight was inevitable, killed one of his oxen, so that his men might have a good feast beforehand and fight on a full stomach. He sent a leg of this ox to Mpende, who had assembled all his available men under arms at a distance of about half a mile from Livingstone's camp. After waiting some time in suspense, two old men made their appearance, and said they had come to inquire who he was. Livingstone replied, "I am a Lekoa."[1] The old men then said, "We do not know that people. We suppose you are a Mozungu,[2] the tribe with whom we

[1] *Koa* or *Kua* (sing. *Lekoa*, pl. *Makoa*) is the name given by the Betshuana to the English.

[2] *Mozungu* or *Muzungu* (pl. *Ba-zungu*) is the name given by the Zambezi people to the Portuguese, white, yellow, and black. The root, *-zungo*, is always the name applied to white men (or civilised black men who are European subjects) by the Bantu tribes of East Africa from the Zambezi to the River Tana, and Zanzibar to Tanganyika.

have been fighting." On Livingstone explaining to
them that he could not be a Portuguese, they allowed
themselves to be convinced, and said, in that case, "that
he must belong to that tribe that loves the black men."
Livingstone gladly replied in the affirmative. The two
old men then returned to Mpende, and, together with
others of his people whom Livingstone had met on
his way and treated with politeness, they spoke up so
strongly in his favour at the chief's council that Mpende
made friends with him and furnished him with canoes
to cross the Zambezi to the south bank.

All along this journey down the Zambezi, Livingstone's men had constantly to supply themselves with
food by their daring deeds as hunters. They scarcely
ever caught sight of an elephant but he was doomed to
die sooner or later under their vigorous attacks. One
little incident, however, connected with their killing of
elephants, deserves mention, as illustrating the way in
which their leader adapted himself to the rules and
regulations of native chiefs whenever practicable. He
had ascertained that on the right bank of the Zambezi
he was in a country where the game-laws were very
strict, and that it was the custom that when game was
killed notice should be sent to the owner of the land on
which it had been killed, and that the meat should not
be cut up until the lord of the manor had appeared and
given permission. The owner of the soil was also en-
titled to a portion of the meat and one of the tusks in
the case of an elephant; in the case of a buffalo, the
left hind leg. Accordingly, when Livingstone's men
had killed an elephant on the south bank of the Zambezi,
near Tshikova, information was immediately sent to the
nearest chief, who despatched his messengers to give the

requisite permission for the cutting up of the carcass, and, in addition, a nice little present to Livingstone's men for their skill as hunters. The elephant was equitably divided into two parts, the natives carried away their share and one of the tusks, and the greatest friendliness ensued.

Pursuing his road towards Tete, Livingstone nearly got into difficulties with a powerful chief called Katolosa, whom he states in his book to be a degenerated descendant of the once-powerful emperors of Monomotapa. Livingstone had studiously avoided the villages of this chief, because he dreaded the heavy road-tax which would be levied on his part; but, in spite of all his precautions, he came into contact with Katolosa's men, who threatened to send information to their chief of Livingstone's attempt to pass through their country without leave. He therefore had to purchase their silence with two small tusks, and was thankful to be let off so easily. This, however, was the last difficulty he encountered in his march towards the east coast, for a few miles farther brought him to the vicinity of Tete, the capital town of the Portuguese on the Zambezi. Before he reached that town, however, he was met by two Portuguese officers and a company of soldiers who had been sent with the materials for a civilised breakfast, and a *machilla*, or sedan-chair, to convey Livingstone in comfort to Tete. His Makololo thought that their leader had been captured by armed men, but their fears were soon allayed; and although Livingstone had been awakened by this party at two o'clock in the morning, he ate ravenously of the meat which had been so thoughtfully sent to him. "It was the most refreshing breakfast I ever partook of; . . . and this pleasure was enhanced by the news that Sebastopol had fallen and the war was finished."

Major Tito Augusto d'Araujo Sicard, the Portuguese commandant of Tete, received Livingstone with great kindness, and did everything in his power to restore him from the emaciated condition to which he was reduced by his exhausting journeys. Livingstone's approach from the interior had been foreshadowed to Major Sicard by the reports of some natives who had preceded him down the Zambezi, and who had said, alluding to his astronomical observations with the sextant and the artificial horizon, that "the Son of God had come, and he was able to take the sun down from the heavens and place it under his arm."

Livingstone had reached Tete on the 3rd March 1856, but his kind host, Major Sicard, would not allow him to proceed immediately to the coast, because it was considered then to be the unhealthy season in the lands bordering the sea. Livingstone spent his time at Tete most profitably in collecting examples of the plants and metals of the district which might prove valuable in commerce. He had arranged with Major Sicard to leave his Makololo behind at Tete whilst he proceeded to England, and this gentleman gave them a large piece of land on which they might build, and where they might cultivate grain and vegetables whilst they maintained themselves with elephant-hunting and wood-cutting. Having settled these affairs, therefore, Livingstone left Tete on the 22nd April, and journeying down the Zambezi as far as Mazaro, which is a little below the African Lakes Company's modern station at Vicente, he crossed overland to the Kwa-kwa River, and descended this stream to Quilimane, following, in fact, the route to the coast which is still the one in vogue, owing to the laziness and want of enterprise on the part of both the Portuguese and the English in developing the direct route from the sea up the Zambezi River.

Livingstone reached Quilimane (which is twelve miles from the sea) on the 22nd May 1856, very nearly four years after he had quitted Cape Town for the Zambezi. He had been three years without hearing from his family, and although there were no letters awaiting him from them at Quilimane, he nevertheless received a packet of newspapers and a letter from Admiral Trotter which conveyed information of the welfare of his family and the news of the world.   H.M.S. *Frolic* had called at Quilimane to inquire for him in the previous November, and her captain had most considerately left a case of wine, to which present her surgeon, with equal forethought, had added a bottle of quinine.   Livingstone's joy, however, on reaching the coast was sadly embittered by the news that Commander Maclure, Lieutenant Woodruffe, and five men of H.M.S. *Dart* had been lost on the bar of the Quilimane River in coming to that place to make inquiries about him.

As these visits of Her Majesty's ships-of-war had unfortunately not coincided with Livingstone's arrival at Quilimane, he was obliged to wait at that unhealthy place for about six weeks, at the end of which time H.M.S. *Frolic* again arrived off Quilimane. She had brought Livingstone abundant supplies for all his needs, and £150 to pay his passage home had been sent him by his kind friend Mr. Thompson, the agent of the London Missionary Society at Cape Town.   The Admiral on the Cape station had also sent him an offer of a passage to the Mauritius, which Livingstone thankfully accepted.

One more sad incident chequered the joy of his returning. He had decided, after much consideration, to take one of his best Makololo head-men with him to England. This man's name was Sekwebu. He pleaded very hard not to be separated from his master, and when Livingstone said to him, "You will die if you go to a country so cold as mine," he answered, "That is nothing ; let me die at your feet." However, the strangeness of the life on the man-of-war and the wearying journey over the waste of waters proved too much for the balance of the poor savage's mind, and he went completely mad. After resisting ineffectual attempts to restrain him, Sekwebu leapt overboard when the *Frolic* arrived at Mauritius, and deliberately drowned himself by holding himself under water by the chain cable.

After some stay at Mauritius, Livingstone started for England by way of the Red Sea, and arrived at London on the 12th December, having attained to lasting fame.

CHAPTER XIII.

THE ZAMBEZI.

BEFORE recounting the reception which Livingstone met with on his return to England after his great journey across the continent up and down the Zambezi, it may be well to give at this juncture a general description of that river, and of the countries through which it flows.

The Zambezi—providing that we consider the Liba branch to be the main river—rises at a point in about 12° S. latitude and 25° E. longitude, on the slopes of a great clump of mountains to which no general name has been given, but which are situated very nearly in the middle of the continent, and are sufficiently remarkable in that they give rise to both branches—the Liba and Kabompo—of the Upper Zambezi, to the Kafukwe or Kafue (one of the Zambezi's most important affluents), and to the Lualaba and Luvira, two great tributaries of the Upper Congo. More than half encircling the high plateau, which is really a broadening-out of the acuter ridges of mountains to the north,[1] the Zambezi-Liba flows first westward, and then south-west, receiving in its turn many little feeders from the Kifumaji marshes and Lake Dilolo, and streams of longer course from the Kioko or Tshibokwe plateau. The Zambezi then flows to the

---

[1] The western edges of this plateau received the names the Piri Hills and the Monakadze Mountains.

south, and, at the southern angle of the parent plateau, receives the Kabompo, which has almost equal claims to be considered the main stream, but that it has not quite such a long course as the Liba. Just below the junction of these two rivers another important but almost unknown stream, the Lungo-e-bungo or Dung-e-ungo, enters the Zambezi, coming from the far-distant west, and rising in the high-lands of Lutshaze and Kioko not very far to the east of Bihe, and therefore not much more than 300 miles from the Atlantic. After the junction of these three great streams (the Liba, the Kabompo, and the Lungo-e-bungo), the united river, which is now a powerful body of water, receives the name of the Liambai, and flows through the exceedingly fertile but swampy Barotse Valley, which appeared to Livingstone to be the bed of an old lake. At the Gonye Falls, however, which may be described as the outlet to this valley, the river becomes much straitened in breadth and compressed within a narrow rocky bed, and from here to near Sesheke its navigability is hindered by frequent rapids, and by the perfectly impassable Falls of Gonye. A little distance beyond Sesheke is the junction of the Zambezi-Liambai with the Tshobe. This latter river, in its upper course, is called the Kwando, and rises in the Lutshaze country, not far from the sources of the Lungo-e-bungo. The Kwando, in its extreme lower coast, appears to be somewhat doubtful in its perennial flow, or at least its visible flow above the surface of its bed. During the height of the dry season, where it passes through the arid country of Mbukushu, it apparently dries up for several months, though the water still continues percolating through the sand, several feet below the bed. It emerges, however,

N

in the Tshobe Marsh, wherein it becomes divided into a network of streams which reunite into one river and enter the Zambezi under the name of both Tshobe and Kwando. After this confluence the Zambezi, which has been further increased in volume by numerous streams flowing from the western versant of the Batoka plateau, turns eastward and rolls on to the Victoria Falls, a zigzag crack in a basaltic ridge. Between Rohlf's Island above Sesheke to a little distance below the Victoria Falls the Zambezi is only navigable in portions of its course; but when the river has broadened out after leaving the tortuous chasm of the Victoria Falls, and has slowed down somewhat from its impetuous rush, it once more becomes navigable, with scarcely any insuperable obstacle, as far as the rapids of Kariba; and even these, Livingstone thought, might be passed when the river was in flood, in which case the navigability would continue as far as the Kebra-basa Rapids, a hundred miles above Tete.

After the Victoria Falls the river continues its eastern direction for over a hundred miles, when it turns to the north-east as far as its junction with the Kafue, a stream of considerable length, which in the direction of its course, as far as it has yet been imperfectly mapped out, offers a curious parallel in miniature to the Upper Zambezi. It is possible that this stream, the Kafukwe or Kafue, *was* the Upper Zambezi in the days before the Liambai had broken through a fissure in the basaltic rocks, and when it flowed into a vast lake which covered all the northern portion of Betshuanaland. After the Kafue confluence the Zambezi takes a more eastern direction, flows round the edge of a very mountainous country, and receives on its left bank the important Loangwa or Aroangoa River.

The Loangwa rises far to the north, on the edge of the Nyasa-Tanganyika plateau, and flows first south, then south-west, and then, with a bold bend and many wiggle-waggles, south again. Mr. Alfred Sharpe has recently navigated it in canoes from a point about 200 miles above its confluence with the Zambezi down to that point where it enters the latter river. From the mouth of the Loangwa the Zambezi flows pretty regularly to the east, without any serious obstacles to navigation (unless it be the Kakolole Rapids when the level of the water is low), until the river enters the deep gorge of Morumbua or Kebra-basa,[1] where it descends nearly a thousand feet in a long succession of cataracts and rapids, covering a distance of twenty or thirty miles. At the end of these falls the river turns to the south-east, and its navigability is resumed, not to be wholly lost (though it becomes somewhat arduous in the gorge of Lupata below Tete) from here to the sea. Just below the important town of Tete, the Rifubwe, which rises in the Kirk Mountains near the shores of Nyasa, enters the Zambezi, and a little farther down the Zambezi receives the Mazoe or Arwanya river, coming from Mashonaland. After its junction with this latter stream the Zambezi begins to open out into a very broad river, strewn with countless islands. Just below the Portuguese town of Sena the Zambezi bifurcates, and one branch (the minor one) flows north-west to the

---

[1] Sir John Kirk tells me, and I think it a most probable explanation of this latter word, that Kebra-basa, which is the common name given to these falls and rapids by the Portuguese, is a misspelling of the Portuguese words *Quebra baço* = "break-the-spleen," which is not a bad word to express the fatigue felt by the native canoe-men in endeavouring to force their canoes up such of the rapids as are not quite impassable.

Shire round the island of Inyangoma.[1] Properly speaking, the Shire River, coming from Lake Nyasa, enters
the Zambezi at the lake-like widening of its northern
branch, the Ziwe-Ziwe, and the two streams united
complete the circuit of Inyangoma Island, and rejoin
the broad main river opposite to the Portuguese settlement of Shupanga. One more important stream (the
Zange) the Zambezi receives, and then the over-full river
begins to give, begins to distribute its waters over the
delta. First of all a kind of leakage occurs on the north
bank opposite Shupanga, and little streams run concurrently with the main river without apparent connection,
but being fed by underground filtration. These gather
strength as they run parallel to the Zambezi, and become navigable at a place called Mopea (four miles from
the Zambezi banks) under the name of the Kwa-kwa,
which stream flows sluggishly to the Quilimane estuary.
No branch, however, visibly leaves the Zambezi till much
lower down, though there was formerly a short direct
outlet communicating with the Kwa-kwa. This is now
a dry grassy creek, except when the river rises in flood
during March and April, at which time there is actually
direct water communication between the Zambezi and
Quilimane. But the first branch of the river which is a
permanent outlet, and is indeed within the tidal influence, is the Tshinde, which leaves the left bank of the
Zambezi at a distance of nearly forty miles from the
sea, and following a very tortuous course, enters the
estuary of Ñañombe. It has recently been discovered
that the Tshinde creek is the best bar of all the mouths
of the Zambezi, and offers the deepest and most navigable
entrance to that river from the sea. This fact was first

[1] This branch is called the Ziwe-Ziwe.

published by Mr. Daniel Rankin in the early part of 1889, but it is supposed to have been known long before to the local Portuguese, and it was certainly suspected by Dr. Livingstone; but the former, for reasons of their own, were not anxious to draw attention to the Tshinde creek, and the latter, through obstacles thrown in his way by the Portuguese, was prevented from exploring this outlet to the great river. The main Zambezi, under the name of Kwama, is five or six miles broad where it enters the sea, but as it has a very shallow and dangerous bar, it is impracticable for navigation. The other mouths are the Inyamisengo or Kongoni, the Santa Catarina, and the Melambe.

The navigability of the river for steamers and steamlaunches may be summarised as follows :—

It is possible for steamers not drawing more than one foot eight inches to navigate the Zambezi from the Tshinde mouth to Tete all the year round, though, during the height of the dry season, the Lupata Rapids below Tete are somewhat dangerous to pass, on account of hidden rocks ; and although this danger is removed in flood-time by the much greater height of the river, the difficulty of passing the rapids is increased on account of the much greater volume of water which is racing down the stream at the rate of six or seven miles an hour. Above Tete the river can be navigated for a short distance farther, until the force of the stream becomes too strong in the vicinity of the Kebra-basa Falls. These cataracts are, as I have said before, completely impassable to any known form of vessel. There is a small strip of navigable river above them until you come to the Kakololo Rapids which I believe can be passed when the river is high. From the Kakololo

there is no serious bar to navigation until you come
to Kariba, where there are more rapids, which are also
said to be passable at flood-time. Beyond Kariba there
are the Kansalo Rapids, not so difficult of passage
except when the river is too low, and then you can
steam or paddle to within a short distance of the Victoria
Falls. There is not much continuous navigation to be
had for a long way above the Victoria Falls until the
cataracts of Gonye have been passed; after which the
Zambezi offers a stretch of unimpeded navigability up
to the junction of the Liba and Kabompo.

Almost all that we know of the geology of the Zambezi
Valley we learn from the works of Livingstone, who is
the only traveller in these regions that has paid any
attention to the subject.

In Lunda the lower part of the Zambezi Valley is
formed of ferruginous conglomerate on the surface.
Farther along its course the land is hardened sandstone
with madrepore holes, banks of gravel, and occasional trap
rocks cropping out. South of 12° N. latitude there are
large patches of soft calcareous tufa, with pebbles of
jasper and agates overlying horizontal trap rocks, amyg-
daloids with analcime; and mesotype through which has
burst the basaltic rock, forming hills and showing that
the bottom of the valley consists of old silurian schists.
In the rapids of the upper part of the Zambezi, before its
confluence with the Tshobe, the rocks, which crop out in
the bed of the stream, and which, for some miles form
its bottom, are of black-brown trap or of hardened sandstone. A certain amount of disintegration in these rocks
is taking place near the water's edge owing to the action
of a kind of lichen, and which, as it were, eats into the
rock and absorbs much stony matter in its tissue.

The banks of the Tshobe are of soft calcareous tufa, and the river has cut for itself a deep perpendicular-sided bed. The plain through which it flows, according to Livingstone, is covered with a deep stratum of tufa, which he takes to be the deposit of an old lake. At the confluence of the Tshobe with the Zambezi there is a dyke of amygdaloid lying across the latter river which contains crystals that are gradually dissolved by the water and leave the rock with a worm-eaten appearance. "It is curious to observe," writes Livingstone, "that the water falling over certain rocks, as in these instances, imbibes an appreciable, though necessarily most minute, portion of the minerals they contain." A large island called Mparia stands at the confluence of the two rivers. This is composed of trap (zeolite, probably mesotype) of a younger age than the deep stratum of tufa in which the Tshobe has formed its bed, for, at the point where they come together, the tufa has been transformed into saccharoid and limestone.

When we come to the Victoria Falls on the Zambezi we arrive at one of the most remarkable sights which any river in the world has to show.

The broad Zambezi, flowing nearly due south and 1900 yards wide, is cleft by a chasm—a crack in its bed—running athwart its course. The whole river plunges precipitously down this chasm to a depth of about 360 feet, or, counting the depth of the water, say 400 feet. The entire volume of water rolls clear over quite unbroken; but after a descent of 400 feet the glassy cascade becomes a seething, bubbling, boiling froth from which spring upwards high into the air immense columns of steam-like spray. On the extreme edge, on the very lip of the chasm, there are four or five raised lumps of rock which have become islands densely covered with trees. To a certain extent they break the uniform descent of the whole breadth of the river. Beginning on the south bank, there is first a fall of thirty-six yards in breadth, and, of course, uniform in depth of descent to the rest of the river. Then Boaruka, a small island, intervenes, and there is only a thin veil of water descending over the rock in front of it. Next comes a great fall with a breadth of 573 yards; a projecting rock separates this from a second great fall of 325 yards broad; farther east stands Garden Island; then comes a good deal of the bare rock of the river-bed uncovered by a descent of water, and beyond that a score of narrow falls, which at the time of flood constitute one enormous cascade of nearly half a mile in breadth. Those falls, however, which are between the islands are the finest, and there is little apparent difference in their volume at any period of the year. Their vast body of water, separating into spurts of comet-like form, encloses in its descent a large volume of air, which, forced into the cleft to an unknown depth, rebounds, and rushes up in a mass of vapour, and forms three to six columns of steam or smoke-like appearance, visible twenty miles distant.[1] On attaining a height of 200 or 300 feet above the islands, this vapour becomes condensed into a perpetual shower of fine rain, which produces and sustains the most exuberant vegetation on the islands and on the neighbouring shores. As might be imagined, the most beautiful rainbows of more than semicircular extent play over the face of the Falls.

[1] From the smoke-like semblance of this vapour and the terrific roar of the descending river has been derived the picturesque native name for the Falls, " Mosioatunya " = " smoke sounds (there)."

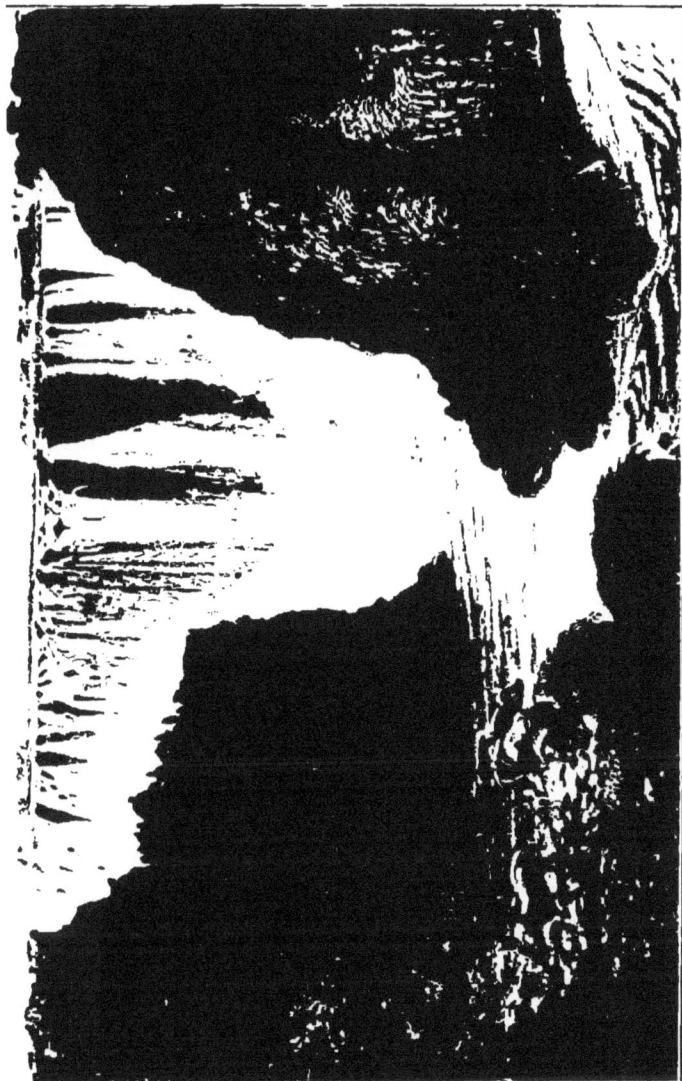

VICTORIA FALLS.

(From Thos. Briggs' Album, by permission of Day & Son.)

After the Zambezi has descended into this gulf, which is nearly twice the depth of Niagara, its wonder does not cease. Garden Island, almost in the centre of the Falls, divides the cascade into two main branches at the bottom of the gulf, which flow round a vapour-hidden mass of rock, and reuniting in a boiling whirlpool, find an outlet nearly at right angles to the fissure of the Falls. This outlet is nearer to the eastern end of the

Sketch Map of the
VICTORIA FALLS
of the Zambezi.

One Mile.

chasm than to its western extremity, and is no more than thirty yards wide. Within these narrow limits the Zambezi, which was over a mile wide when it plunged down the Falls, rushes and surges south through this extremely narrow channel for 130 yards, then abruptly turns and enters a second chasm somewhat deeper and nearly parallel with the first. Abandoning the bottom of the eastern half of this second chasm to the growth

of the large trees, it turns sharply off to the west, and
forms a promontory of over 1000 yards long, by 400
yards broad at the base. After reaching this base the
river runs abruptly round the head of another promontory, and flows away to the east in a third chasm;
then glides round the third promontory, much narrower
than the rest, and away back to the west in a fourth
chasm; and after that it rounds still another promontory,
and bends once more in another chasm towards the east,
after which the extraordinary zigzags of this gigantic
yet narrow trough become softened down into a wider,
less abysmal gulf, which broadens and straightens as the
river flows eastward in an easier descent.

In the abrupt turnings of the sharply-cut trough the
promontories of rock are flat and smooth, and reduced
to quite a narrow ledge at their extremities, so that it
would be dangerous to walk to the end. But the remarkable feature of these rocky zigzags is, that their
surface is almost on a general level with the upper bed
of the Zambezi above the Falls. In fact, one can imagine
that, before this strange crack in the basaltic rock was
formed in the bed of the Zambezi, the river flowed in
undiminished breadth over the basaltic bottom, which
had not then been riven with a zigzag chasm 400 feet
in depth and thirty to forty feet broad.

Below the Victoria Falls the formation of the Zambezi Valley is mostly white mica schist and gneiss. This
is succeeded by black mica with out-cropping granite,
and to the north of the Zambezi, in the Batoka country,
this granite may be seen thrusting up great masses of
mica schist and quartz, and making the strata fall over
them on each side, "like clothes hung up on a line,"
the uppermost stratum being always pink marble dolo-

mite or bright white quartz. In one or two places near the valley of the Kafue there are hot springs and conical hills of igneous rocks. Beyond the confluence of the Kafue with the Zambezi the rocks are igneous, and contain specular and magnetic iron; there are also veins of finely laminated porphyry and granite. More hot fountains appear in this district. Near the confluence of the Zambezi and the Loangwa the rocks are of various-coloured mica schist, and parallel with the Zambezi lies a broad belt of gneiss with garnets in it. It stands on edge, and several dykes of basalt with dolomite have cut through it. The surface-soil in this district contains so much comminuted talc and mica from the neighbouring hills that "it seems as if mixed with spermaceti." [1] Between Tete and Zumbo the rocks are mainly sandstone overlying coal; trap dykes, syenitic porphyry dykes, black vesicular trap (penetrating the clay shale of the country and converting it into porcellanite and partially crystallising the coal). On this sandstone lie fossil palms and coniferous trees (*Araucaria*), converted into silica.

At the Kebra-basa Rapids the chief rock is syenite, some portions of which have a beautiful blue like *lápis-lazúli* diffused through them: blocks of granite also abound of a pinkish tinge; and these, with metamorphic rocks contorted and thrown into every conceivable position, "afford a picture of dislocation or unconformability which would gladden a geological lecturer's heart." [2] In the dry season the stream of the Zambezi runs at the bottom of a narrow and deep groove in this gorge of Kebra-basa, the sides of which are polished and fluted by the whirling action of the water in flood.

1 Livingstone.   2 Ibid.

The breadth of the groove is often not more than forty to sixty yards, and it has some sharp turnings, double channels, and little cataracts in it. The depth of the river here in flood-time is more than seventy feet. Huge pot-holes as large as draw-wells have been worn in the sides, and are very deep. Some of these holes have been worn right through, and only the side next the rock remains.

Below Tete igneous rocks crop out again with hot fountains, and this formation would seem to extend northwards along the valley of the Rifubwe to the west shores of Lake Nyasa, and down the Zambezi to near Sena, after which we come to a region of calcareous tufa which shows signs of having been at one time an inlet of the sea.

Throughout all this Zambezi region iron seems to be present in greater or less quantities. Gold is found in the river-valleys and rocks from Zumbo to Sena, and in the regions to the north and south of the Zambezi Valley; in fact, in a regular belt running north and south from the Transvaal to Tanganyika. Copper also is present, and is to a certain extent associated in locality with the gold.

Livingstone considered that there was a vast coal-field stretching from the Zambezi between Tete and Zumbo to the banks of the Rovuma River in the north-east. This supposition is strangely borne out by the more recent discoveries of coal on the west shore of Lake Nyasa. The conjunction of coal and iron he considers auspicious for the future development of industries and manufactures in these lands. He also points out the abundance of pink and white marble dolomites along the course of the Zambezi between Zumbo and Tete, and the utter ignorance of the Portuguese that by burning these substances they might obtain lime, for which at the time of his visits to the Zambezi they had to send all the way to Mozambique. It is interesting to note, in connection with this, that the African Lakes Company has obtained excellent lime from the marbles found in the Shire Highlands and on Lake Nyasa.

The researches of Sir John Kirk, Dr. Peters, and a few others have shown that the *flora* of the Zambezi Valley is as rich in genera and species as almost any part of Africa; yet, except in the extreme upper portion of the Zambezi course, where it flows through the Lunda country, there are but few fine forests along its banks; that is to say, forests of the West African character of tropical vegetation. In fact, as regards both *flora* and *fauna*, that part of the Upper Zambezi which goes by the name of Liba may be said to be within the West African sub-region, while the whole remainder of the lands through which the river flows belong, in the character of their *flora* and *fauna*, to the more generalised, less forested Ethiopian subdivision.

On those parts of the river which have a sluggish course through tracts of marsh, the beautiful papyrus grass may be seen growing, often over immense areas; and in all the little sheltered bays and inlets and side-marshes of the river that curious large duck-weed, the *Pistia stratiotes*, is found. This plant is exactly like a lettuce in superficial appearance. As it grows it sends out a strong horizontal side root, from which springs up another plant, and this again gives rise to a third, and so on; so that in time, if left undisturbed, this *Pistia stratiotes* forms a regular mat of vegetation on the surface of the water, which effectually impedes the progress of a boat and becomes a very serious obstacle to the paddles or screw of a steamer. Yet, as it is a most delicious shade of pure, pale green, with a faint bluish bloom on it, the appearance, to an artist, of one of these quiet inlets of the river, looking like a perfectly flat lawn of compact uniform lettuces, is very pretty, especially with the dainty chocolate-coloured jaçanás (*Parra Africana*) walking over its surface with their spider-like toes. These masses of huge duck-weed, however, are never met with where there is a strong stream, and the annual floods of the Zambezi constantly break up their floating fields of vegetation and sweep them down over the rapids and cataracts into the more sluggish reaches of the lower river, where they become matted together, and with the grasses and other aquatic plants, which grow on and amid them, form those curious floating islands of vegetation which are carried out to sea from the mouths of the big Tropical African rivers. Several other *Cyperus* grasses besides the papyrus grow in abundance along the Zambezi, and for miles and miles along its banks you see serried ranks of reeds of the genus *Andropogon*. These reeds bear large heads of creamy-white flower-tufts, almost as big as those of the pampas grass, and as the wind blows across the marshes it sways them into wave-like undulations, whereon the great white heads of blossom appear like flecks of foam cresting the billows of shining green leaf-blades beneath. These grasses, however, cease to inspire one with admiration for their beauty when it is a question of forcing one's way through them on land or in canoes, in which case they call forth execrations, from the sword-like nature of their long stiff leaves. These not only prick you with their points, but their edges are of razor-like sharpness, and if drawn quickly across the surface of the skin will cut severely.

Considerable portions of the lands bordering the Zambezi, especially from its source to the Victoria Falls, and from Tete to the Delta, are admirably suited in their natural conditions to the cultivation of rice, and already in most parts of the Lower Zambezi this grain (introduced by the Arabs and the Portuguese) is grown to a considerable extent by the natives. Under careful management its cultivation might be increased to an enormous extent, and if the right sort of rice were planted, the Zambezi would become one of the greatest and most profitable rice-growing districts in the world. The rice grown by the Arabs on the shores of Lake Nyasa is of the best possible quality. Other cultivated grains in this region are the *Holcus sorghum*, the *Pennisetum*, and maize, which is grown almost everywhere and thrives exceedingly. Livingstone speaks of wheat being cultivated in places by the Portuguese, but I have never seen any corn myself that has come from the Zambezi. On the high-lands on either side of the river-valley there is no doubt wheat might be grown with very great success. In the same latitudes, and in much the same sort of country, on the Wila plateau behind Mossamedes, the Boers have succeeded in growing crops of wheat of Scriptural abundance. A species of bamboo is noticed by Livingstone on the hills bordering the Upper Zambezi.[1]

[1] No doubt the same species which reappears in the Shire Highlands to the south of Lake Nyasa, and again in the mountains at the north end of that lake, and in those bordering on the south end of Tanganyika. The bamboos, though they have several species of their genus indigenous to Africa, are not nearly as widespread or common in that continent as they are in Tropical Asia.

In variety of species and genera the palms of the Zambezi are not remarkable, though they make up for this somewhat by the abundance in numbers of the few kinds which are found there. The commonest genus is the *Borassus*—the well-known fan-palm. It is represented by one or two species, and the *Hyphæne* palm appears to be found in this region in the form of the *Hyphæne ventricosa*. A wild date (*Phœnix spinosa*) is very commonly met with, generally growing as a low bush. Of course, the coco-nut palm is found in the Delta and up as far as Tete, in the vicinity of human habitations, but it is not a native of the country, or even of the East African sea-coast, whither it has been brought by the Arabs and Portuguese. It is possible that a species of *Calamus* climbing-palm may be found in the forest region of the Upper Liba, but its existence has not yet been definitely reported. Livingstone mentions the Oil-palm, however, as penetrating to this upper portion of the Zambezi watershed, and I have myself seen a species of *Elaïs* in the Zambezi Valley, though whether it was the well-known *Elaïs guineënsis* I was not able to determine. Practically speaking, as far as the average unobservant traveller is concerned, the only kinds of palm to be commonly seen in the Zambezi Valley are the *Borassus* and the wild date.

Cycads are not infrequently found in the vicinity of the Zambezi, from Tete to the confluence of the Kabompo.

Aloes, dracænas, and lilies are abundantly represented by numerous—and in the case of the lilies—very beautiful species. *Crinum* is the commonest lily genus, and has species that are white, pink and white, and even scarlet in their blooms. To see, as one may do towards the close of the rainy season, fields near the river's bank or glades in the forest an almost uninterrupted sheet of lily blooms for several acres in extent, is a sight so lovely that you pardon Africa all its sins on the spot. A wild species of *Musa* (plantain) is found in the Zambezi regions. I do not know whether it is *Musa ensete* or another kind closely allied to it. Its hard, round, black seeds are frequently converted into ornaments by the natives.

After the first rains the Zambezi Valley and all the countries near it, no matter how rocky or stony their nature, are covered with innumerable blooms of various species of *Amomum*, which grow close to the ground, blossom before the appearance of the leaf-shoots, are of the size and somewhat of the appearance of extremely large crocuses, and, like the varieties of cultivated crocus, are an intense purple, a bright yellow, pure white, or pale mauve in colour. The flowers are afterwards succeeded by large bright red seed-pods, which contain the " grains of Paradise " so much sought after for making spices.

This part of Africa is not remarkably rich in the variety of its orchids, and those genera which are represented are chiefly of a terrestrial, not an epiphytic nature (except, of course, in the forest country of the Lunda, where parasitic orchids abound). The orchids chiefly found in the Zambezi countries belong to that beautiful genus *Lissochilus*, which presents us here with some five or six different species bearing flowers of mauve-red, mauve and white, mauve and green, white, and yellow colours. A beautiful species of *Eulophia*, which has flowers of a vivid orange colour, is also terrestrial, as are the various kinds of *Habenaria*, *Satyrium* (one of which has flowers of an ultramarine blue), and *Disa* which are found on the

o

islands or in the marshes of the Zambezi Basin. A few
species of *Angræcum* are found as epiphytes among the
trees near the sea-coast.

The *Gladioli* are numerous and beautiful, the flowers
in some species being of strange, indefinable tints of
flame-colour and grey-purplish-green.

The chief trees of commercial value or remarkable
appearance found in the Zambezi Valley are several
kinds of *Vitex* (some of which bear seeds containing a
valuable oil); fig-trees with pendulous roots from the
branches and a viscous sap which produces rubber;
Candelabra *Euphorbias ;* various kinds of ebony (*Dios-
pyros*) *;* Baphias, with timber of a bright red colour;
Copaifera guibourtiana (yielding a valuable gum), and
C. Mopane, the "iron-wood" tree found all over the
Zambezi Basin, but especially abundant in dry plains,
where it forms monotonous shadeless forests; *Trachylobium hornemannianum*, which produces the copal gums
of commerce; the Tamarind, with its delicious acid
fruit; Parinariums, with edible drupes ; many Acacias *;*
and Papilionaceous trees, such as *Lonchocarpus*, growing like a laburnum and decked with masses of violet
blossom. There are also the lofty *Erythrophlæum* (from
whose bark is obtained a violent poison), the *Sterculia*,
and the *Eriodendron*, with their buttressed trunks and
crowns of deciduous foliage.

Numerous creepers and *Convolvuli* behang the forests,
most of them producing the most gorgeous show of
vivid-coloured flowers. One of these twining plants,
the *Landolphia florida*, is a source of rubber-supply. I
might note, amongst other useful plants and shrubs of
the Zambezi district, the indigo, the various species of
wild cotton, the coffee-shrub, the castor-oil plant, and

the hemp-producing *Hibiscus*. Whatever this region may have to complain of in sparseness of forests, it can vie with any country in the world for the beauty and vivid colouring of its flowers. It is also likely to find a market for the valuable drugs which are to be obtained from many of its trees and plants.

As regards the zoology of the Zambezi Basin, Livingstone well remarks that there are few parts of Africa which are so remarkable for the abundance of beasts, birds, and fishes as the Zambezi Valley and its waters. Especially numerous are the water-fowl in those countries bordering the river's course where the lands are open, flat, and swampy, such as the Barotse Valley and the lower part of the Zambezi from Tete to the sea. Here are the ideal haunts and homes of pink and white Tantalus storks; of the tall, green-black and white and concave-billed jabiru; of the bald-headed, naked-cropped, disreputable marabu; of darters and cormorants and grey-white pelicans; of chocolate-coloured jaçanás; of substantial-looking spur-winged geese, knob-nosed geese, yellow-brown Egyptian geese, tree-ducks, and African teal; of the filthy-feeding, chocolate-brown *Scopus umbretta;* of stilt-plovers, yellow-wattled lapwings, and big blue-green, red-beaked rails; of giant herons, white egrets, tiger-bitterns, dark-purple herons, fawn-coloured and blue-grey night-herons; of spoonbills; of the Sacred Ibis of the Upper Nile, with its naked head and neck of inky-black, its back plumes of the same tint, and its remaining plumage of snowy-white, and of the Hagedash Ibis (whose colours are a gorgeous, glossy, blue-grey-red and golden-green); of red-beaked screaming terns, and scissorbills ; of the black and white fishing-vulture, and the splendid white-headed, chocolate-bodied fish-eagle,

whose cheerful screams are the dominant note throughout the land; of the lovely, crested peacock crane (one
of the most beautiful of birds); of the huge Demoiselle
crane of ultra-elegant shape and uniform dove-grey
colour; and of other coursing, stalking birds who frequent the reclaimed grass flats in preference to the
permanent swamps.

Francolins and guinea-fowl abound along the banks
of the Zambezi; fruit-pigeons and blue-green or grey
touracoes hide in the bushy trees which border the
river's brim. The beautiful *Narina trogon*—the only
genus of the *Trogonidæ* found in Africa—is frequently
met with in the Zambezi forests, and is a strikingly
gaudy bird, with its scarlet-crimson breast and iridescent emerald-beryl-green back. Another lovely bird-
form particularly common in Zambezi is the crimson
bee-eater,[1] which is of the same gorgeous combination of
crimson and green as the *Narina trogon*. Of this bee-
eater Livingstone writes : " It loves to breed in society.
The face of a sandbank is perforated with hundreds of
holes leading to the bee-eaters' nests, each one of which
is about a foot apart from the other, and as we pass
them the birds pour out of their hiding-places and float
overhead."

Other interesting birds common in the Zambezi countries are the honey-guide,[2] which chirrups in front of men
till it leads them to the place where the wild bees have
stored their honey (a piece of the comb is then tossed to it

---

[1] *Merops bullockoides.* I have seen a little colony of a hundred or
so of these birds perched on the branches of a low shrub near the river-
side, and said to my companions, " Just look at the splendid mass of
flowers on that tree," when, at the sound of my voice, the flowers
suddenly flew away and left the branches bare and uninteresting.

[2] *Indicator.*

as a reward), and the rhinoceros and buffalo birds,[1] which are severally a starling and a weaver-bird, and which, in their special relations with the rhinoceros and the buffalo, exhibit other quaint instances of profitable partnerships between diverse animal forms, such as we see in dog and man, honey-bird and honey-loving man, the spur-winged plover and the crocodile, the pilot-fish and the shark. While acting the part of guardian spirits to the rhinoceros and buffalo, these birds at the same time feed on the parasites which infest their large friends. When the buffalo is quietly grazing, the red-billed weaver-bird may be seen hopping on the ground snapping up insects and other food, or sitting on the buffalo's back picking off the ticks with which its skin is infested. The sight of this bird being more acute than that of the buffalo, it is soon alarmed by the approach of danger, and, by flying up, apprises the buffalo of its suspicions. When the big beast gallops away from the approach of the slinking lion or the human hunter, the little weaver-bird sits calmly on its back and is borne off to fresh fields and pastures new. The other bird, the *Buphaga Africana*, which attends the rhinoceros, is such a faithful satellite that he furnishes a simile for loyal dependence to the Betshuana, who, when they wish to express their complete subservience to another person, address him as "my rhinoceros," comparing themselves to the rhinoceros-bird. "This bird," says Livingstone, "cannot be said to depend entirely on the insects on that animal, for its hard, hairless skin is a protection against all except a few spotted ticks; but it seems to be attached to the beast, somewhat as the domestic dog is to man; and

---

[1] *Buphaga africana* and *Textor erythrorhyncus.* The first-named is a peculiar starling, and the second a red-billed weaver-bird.

while the buffalo is alarmed by the sudden flying up of its sentinel, the rhinoceros, not having keen sight, but an acute ear, is warned by the cry of its associate, the *Buphaga africana*. The rhinoceros feeds by night, and its sentinel is frequently heard in the morning uttering its well-known call, as it searches for its bulky companion. One species of this bird, observed in Angola, possesses a bill of a peculiar scoop-shaped form, which is intended only to tear off insects from the skin ; and its claws are as sharp as needles, enabling it to hang on to a beast's ear, while performing a useful service within it. This sharpness of the claws allows the bird to cling to the nearly insensible cuticle without irritating the nerves of pain on the true skin, exactly as a burr does to the human hand ; but in the case of the *Buphaga africana* and *Textor erythrorhyncus*, other food is partaken of, for we observed flocks of them roosting on the reeds, in spots where neither tame nor wild animals were to be found."

To some extent the Zambezi acts as a boundary in the distribution of certain animals, but it would seem as though this were rather owing to the agency of man, who has possibly broken the continuity of the *habitat* of beasts and birds of the chase, for many of them are of a nature to be scarcely checked in their range from north to south by the intervention of a river which at certain times of the year they could swim or ford. In the case of the ostrich, however, it is just possible that the Zambezi, ever since it took to flowing into the Indian Ocean, may have served as a complete barrier in obstructing the range of this bird from the south northwards ; because I believe that ostriches would not be able to cross any depth of water, and as they equally object to a densely-forested country, they could not overcome this obstacle by going round the sources of the Zambezi, as to do so they must pass through the dense forests of Lunda.

The range of the ostrich in Africa is a very curious problem. In the desert regions of Northern Africa and Arabia, from, roughly speaking, the southern slope of the Atlas Mountains and the shores of the Mediterranean to the Upper Niger, the countries of Bornu, Wadi, Darfur, and the valley of the Nile as far south as about 10° S. latitude, and then skirting the north of Abyssinia to the Red Sea and the Persian Gulf, we have the common ostrich.[1] In the eastern horn of Africa (Somali- and Galla-lands), and down through the country between Victoria Nyanza and the Indian Ocean as far south as the lands of Wunyamwezi and Ugogo, there is a second species of ostrich, *Struthio danaoides,* which is distinguished from the common species, *S. camelus,* by the colouring of the soft parts and naked skin, and the size and markings of the egg; also, it is generally believed, by the poorer character of the plumes. After this there is, as far as we yet know, a gap in the continuous distribution of the ostrich, which has not yet been found in the lands to the east and west of Lake Nyasa, or in Western Africa between the twelfth degree of latitude north and south of the equator. In the interior of South-West Africa, behind Mossamedes and Benguela, and on the south bank of the Zambezi, from the confluence of the Tshobe to the Indian Ocean, and thence right away to the extremity of South Africa, the ostrich

---

[1] This bird ranged over much of North-Western India and Persia, and as far north as the confines of Armenia down to the historical period.

reappears, and in the form of the common species, *S. camelus*, not in that of its nearest neighbour, *S. danaoïdes*. What has caused this curious break in the range of the ostrich? Why should it be found on the south bank of the Zambezi and not on the north, in a country precisely the same in its natural features? Why should it inhabit Wunyamwezi, and yet not frequent the very similar lands to the east of Lake Nyasa? These are questions which, with our present imperfect knowledge of the countries they affect, it is not easy to answer.

To a certain extent the rhinoceros is affected much in the same way by the Zambezi in its area of distribution. The white species (*Rhinoceros simus*—now, alas! extinct) was never met with north of the Zambezi; and the common black species (*R. bicornis*) is, Livingstone thought, also absent from the lands lying immediately to the north of the Zambezi, though this dictum has since been disproved in its sweeping character by other travellers, such as Mr. Richard Crawshay and myself, who have certainly seen the rhinoceros in the country to the west of Lake Nyasa and near the south end of Tanganyika, though it is far from common in those regions. The existence of the rhinoceros has not yet been reported in that wide stretch of country between Lake Nyasa and the Indian Ocean, though the beast has been met with frequently throughout the countries which separate Tanganyika from the Zanzibar coast. From here the rhinoceros, in its area of distribution, stretches up through the lands eastward of the Victoria Nyanza (wherein it is particularly abundant) into the Egyptian Sudan, Somaliland, Abyssinia, Arabia, Darfur, Wadai, Bornu, Sakatu, and (it is said) into a portion of the country enclosed by the bend of the Upper Niger.

I do not think it is known in Senegal, but as in other respects Senegal belongs to the Ethiopian sub-region and not to the West African, I should never be surprised to hear of the rhinoceros being found there.

Another big beast that is checked in its range by the Zambezi is the giraffe. The distribution of this modern representative of the *Sivatherium* follows very closely that of the rhinoceros. Wherever you meet with the rhinoceros, you are almost certain to see the giraffe. Livingstone supposes that this latter beast is not found on the north side of the Zambezi, and perhaps he is right as far as regards the vicinity of the river (though it is exceedingly abundant on the south bank); but Mr. Alfred Sharpe, a good observer and sportsman, has recently informed the present writer that he has seen the giraffe in the lands near the middle course of the Loangwa, and between that river and Lake Nyasa. It has been also said that the giraffe is met with at the back of Moçambique, but no proof of this assertion has been given. The nearest district to the Zambezi coming from the north in which I myself have ever found traces of the giraffe was in the country near Lake Rukwa, considerably to the north of Lake Nyasa.

There are also a few other forms, chiefly rodents, which are met with on the south bank of the Zambezi, and thence right away to the extremity of South Africa, but not on the north side of that river. The Cape hunting-dog (*Lycaon venator*), though not absent, is far rarer on the northern side of the Zambezi. The gemsbok (*Oryx gazella*) is not found on the north bank of the Zambezi, and indeed going northwards no other species of *Oryx* appears until you reach the northern parts of Wunyam-wezi and meet with *Oryx beisa*. There are numerous other mammals (which perhaps it would be tedious to catalogue) that share this peculiarity of distribution with the ostrich, rhinoceros, giraffe, hunting-dog, and oryx. There is, in fact, a distinct gap in the continuous area ranged over by these genera and species, which extends northwards of the Zambezi from the boundary of the West African region to the south end of Tanganyika, and right across from there to the Indian Ocean. The only plausible reasons I can suggest to explain these facts are, firstly, the alteration of the course of the Zambezi, which, from flowing due south into a large inland lake (of which Ngami and the salt-pans are the nucleus), was suddenly diverted into its present channel across the continent into the Indian Ocean; and, secondly, the disturber of all things, man. The Arabs, it must not be forgotten, introduced firearms into East - Central Africa, and especially the Nyasa region, nearly a hundred years ago, and for a much longer time north of the Zambezi than south of it the people have been pursuing the big game with superior weapons.

The marshes of the Upper Zambezi and the Tshobe shelter two very remarkable antelopes which have become specially adapted to an aquatic life. Except in the community of habits and special fitness for an amphibious existence, they are not connected one with another by descent or affinity, for one of them, the " letshwe " (*Cobus letshwe*) belongs to the great gazelline sub-family of ring-horned antelopes, goats, and sheep; and the other, the " nakoñ " (*Tragelaphus spekii*), belongs to the same group as the eland, kudu, and other *Tragelaphinæ*, which are ruminants more nearly allied to the oxen in some respects than to the ring-horned antelopes.

The *Cobus letshwe* is replaced on parts of the south bank of the Tshobe by a nearly-allied species, the "mpuku" (*Cobus vardoni*), not of such a wholly water-loving character as the "letshwe." This latter animal is usually to be seen standing knee-deep or even up to its belly in water, cropping the grass above the water's surface, or else lying just on the water's edge. When the letshwes run they stretch out their noses and trot; but on being pressed they break into a springing gallop, now and then bounding high into the air. Even when in water up to their necks they do not swim, but get along by a succession of bounds, making a tremendous splashing, though not as fast as the natives can paddle; and when the country is flooded great numbers are driven into deep water and speared. The feet of the letshwe do not show any marked adaptation to an aquatic life. The hoofs are small, and the skin above the toes is covered with hair. But in the *Tragelaphus spekii*, as in the allied species, *T. gratus*, the under-side of the foot is naked, the false hoofs are much prolonged, and the front hoofs are greatly enlarged, lengthened, and flattened, so that the animal is a clumsy walker. The nakoñ, or *Tragelaphus spekii*, is chiefly limited in its distribution over South-Central Africa to the Upper Zambezi, the Tshobe, and the districts about Lake Ngami, though it reappears again in the marshes of Bangweolo and of the Victoria Nyanza, where it was discovered by Speke. The hair is long and silky, and of a uniform greyish-brown, altogether devoid of those spots and stripes which are so characteristic of the *Tragelaphinæ*, though Mr. Selous tells us that the young of the nakoñ, especially in the fœtal stage, are spotted and striped like a bush-buck. Livingstone says of it: "This

animal has more of 'paunchiness' than any antelope
I ever saw ; " and Selous remarks that it is a very thick-
set, clumsy-looking beast. The hair, though long, would
seem to be rather sparse, and it would appear that this
creature is gradually becoming more adapted to a water-
life by losing its hair, after the fashion of other water-
loving mammals, such as the hippopotamus, manatee and
porpoise, the river-pigs, and the elephant. The gait of
the nakoñ on land closely resembles the gallop of a
dog when tired. It feeds by night, and lies hid among
the reeds and marshes all day ; when pursued, it dashes
into sedgy places containing water, and immerses the
whole of its body, leaving only the tips of the nose and
the points of the horns exposed.

In the countries bordering the Liba and in part of
the Barotse Valley the prevailing species of eland
(*Oreas canna*) would appear to be the striped or Derbian
eland, which is the only form of this antelope met with
in Western Africa, the dun-coloured variety being the
prevailing form in East and South Africa. Almost all
the South and East African antelopes are represented
abundantly in the Zambezi Basin, with the exception I
have already cited of the *Oryx gazella*, which is only
found to the south of that river. The hippopotamus still
infests in great numbers every stream or piece of water
which is deep enough to submerge its great body during
the day-time. Livingstone makes some very interesting
and true remarks about their habits : " In reaches of
still, deep water very large herds of hippopotami are
seen, and the deep furrows they make, in ascending the
banks to graze at night, are everywhere apparent. They
are guided back to the water by the scent, but a long-
continued, pouring rain makes it impossible for them

to perceive by that means in which direction the river lies, and they are found standing bewildered on the land. The hunters take advantage of their helplessness on these occasions and kill them. It is impossible to count the numbers in a herd, for they are almost always hidden beneath the waters ; but as they require to come up every few minutes to breathe, when there is a constant succession of heads thrust up, then the herd is supposed to be large. They love a still reach of the stream, as in the more rapid parts of the channel they are floated down so quickly, that much exertion is necessary to regain the distance lost by frequently swimming up again, and such constant exertion disturbs them in their nap. The males are of a dark colour, the females yellowish-brown. There is not such a complete separation of the sexes among them as among elephants. The young hippopotamus when very small takes its stand on the neck of the dam, and the small head rising above the large one comes sooner to the surface. The mother, knowing the more urgent need of air for her calf, rises more frequently above the water when it is in her care."

The lion, leopard, cheetah, serval, fierce wild cats ; the civet, genet, and ichneumon; the jackal, the spotted hyæna ; the long-nosed elephant-shrew, and most of the small African carnivores and insectivores are found abundantly throughout the Zambezi Basin. An otter (*Lutra inunguis*) is very common in the Tshobe and parts of the Upper Zambezi. The *Orycteropus* or ant-bear (an edentate) is met with abundantly in the countries to the south of the Zambezi, but is not so common on the north bank.

This river and all its affluents swarm with fish of the usual African fresh-water genera. Livingstone states, however, that the fish are more numerous and varied in character in the Zambezi above the Victoria Falls than below them. He cites the native names of about twenty varieties, few of which, however, are identified by any scientific name. We know, however, that siluroids, cyprinoids, murænoids, scavoids, clupeoids, and chæto-dontoids frequent the waters, together with a *Clyostinus*, a *Malapterurus*, and a *Clarias*. That remarkable ganoid, *Polypterus*, however, so common in the Nile, Congo, and Niger, is apparently absent from the Zambezi; but in all the muddy creeks and pools the still more interesting *Protopterus* or "mud-fish" (which is a living link between the fish and the amphibia) is found, and falls an easy prey to the natives, who, when the waters dry up, capture these *Protopteri* in their mud-burrows.

The abundance of piscine food naturally explains the swarms of crocodiles (chiefly, if not entirely, of the one kind, *Crocodilus vulgaris*, the common crocodile of Africa), and possibly also of the large *Varanus* lizards, which are almost as aquatic as the crocodile, and, though they also feed on eggs and small mammals, are nevertheless very partial to fish.

In the basin of the Zambezi the indigenous human inhabitants, as far as we know, belong exclusively to the Bantu family of negroes, the only exception to this being possibly a few Bushmen who may approach the Zambezi districts from the west or south. There are also, of course, the Portuguese half-breeds, who are found chiefly along the course of the Zambezi, between Zumbo and Sena, and a few white Portuguese, English, French, Dutch, and Poles, who, mostly since Livingstone's day, have settled at a few points on the river as missionaries or traders.

The principal Bantu tribes inhabiting the basin of this river may be catalogued from its source downwards to the sea in the following order :—

There are first of all the Ba-lunda, or A-lunda (as they generally call themselves), who dwell in the lands near the sources of the Liba. These people belong to a very widespread race, and speak a Bantu dialect which extends its affinities from Lake Moero and the Lualaba to the River Kwango and the frontiers of Angola.[1] For some centuries, apparently, there has been a sort of central rule throughout the vast Lunda countries, though both the dynasty and the seat of government have frequently changed, and subsidiary satraps have become in time independent monarchs. The paramount chief of the A-lunda is the personage known as "Mwata-yanvua,"[2] or, as Livingstone calls him, "Matiamvo." The territory more immediately ruled over by this monarch lies between the Kasai and the Kwango, and is bounded on the north by about the sixth degree of south latitude, and southwards by the Zambezi watershed.[3] The A-lunda appear to be usually a placable, industrious people, not wholly savages by any means, but, like most tribes dwelling in a forest country, very superstitious, and holding a more definite religion than the Bantu races

[1] Major H. de Carvalho, who visited Lunda in 1887, wrote on his return (1889) an admirable treatise and practical grammar of the Lunda tongue. I wish the Belgian officers on the Congo were as industrious as the Portuguese in collecting linguistic information.

[2] This is the correct form of the name, but it is ordinarily spelt and pronounced "Mwata-yanvo."

[3] The Mwata-yanvua's kingdom for a century has been to a certain extent under Portuguese influence ; but in 1887 a Portuguese expedition, under Major Henrique de Carvalho, proceeded to the Mwata-yanvua's capital, and concluded a treaty with that monarch, which placed his kingdom under Portuguese protection.

farther east and south. Below the A-lunda are the
various tribes of the Baloi or Barotse (as they are called
by their old conquerors, the Makololo), who in race and
language are closely akin to the A-lunda and Ambonda
of Angola. Settled among them as conquerors in
Livingstone's time were small colonies of Makololo, a
Betshuana people from the south, but these are now
all either absorbed or expelled. West of the Tshobe-
Kwando there are tribes related in race and language
to the Ova-herero group. South of the Tshobe, the
sparse population is mainly composed of Betshuana and
Bayeye, who apparently belong to a group related to
the Barotse. The people of the Barotse Valley and the
Bayeye are exceedingly dark in the colour of their skins,
as compared to the much lighter Betshuana, who owe
their greater yellowness of complexion, no doubt, to an
admixture with the Hottentots and Bushmen. No
doubt the black skin of the Barotse comes to a great
extent from their living in a hot, marshy valley. On
the north bank of the Zambezi, the prevailing type
between the Tshobe confluence and the Kafue is the
Batonga or Batoka, a tribe which of late has attained
rather a bad character for their quarrels with Dr.
Holub and the murder of several inoffensive Jesuit
missionaries. Of these people, Livingstone says that
those who dwell near the banks of the Zambezi are very
dark in colour, while such sections of the tribe as inhabit
the high-lands to the north are a light brown. They
have an unsightly custom of knocking out the two front
incisor teeth at the age of puberty. This is done in
both the sexes, and the under-teeth, being relieved from
the attrition of the upper, grow long and somewhat
bent out, and thereby cause the under-lip to protrude

in a most unsightly way. When questioned by Livingstone respecting the origin of this practice, the Batoka
replied that their object was to be like oxen, and those
who retained their teeth they considered to resemble
zebras. It is curious, however, that among many of
those tribes of savage or semi-savage men who knock
out, chip, file, or discolour their teeth, the ostensible
reason usually given for these practices is, that they
thereby distinguish the human being from the brute.
Thus, the natives of the Malay Peninsula and of other
parts of Eastern Asia who blackened their teeth stated
as their reason for doing so their dislike to having white
teeth like dogs.

Neither the Batoka nor the Barotse practise circum-
cision.

Among that section of the Batoka or Batonga[1] (as
they are there called) who dwell to the east near the
Kafue, it is the custom for the men to go absolutely
nude, though they cover their bodies with a coat of red
ochre. The women, on the other hand, were more
scrupulously clothed than any other of the neighbouring
tribes. As to the men, Livingstone writes : " They
evidently feel no less decent than we did with our clothes
on. . . . I asked a fine, large-bodied old man if he did
not think it would be better to adopt a little covering.
He looked with a pitying leer, and laughed with surprise
at my thinking him at all indecent; he evidently considered himself above such weak superstition."

These Batonga have also an odd mode of salutation,
which custom, however, extends right away to the tribes
to the west coast of Nyasa. They throw themselves on

[1] The local name of these people is Bawe or Baenda-pezi = "go-
nakeds."

P

their backs on the ground, and, rolling from side to side, slap the outside of their thighs as expressions of thankfulness and welcome.

Behind the Batoka, along the upper course of the Kafue and between that river and the Loangwa, are the cantankerous, treacherous, quarrelsome people known as the Ba-shukulompo, or Ma-shukulumbwe. With these people Livingstone did not come much into contact, as he scarcely entered their country, but they have since been visited by other travellers, who have always been repelled by their attacks. Not much is known about them, but they are supposed to be midway in race and language between the Ba-bisa of Bangweolo and the Batoka.

On the south bank of the Zambezi, opposite the Batoka, there are the various tribes of the Ba-nyai, who are of a light coffee-and-milk colour, and are, therefore, considered to be handsome people throughout the whole country. As they draw out their hair into small cords a foot in length and entwine the inner bark of a tree inside each cord and dye the ends red, many of them reminded Livingstone of the ancient Egyptians. The great mass of hair which they possess reaches to the shoulders, but when they intend to travel they draw it up to a bunch and tie it on the top of the head. They are cleanly in their habits.

North of the Zambezi for some little distance to the east of the Loangwa River and along the banks of that stream for about half of its course the people are called Basenga. They appear to be rather a mixed tribe, and of late they have been nearly exterminated by the ruthless attacks of the black Portuguese slave-hunters and by the raids of the migratory Zulus who have

crossed the Zambezi. In language the Basenga seem
to be just midway between the people of Nyasa and of
the Zambezi about Tete on the one hand, and the
Ba-bisa of Bangweolo on the other. Near the Kebra-
basa Rapids there is the small tribe of Badema, who,
together with the people on both sides of the Zambezi,
as far as its confluence with the Shire, are of the same
race and speak the same language, practically, as the
Mañanja, A-nyanja, Wa-tshewa, A-maravi, and A-tonga,
who dwell farther to the north, along the Shire Valley,
and on the south-east and west shores of Lake Nyasa.
South of this group, which may be called generally the
"Nyanja" people, you have the Mashona, the Barue,
the Bateve, and various other tribes about whose languages little is known, but who are supposed to be
related to the Zulu group.

The Mashona and the Banyai countries, to the south
of the Zambezi, are ruled over by some 30,000 or 40,000
Zulus—the Amandabele or Matabele, who migrated to
these high plateaux of Mashonaland from the Transvaal
some seventy years ago. At various periods hordes of
these same Zulus have crossed the Zambezi to the north
and have settled in the Busenga and Angoni countries
to the west of Lake Nyasa, and have extended their
raids right up to the Nyasa-Tanganyika plateau, and
even to the east shore of Lake Tanganyika. Although
they are fast becoming mixed in blood and language
with their serfs, the Senga and Nyanja people, they
still retain to some extent the Zulu tongue.

Along the banks of the Zambezi from Tete to the sea
a special race and language have sprung up since the
Portuguese have held dominion over that portion of the
river. These are the A-tshigunda people, who speak the

Tshigunda dialect, a kind of *lingua franca* which is merely composed of a mixture of languages of the principal tongues bordering the Zambezi with the Tshi-nyanja element as the dominant one. The people themselves are a fine-looking lot, ordinarily of good stature, handsome features, and full beards. Though quite black in complexion, they are nevertheless strongly tinctured with Portuguese blood, though the intermixture no doubt dates from the early days of Portuguese colonisation. The real origin of these people was the heterogeneous collection of slaves from all parts of Africa which the Portuguese placed on their plantations and with many of whom they interbred.

To the north of the Zambezi Delta, in the Quilimane district, there is a race of people who speak a dialect of Makua, and are closely related to the tribes of the Moçambique province. In the islands of the Delta, and to the south of it, you have the A-tshigunda, and tribes related to the Zulu stock.

The Portuguese rule on the Zambezi is only of a settled, effective character as far up as Tete, but the Portuguese Government recently resumed the occupation of Zumbo, which had been totally deserted in Livingstone's day. Tete is, however, a considerable town, and can boast of a certain amount of civilisation. It has churches and shops, a fort and a garrison of black soldiers, with a white commander and non-commissioned officers.

In an unhealthy locality near the big island of Inyangoma, formed by the Zambezi and the Shire, is the town of Sena, which was the first place on the Zambezi occupied by the Portuguese towards the close of the sixteenth century. It is remarkable to note that when

the Portuguese first arrived there they found a good
many Arab traders settled at that place, whose presence
on the Zambezi would almost seem to have continued
from the establishment of the powerful Arab sultanates
of Kilwa, Moçambique, and Sofala, which were founded
in the eighth century, if even they did not date from
earlier days. I think it not improbable that the remarkable ruins of stone buildings which have been
found in various parts of Mashona-, Matabele-, and even
Betshuana-lands are to be attributed to these early Arab
gold-seekers or to Persians who immediately preceded
them rather than to the Phœnicians.[1] The name Zim-
babye or Zimbawe given to some of these ruins simply
means " stones " in the local dialects. From the resemblance which much of that stone-work bears to old Arab
buildings in Eastern Arabia, I am further inclined to
hold his opinion, that the Arabs who strongly held the
nearest approach from the sea to Mashonaland made
settlements inland for mining purposes, and built these
stone walls, turrets, and round towers for smelting
purposes, and for their protection from the natives,
who were probably in those days savages of the wildest
description.

The Portuguese civilisation is seen at its best on the
extreme Lower Shire, near its confluence with the Zambezi, in the establishment of neatly-built civilised dwell-
ing-houses and telegraph stations. They have now a
telegraph-wire from the British boundary at the junction
of the Ruo and the Shire to Quilimane on the coast.
There is a small Portuguese settlement called Mopeia,
on the Kwa-kwa river, about four miles from the

---

[1] Certainly not to the Portuguese, for many good reasons too long
to recapitulate here.

Zambezi. In the delta of the Zambezi, a place called Conceição, on the Nyamisengo or Kongoni mouth, some plantations along the Tshinde Creek, and a small garrison at the Tshinde mouth are at present the only signs of Portuguese colonisation. The real capital, however, of the Zambezi regions is the important town of Quilimane (Kilimane), on the estuary of the Kwa-kwa River. This is a very well-built, civilised-looking settlement, with a fine esplanade along the river-side, handsome public buildings, broad, clean streets, big churches, a club and hotel, and well-planted public gardens. It is the most go-ahead place in the Portuguese East African possessions, except, of course, Delagoa Bay.[1] As, however, Quilimane is built in the middle of a mangrove marsh, it swarms with mosquitoes, and is not very healthy.

Taking it all in all, the Zambezi Basin is one of the richest districts in Africa, as regards the fertility of its soil, the value of its mineral deposits, and its amazing abundance of animal life. It compares, however, unfavourably with the Nile, the Niger, and the Congo for navigability; and although not worse, it is certainly no better than the two last-named rivers in the unhealthiness of its climate.

[1] Where the progress, however, is only evident among the Germans, Dutch, and English who reside there.

CHAPTER XIV.

LIVINGSTONE RETURNS TO ENGLAND.

LIVINGSTONE was to have been met at Southampton on his return to England by his wife and a large number of friends, but unfortunately an accident occurred to his steamer in the Mediterranean off the island of Zembra, to the south of Sicily. The shaft of the engine broke, and the ship was drifting hopelessly towards the rocks of the island, but, fortunately, just as they were preparing to leave the ship in the boats, a wind sprang up and swept the vessel out of danger into the Bay of Tunis. From here the passengers were sent on to Marseilles, and Livingstone proceeded home *via* Paris and Dover, where he landed, and journeyed as quickly as possible to Southampton, by way of London, to meet his wife.

On the 15th December 1856 the Royal Geographical Society held a special meeting to welcome him. Sir Roderick Murchison was in the chair, and among the large audience were some of Livingstone's previous fellow-travellers, Captain Steele,[1] Major Vardon, and Mr. Oswell. At their anniversary meeting in the month of May 1855, the Royal Geographical Society had already awarded to Livingstone their Victoria gold medal for his journey from the Cape to the Zambezi,

[1] Afterwards General Sir Thomas Steele.

and thence to Loanda, and this was now presented to him, its presentation being preceded by an eloquent and kindly speech on the part of Sir Roderick Murchison.

After this, meeting succeeded meeting. The London Missionary Society received him, with Lord Shaftesbury in the chair; and later on, at the very beginning of 1857, there was a more general assembly at the Mansion House, at which full expression was given by many persons of distinction to the impression which Livingstone's quiet, daring, fruitful work and modest demeanour had made on the British public.

Soon the stream of popular favour made Dr. Livingstone the lion of that season of 1857. He had received both the freedom of the City of London and of Hamilton[1] (which, as he humorously remarks, "insured him protection from the payment of jail fees if put into prison "), of Glasgow and of Edinburgh. The Prince Consort granted him an interview very early in the year; he received testimonials and addresses from all manner of societies; a sum of £2000 was raised by public subscription in Glasgow and presented to him in the autumn. In Dublin he was fêted at a meeting of the British Association for the Advancement of Science, at Manchester he was welcomed at the Chamber of Commerce, and even little Blantyre, his native village, gave him a public reception.

Oxford conferred on him the degree of D.C.L., Glasgow had made him an LL.D., and the Royal Society elected him a Fellow. At Cambridge he received a most encouraging reception, and in his lecture there practically started the Universities' Mission to Central Africa, which has since done such good work at Zanzibar and on Lake Nyasa.

---

[1] In Lanarkshire, where his relations and family were living.

Had Livingstone been a Frenchman or a German, a Belgian or a Portuguese, an Austrian or an Italian, or, in fact, had he belonged to any nation but England, which had instituted orders of merit and distinction, he would, no doubt, have received some decoration from his Government; but in those dark days of 1857 it was not within the mental scope of the statesmen then in power to conceive that a mere ex-missionary, a mere explorer of a half-savage continent—although he might receive from some bland Minister a little good-natured, kindly recognition of his existence—could be placed on the same level as, let us say, the *Chargé d'Affaires* at the Grand-Ducal Court of Pumpernickel or the Colonial Treasurer of Barataria. However, the commercial spirit of the country having been attracted towards these new lands of the Zambezi, a movement was set on foot, starting from the British Association meeting at Dublin, and swelling with concurrence and support from Manchester, Glasgow, Edinburgh, Leeds, Sheffield, and other manufacturing towns, and Her Majesty's Government of that day was induced to appoint Livingstone to be H.M. Consul, at £500 a year, for the Zambezi, and to equip an expedition under his command for the thorough exploration of that part of South-Eastern Africa through which the Zambezi flows.

Before taking service under the Government, Livingstone had gently severed his connection with the London Missionary Society, with no feeling of aught but friendliness on either side. The Directors of that Mission fully realised that the scope of Livingstone's work was of a vaster kind than could be controlled by their modest means and organisation, so that in the autumn of 1857 he ceased to be officially a missionary, although he remained a missionary in spirit to the end of his days in propagating, wherever he went, the best precepts of Christianity, especially as regards the duty of man towards man. Nevertheless this public intimation of his having changed his ostensible career drew down on him not a few protests from narrow-minded souls. To one, a lady, he wrote this excellent reply (I quote from Dr. Blaikie) :—

" Nowhere have I ever appeared as anything else but a servant of God, who has simply followed the leadings of His hand. My views of what is *missionary* duty are not so contracted as those whose ideal is a dumpy sort of man with a Bible under his arm. I have laboured in bricks and mortar, at the forge and carpenter's bench, as well as in preaching and medical practice. I feel that I am 'not my own.' I am serving Christ when shooting a buffalo for my men, or taking an astronomical observation, or writing to one of His children who forget, during the little moment of penning a note, that charity which is eulogised as 'thinking no evil;' and after having by His help got information which I hope will lead to more abundant blessing being bestowed on Africa than heretofore, am I to hide the light under a bushel merely because some will consider it not sufficiently, or even at all, *missionary?* Knowing that some persons do believe that opening up a new country to the sympathies of Christendom was not a proper work for an agent of a missionary society to engage in, I now refrain from taking any salary from the Society with which I was connected, so no pecuniary loss is sustained by any one."

In February 1858 Dr. Livingstone received a formal

commission from the Queen, countersigned by Lord
Clarendon (the Secretary of State for Foreign Affairs),
which appointed him to be H.M. Consul at Quilimane
for the East coast of Africa to the south of the dominions of Zanzibar, and for the independent districts
in the interior, as well as commander of an expedition to
explore Eastern and Central Africa. Having accepted
the appointment, Livingstone set to work during the
remaining months of his stay in England to organise
this expedition. A paddle-steamer of light draught was
procured for the navigation of the Zambezi, and the
various officers of the expedition received their appoint-
ments. The Admiralty was represented by Commander
Bedingfield, R.N.; the post of secretary and general
assistant was bestowed on Charles, the brother of
Dr. Livingstone.

The most important person in the expedition, however, after Dr. Livingstone, was John Kirk, an enthusiastic and ambitious young doctor and naturalist from
Edinburgh, who, after obtaining his degree in the
Edinburgh University, started for the Crimea, and was
appointed physician to the British hospital at Renkioi
in the Dardanelles, in which capacity he so far distinguished himself, that he found it not difficult to
obtain one of the leading positions in Dr. Livingstone's
expedition to the Zambezi. To this post he was appointed
almost more as naturalist than as physician, because
he had already evinced considerable qualifications as a
botanist. His was the one appointment in this expedition which proved an unqualified success. Others
failed from want of capacity, or bad temper, or weak
health, or else circumstances were adverse to the display of their good qualities. Richard Thornton, for

instance, who was appointed to be the practical mining geologist under Livingstone, did not quite hit it off with his leader. He did very excellent surveying work —in fact, almost all the surveying work that was done—on the Zambezi, but he disagreed with Livingstone, and had to leave; and although he afterwards rejoined the expedition, he had during the interval ex-

SIR JOHN KIRK.
(*From a photograph by Maull and Fox*).

hausted his strength in remarkable explorations of Mount Kilima-njaro with Baron von der Decken, and in making an arduous overland journey from the Shire to the Zambezi his health gave way, and he died of fever. Mr. Thomas Baines, who was appointed artist and storekeeper (a strange conjunction !), was a rather remarkable,

self-educated man, who had greatly distinguished himself in exploring North-West Australia.   Finally, Mr.
George Rae was appointed ship's engineer, and proved
himself to be an excellent choice.

All these people, and all who might be afterwards
engaged in the service of the expedition, were required
to implicitly obey Dr. Livingstone's directions as leader.

Livingstone was on very friendly terms with the
Portuguese ambassador in London, the Conde de Lav-
radio, who expressed a strong desire—and, I think, a

R. THORNTON.

genuine one—to help him in his work.   Livingstone
was naturally anxious to get the material assistance of
the Portuguese Government in furthering the aims of his
expedition, and it was at first thought he would do well
to go to Lisbon to make his request at headquarters.   The
Prince Consort had promised to use his influence with
his cousin, the King of Portugal,[1] but yellow fever and

---

[1] This monarch was the young and gifted Dom Pedro V., whose all-
too-short reign showed him to be one of the most promising and en-
lightened sovereigns who have sat on the Portuguese throne.

the fear of delays—for Livingstone was fretting with impatience to be off—caused the project of visiting Lisbon to be abandoned. The Portuguese ambassador returned to London before Livingstone left, and proposed to him that representatives of the Portuguese Government should accompany his expedition, an idea to which—no doubt rightly—Lord Clarendon strongly objected. Finally, the suggested Portuguese co-operation was reduced to the furnishing to Livingstone of letters of introduction to the Portuguese governors at Moçambique and Quilimane. Livingstone complained afterwards that these letters were neutralised by the sending out of secret instructions to the officials in question, who were thus directed to assume a neutral attitude, and neither to assist nor hinder Livingstone's expedition. For this apparent duplicity of conduct the Portuguese Government have been severely blamed by many of Livingstone's friends, and by those who have written on the subject of his work in Africa. In this matter I think the Portuguese have had hard measure meted out to them. What should surprise one in reviewing the question at a later date, and with the fuller knowledge of the views entertained by the British nation at the time when Livingstone was starting on his second journey to the Zambezi, is that the Portuguese offered no hindrance or objection to the exploration of these regions. The rights of the Portuguese Government to almost any part of the Zambezi were openly scoffed at in England, and a general impression had got abroad that if the Zambezi were found as navigable as Livingstone hoped, and its lands of a fairly healthy character, in some way or other that district might be added to the British Empire. I do not suppose for a moment that this impression was induced by anything said, or done, or written, or even hinted at by Her Majesty's responsible advisers; but it was put forward in the plainest words by people of high position and notoriety in England, who, though not in any way connected with the Government, were supposed to speak with a certain amount of authority. Under these circumstances, can it be wondered at that the Portuguese did not actively assist the progress of Dr. Livingstone's expedition, which, had it proved as successful as at first anticipated, might have resulted, especially at that juncture, in the abstraction from Portuguese rule of all, or nearly all, the Zambezi countries? I am not venturing to decide as to the validity of the Portuguese claims to both banks of the Zambezi, or to any part of it which was not actually held by them; indeed, Dr. Livingstone was able to show, on his return from his first journey, that the south bank of the Zambezi between Tete and its mouth was entirely dominated by Zulus. Still, the Portuguese had claims and pretensions there several centuries old, and felt, no doubt, quite as sentimental about them, as we did about our equally vague rights to the Zanzibar coast when the Germans started to secure it. Under these circumstances, it is ridiculous to blame the Portuguese for not assisting Dr. Livingstone. It is rather to their credit that they did nothing to oppose him.

The Portuguese have no doubt claimed far more of Africa than they had any right to possess either by occupation, or conquest, or means of utilisation. They have hampered the commerce of their colonies by absurd tariffs; they have shirked the question of the entire suppression of slavery a little more than we have done in our West African colonies; in short, their little nation

of under 5,000,000 has attempted a task commensurate
with the capacity of a first-class power, and has left it
uncompleted through insufficient resources. But this
much must be said for them, that, with all their distrust
of our pushing ways and unfriendly zeal, they have never,
to my knowledge, put obstacles in the way of British
travellers exploring their territories, or the lands they
claim as theirs. Their kindness to Livingstone stands
on record; the same kindness and the same facilities
have been shown to many other travellers, like Arnot,
Lord Mayo, O'Neill, Elton, and myself. We should
probably have met with very different treatment under
the same circumstances at the hands of Frenchmen,
Dutchmen, Germans, or Russians.

Lord Palmerston was too busy to enter deeply into
Livingstone's schemes, but Lord Clarendon threw himself heart and soul into the planning of this expedition. Africa was new then, and had just begun to
attract attention. Not even our disastrous Niger expeditions, with their loss of life and poor results, had
checked that belief in the possibility of opening up
Tropical Africa, which during the "fifties" reached a
blaze of indiscriminating enthusiasm. The cold fit of
discouragement and withdrawal was to follow in the
next decade, and Lord John Russell, who succeeded Lord
Clarendon as Foreign Secretary, was to be its chief
exponent. [1]

Livingstone never forgot the kindness and encouragement shown him by Lord Clarendon, and he repeatedly
recurs to it in his private letters and published writings.

---

[1] There was, of course, the short interval between Lord Clarendon and Earl Russell, in which the Earl of Malmesbury was Foreign
Secretary.

He attached this nobleman's name to one of the highest and most notable mountains in South-Central Africa (Mount Tshiperone), which he named Mount Clarendon. This latter name ought, I think, to be retained by the British in Nyasaland as an historical landmark, and a memorial to the first Foreign Secretary who took any intelligent interest in Africa.

Before leaving for the Zambezi, Livingstone was received by the Queen at a private interview, an honour which afforded him much gratification; for, as he informed Her Majesty, he would now be able to tell the people of Africa that he had seen his "Chief," the fact of his not having done so hitherto being a subject of much surprise to them, who are accustomed to ready access to their monarchs.

The Royal Geographical Society took leave of him in a splendid banquet held at the Freemasons' Tavern (which seems to have been the Savoy Hotel of its day), and attended by nearly 350 guests, including the Ministers of Sweden, Norway, and Denmark, two dukes, two earls, and two bishops.

CHAPTER XV.

THE SECOND ZAMBEZI EXPEDITION.

LIVINGSTONE left Liverpool for the Zambezi *viâ* Sierra Leone and the Cape of Good Hope on the 10th March 1858. He travelled on board H.M.S. *Pearl*, a steamer affected to colonial purposes, which on this occasion was destined to carry out to the Zambezi a steam-launch in sections called the *Ma-Robert*.[1] Mrs. Livingstone accompanied her husband, together with her youngest child, Oswell. She intended to accompany him on his second expedition to the Zambezi, a rather foolish plan at the best, especially as she was expecting to give birth to another child; but after leaving Sierra Leone (where they had stopped to engage twelve Krumen), it was decided by Livingstone that his wife and little son should be left at Cape Town to go thence to Kuruman, where Mrs. Livingstone could receive proper attention during her confinement and wait until it was convenient to join her husband on the Zambezi.

The *Pearl*, with Livingstone's expedition on board, arrived off the Zambezi Delta on the 15th May. It was decided at first to attempt the entrance of the River Luawe (sometimes called the West Luabo, and supposed by the Portuguese at that time to be one of the mouths

---

[1] The Betshuana name for Mrs. Livingstone; literally, "the mother of Robert"—Robert being the name of her eldest son.

of the Zambezi), but this opening was found to be an independent and deceptive river, which, in spite of a broad and deep entrance, had but a short course and no connection with the Zambezi. However, inside the Luawe bar the sections of the *Ma-Robert* were put together, and this being done partly on a Sunday, a few foolish fanatics at Cape Town and in Britain actually criticised Livingstone for permitting work on the Sabbath, objurgations to which he made the very sensible reply (in referring to this and other occasions whereon he had to order work to be done on a Sunday), that "it is a pity some people cannot see that the true and honest discharge of the common duties of everyday life is Divine service."

Finding the Luawe no good, Mr. Francis Skead, the surveying officer lent to the expedition,[1] made a careful examination of three other mouths of the Zambezi. By some strange oversight, he did not examine the Tshinde or Ñañombe mouth (which has since been found to be the best entrance to the main river), but he decided on the next best, the Kongoni, or Nyamisengo, up which the *Pearl* made a successful journey, and passing through the narrow, winding, natural canal which communicates between the main Zambezi or Kuama and the Nyamisengo Creek, entered the former river about ten miles above its chief outlet into the sea.

Steaming on up the main Zambezi to what is now Expedition Island, nearly opposite the embranchment of the Tshinde Creek (which Livingstone noticed, and which he opined was the "secret canal" known only to the Portuguese slavers), the voyage of the *Pearl* came to an

---

[1] Mr. Skead was, and is still, I believe, Government Surveyor at the Cape of Good Hope.

end, as it was thought that her considerable draught of water would not permit her to ascend the river any higher with safety. Accordingly, the goods and stores of the expedition were landed on this island, and so arranged that the *Ma-Robert* and a pinnace could convey them by degrees higher up the river. With the departing *Pearl*, Commander Bedingfield left the expedition owing to a disagreement with Livingstone which occurred in connection with the landing of the stores on Expedition Island. At first Livingstone was disinclined to accept his resignation, but as Commander Bedingfield persisted in tendering it, Livingstone had no option but to acquiesce in his withdrawal. This early *contretemps* in the history of the expedition vexed Livingstone sorely, but he justified himself at considerable length in his despatches to the Foreign Office. After a careful inquiry into the whole affair, Lord Malmesbury (who had succeeded Lord Clarendon as Foreign Secretary) wrote to Livingstone to the effect that, having consulted with the Admiralty, he was satisfied as to the propriety and fairness of Livingstone's action in this unfortunate misunderstanding.

After Commander Bedingfield's departure, Livingstone took his place as skipper of the *Ma-Robert*, and in spite of his inexperience in such functions, managed to acquit himself pretty well. His first object was to proceed to Tete to pick up his Makololo followers who had been left behind there. The journey thither in the *Ma-Robert* was somewhat hampered by a war in which the Portuguese were engaged with a bloodthirsty, wicked half-caste named Mariano.[1] This man, whose descendants still continue to give the Portuguese trouble, had

[1] Better known by his native name of "Matakenya."

built a stockade near the mouth of the Shire. However, Livingstone passed the war unscathed, and was even able to render some assistance to the Governor of Quilimane, who had been fighting with Mariano at Mazaro. The Zambezi expedition stopped for a little while at Shupanga, nearly opposite the mouth of the Shire. Here Kirkpatrick, of Captain Owen's Surveying Expedition, was buried in 1826, and afterwards, in 1862, Mrs. Livingstone. The Portuguese at Shupanga were very friendly, and rendered much assistance in having wood cut for the steamer.

A start was made from here for Tete on the 17th August, a visit paid to Sena (which had, however, to be reached on foot, as, owing to the shifting of the river's course, it is now situated a few miles from the deep channel of the Zambezi), and finally, after passing successfully the rapids of Lupata, Tete was reached on the 8th September.

Here Livingstone received an enthusiastic reception from his Makololo. Thirty of the hundred and odd men whom Livingstone had left behind him at Tete to await his return had died of smallpox; six more had been murdered by another of the rascally black Portuguese named Bonga. From Tete three several visits were paid to the Kebra-basa Rapids, which were proved to be an effectual bar to the continuous navigation of the river at all seasons of the year, though Livingstone in the *Ma-Robert* ascended the Zambezi without much difficulty to within a short distance of the Kebra-basa gorge. Livingstone, however, would not give up hope of passing through this torrent of whirling water, and attributed his failures to the weakness of his wretched little steamer the *Ma-Robert*. He therefore made strenuous applica-

tions to Her Majesty's Government for a more suitable
vessel; at the same time, and in case these applications
failed in their effect, he asked his friend, Mr. James
Young, to get him a steamer built at his (Livingstone's)
own expense.

The fact was, that the *Ma-Robert*, which had promised
so well at first, had gradually turned out to be an utter
failure. Dr. Blaikie describes her bad qualities very
tersely : " Her consumption of fuel was something enormous ; her furnace had to be lighted hours before the
steamer was serviceable. She snorted so horribly that they
called her 'The Asthmatic,' and, after all, she made so
little progress that canoes could easily pass her. Having
taken much interest in the purchase of the vessel, and
thinking he was getting a great bargain because its
owner professed to do so much through ' love of the
cause,' Livingstone was greatly mortified when he found
he had got an inferior and unworthy article ; and many
a joke he made, as well as remarks of a more serious
kind, in connection with the manner which the ' eminent
shipbuilder had taken to show his love.' "

Pending the arrival of the new steamer hoped for,
Livingstone resolved to spend his time in exploring the
Shire and hunting for the Great Lake which was reported
to be the source of that river. The first trip up the
Shire was made in 1859. At that time the Mount
Morambala and the Morambala Marsh were pretty well
the limits of Portuguese exploration on that river. Beyond Morambala, Livingstone was told that he would be
stopped by the abundance of the *Pistia stratiotis* weed
blocking up the channel, and by the poisonous arrows
of the hostile natives, who were so firmly resolved to
resist the encroachments of slavers that they opposed

all strangers passing up the river. However, Dr. Livingstone and Dr. Kirk managed to appease the suspicions of the Mañanja people who dwell on the banks of the Shire above Morambala, were not stopped by the duckweed, and navigated the river for some 200 miles, until they found themselves at the foot of impassable rapids and cataracts where their first journey up the Shire came to an end, for they had reached a country where white men had evidently never been seen before, the natives mustered in large numbers, and seemed inclined to be hostile; so it was deemed best to return once more to Tete and make preparations for a more careful overland journey to the Big Lake. Livingstone named these cataracts after Sir Roderick Murchison, and this name they have retained ever since.

In the month of March in the same year (1859) Livingstone and Kirk again started for the Shire, and landing at the village of a chief called Tshibisa (who dwelt at a place near the modern settlement of Katunga, or "Blantyre Port"), they left the steamer in charge of Quartermaster John Walker and Able-seaman Rowe, and started to walk overland to the "Nyanja-nkulu," or Great Lake, of whose whereabouts they kept receiving such misleading accounts; for, inasmuch as the term "Nyanja" is applied in that country to all rivers, lakes, and marshes of any magnitude, the land was simply full of "Nyanjas" in all directions. This journey, however, resulted in the discovery of Lake Shirwa, a salt-lake which lies to the east of the Shire Highlands, and south of the real Lake Nyasa. This was a somewhat disappointing discovery, as this small, bitter lake did not fulfil their expectations of the great Nyanja traditionally reported. The *Ma-Robert* returned to Tete on the

23rd June, and there underwent the repairs which this wretched little vessel was always needing.

The *Ma-Robert*, in fact, was an experiment, and an unsuccessful one. She was built of thin steel plates, only a sixteenth of an inch in thickness, in which some chemical action of the water caused minute holes to appear. These holes expanded in time into little stars, with wide cracks radiating in all directions. The bottom of the ship soon became like a sieve, completely full of holes, which leaked perpetually. Frequently the cabins were nearly flooded; for, in addition to the leakage from below, rain poured through the unsound roof, and umbrellas had frequently to be used by the occupants. The method of coupling the compartments was also an imperfect one, and the action of the hinder compartment on the middle one pumped up the water of the river, and sent it in streams over the floor and lockers, where lay the cushions which did double duty as chairs and beds.

After the necessary stay at Tete, the *Ma-Robert* proceeded to Kongone to meet one of Her Majesty's ships which was expected to arrive with stores. Whilst Livingstone and Kirk had been away exploring the Shire, Charles Livingstone had been in serious disagreement at Tete with two other members of the expedition, Thornton and Baines, and both of these persons were dismissed by Livingstone with some harshness and unfairness. He seems, in fact, to have become at this juncture slightly impatient and irritable in disposition, and too much disposed to believe unquestioningly the reports furnished to him about Baines and Thornton without taking into consideration the pleas which they themselves had to offer. The cause of quarrel with Thornton is not very clear, and Livingstone so far

admitted himself in after-days to be in the wrong that
he re-employed Thornton in the expedition, and paid
him that amount of his salary which had been stopped.
The reason of Baines' dismissal was an inadequate one.

THOS. BAINES.

*(From the frontispiece of " The Gold Regions of South Eastern Africa," by
permission of Mr. E. Stanford).*

On journeying up the Zambezi in the *Ma-Robert*, Baines
had become exceedingly ill, and was left at the house
of the Portuguese Commandant at Tete to be nursed.
Here he met with such extraordinary kindness from

that most amiable and worthy man, Major Tito Sicard, that he cast about for some means of bestowing on his host a mark of his gratitude. Being an artist, it occurred to him to paint Major Sicard's portrait. Baines had, among the stores entrusted to his keeping, a quantity of canvas, oil-paints, and other artist's materials, which he was supposed to use for painting scenes and incidents of the expedition. He therefore used a small piece of canvas and a trifling proportion of the oil-paints in painting the portrait of his Portuguese entertainer. Further, it was alleged—and admitted by Baines—that he had given one or two loaves of white sugar to Major Sicard. For these trivial reasons he was charged by Mr. Charles Livingstone with embezzling the goods of the expedition ! Dr. Livingstone supported his brother in the matter, and Baines had to go.[1]

It was also decided to send away the Krumen who had come from Sierra Leone, as they were found to be bad walkers, and of little use except on board the steamer.

[1] It is quite time justice was done to the memory of poor Thomas Baines, especially in these days when his gold-discoveries in the Transvaal and Matabeleland are revolutionising the history of South Africa. He was born at King's Lynn in 1822, and was brought up as a painter of heraldic devices in a coachbuilder's establishment. He was full of artistic talent, but never had any training, so that his drawings and paintings were always of a crude, conventional description. He had a great desire to travel, and as soon as he was able to do so he started for Cape Colony (in 1842), where he made many friends, but where he found art then, as now, at a discount. However, by painting studies of African landscapes, natives, and animals, and by teaching drawing, he was enabled by degrees to earn a living. His adventurous nature urged him farther and farther into the interior, and, besides minor explorations, he took part in several of the Kaffir wars, where he distinguished himself by considerable bravery. When he returned to England he managed to get attached as artist to the exploring expedition which was to visit Northern Australia under the leadership of Mr. Gregory. Here he attained some notoriety by

NYASA AND THE SHIRE HIGHLANDS

Scale 1:4000000   Statute Miles.   George Philip & Son.

In the middle of August 1859 another start was made to discover Lake Nyasa. They proceeded, as before, up the Shire to Tshibisa's, where Dr. Livingstone, Dr.

making a risky voyage in a small schooner from Victoria River in North-West Australia to Java, in order to procure fresh provisions for the expedition. After returning to England on the termination of this journey, Baines, who had greatly distinguished himself, was presented with the freedom of his native town, King's Lynn, and was selected, later on, to accompany Dr. Livingstone's expedition as artist and storekeeper. Unfortunately, he found it from the very first hard to get on with Charles Livingstone, who certainly, from all accounts, appears to have been a somewhat unamiable colleague. The accusation of embezzling was brought against him for painting Major Sicard's portrait, Dr. Livingstone was not satisfied with his explanation, and Baines was therefore dismissed from the expedition, boiling over with anger at the way in which he had been treated. He challenged the strictest inquiry into his conduct from his accusers, but was refused it. He appealed to Earl Russell and to the Council of the Royal Geographical Society, but without effect. He then resolved to await a dispassionate inquiry into his case by public opinion, and in time, when all the facts came to be known, public opinion reinstated him as an honourable man.

He joined an expedition under Chapman to the Zambezi in 1861, in the hope of meeting Livingstone and personally confronting him on the Zambezi, but the meeting never occurred. This expedition of Baines and Chapman went from the west coast overland to the Victoria Falls, and was in many respects a remarkable journey. Baines painted a series of pictures of Zambezi scenery, which are not without merit as careful delineations of nature, but are rather unpleasing in style from an artistic point of view.

On his return from this journey Baines again revisited England, and for some time prepared his sketches and paintings for publication and exhibition in a studio lent him by the Royal Geographical Society in Whitehall Place. In 1868, accounts having reached England of the discovery of gold at Tati by Karl Mauch and Mr. Hartley, Baines was sent out by a company formed in London to explore for gold and obtain concessions for working the mines from native chiefs. He proceeded to Matabeleland, and there made friends with the redoubtable Lobengula, who has prominently figured in South African history of late. Lobengula granted him important concessions north of the Tati, but little came of this, as the directors at home lost heart, and failed to provide the proper capital or machinery far extracting gold from the rocks. In the biographical sketch written of him by Mr.

Kirk, Charles Livingstone, and Rae landed, and started on their journey overland with thirty-six Makololo porters and two native guides. They ascended the beautiful Shire Highlands, passed round by Mount Zomba and Lake Shirwa, and then rejoined the Shire, the left bank of which they followed till they came to the small Lake Pamalombwe, into which the Shire

SHIRE HIGHLANDS.

broadens soon after leaving Lake Nyasa. The party stopped at the village of a chief called Mwana-mwezi,

Hall in 1877, it is correctly prophesied that "a day will and must come when great and powerful communities will exist in these wealthy and fertile countries (i.e., Matabeleland and Mashonaland); but Baines' reward was only the fame of being the pioneer to point the way to them, and for him that was reward sufficient."

Eventually, after many checks and disappointments incurred by the poor amount of support that he met with in his enterprise, Baines fell ill, and succumbed to a long attack of dysentery, dying on the 8th April 1875.

which was a day's march distant from the shores of
Lake Nyasa. Here, on inquiring, they were told, much
to their dismay, that no "lake" had ever been heard of
there; that the River Shire stretched on as they saw it
now to a distance which it would take "two moons"
(months) to cover, and then came out from between
perpendicular rocks which towered almost to the skies.
This information was not as false as it appeared at first
sight to Dr. Livingstone and his companions. The
word "Shire" is not apparently known to the natives
of the upper river. It is a word of somewhat doubtful
origin, and adapted from the Portuguese. The native
name generally applied to the river is "Nyanja," or
sometimes "Gombe" (which really means "river-side").
To the natives of the upper reaches of the Shire the
river and the lake seem one, and are called by one and
the same name, Nyanja; therefore, in telling Dr. Livingstone that the Nyanja (which he took to mean actually
the River Shire) extended two months' journey to the
north and came from perpendicular rocks, they merely
meant that Lake Nyasa was about that distance along,
in their rough computation, and the perpendicular rocks
at the end of it were simply the extraordinary and
precipitous Livingstone or Ukinga Mountains.

However, on the matter being more clearly explained
to them, they admitted that the lake itself, the broader
"Nyanja," was but a day's journey to the north.

Livingstone and his party arrived on the southern
shores of Lake Nyasa, in that south-eastern gulf whence
flows the River Shire, at noon on the 16th September
1859. They were, as far as we know with any certainty,
-the first white men who stood on the shores of Nyasa.
It has, however, been asserted that in the year 1846 a

Portuguese named Candido de Costa Cardoso reached the
south-western shores of Lake " Maravi," as the rumoured
Lake Nyasa was called, in forty-five days' march from
Tete ; but this statement rests on the slight foundation
of his vague statements to Livingstone in conversation :
statements which, while showing that, like other Portuguese traders in the country, he knew of the existence of
Lake Nyasa by native report, yet fail to prove that he
actually reached its shores and did not merely visit
Lake Pamalombwe or a broad part of the Shire River,
or catch a distant glimpse of the expanse of Nyasa from
the heights of the Angoni country. Besides, the Portuguese in question might not have been a white man, but
only one of those mulatto half-castes who range over
Africa, and whose discoveries are worth no more than
the raids of the Zulu or an Arab's trading journey.
The honour, however, which fell to the lot of David and
Charles Livingstone, John Kirk, and Edward Rae was
very nearly being snatched from them by a German.
Dr. Ernest Roscher, an ardent explorer of the careful
type of Barth, Nachtigal, and Junker, had started from
Kilwa and marched across along the Arab route to Lake
Nyasa, finally reaching the shores of that lake at a place
called Lusewa,[1] arriving here, as far as we know, on the
19th November 1859, two months after Livingstone's
discovery. At Lusewa he resided for some time, but
when he turned his steps back to the coast, however, he
was murdered at a place three days distant from the
shores of Lake Nyasa by some of those thoroughly bad
Yao people who are constantly attacking and massacring
strangers passing through their country. Upon repre-
sentations being made to the Sultan of Zanzibar, pres-

[1] For a long time this name was incorrectly written Nussewa.

LAKE NYASA.

sure was brought to bear by the Sultan's envoys on the
Yao chiefs who were responsible for this crime, and the
so-called murderers of Dr. Roscher were sent to Zanzibar
and executed. It is not improbable, however, that for
this purpose the chiefs selected one or two miserable
slaves and sent them to be sacrificed in the place of the
real murderers.

Livingstone's stay at the lake on the occasion of his
first visit was necessarily short. He felt anxious about
the safety of those who were left on board the steamer,
and hastened back to Tshibisa's village. His party arrived
at this place on the 6th October in a somewhat exhausted
condition, which arose more from a mistake on the part of
their cook (who half-poisoned them) than from the usual
fatigues of travelling. In fact, throughout Livingstone's
journeys, more especially from this time forth to the end
of them, one is more and more struck with his heed-
lessness as to the quality and preparation of the food
that he and his companions ate; a most fatal mistake,
for in Africa the great secret of maintaining one's health
is to eat as good food as can be got, and to have it as
daintily and carefully cooked as may be possible under
the circumstances. To maintain that a traveller cannot
do this is ridiculous. By taking a little extra care and
trouble it *can* be done, especially if the European himself has taken the trouble to learn as much about the
theory of cooking as he should about medicine or
mapping. With a little instruction and oversight from
the white man, the worst native cooks can be made to
prepare a passable meal, and it is absurd to maintain
that daintiness in eating is incompatible with useful
work. As Stanley once remarked, " A dead missionary
is no more good than any other dead man." What we

want in Africa is working men, not martyrs, and if you
want to retain your health and strength in the exhausting life, you must live comfortably. I have generally
found that the discomforts of Africa mainly arise from
carelessness and neglect of detail on the part of the
traveller who suffers from them. Had Dr. Livingstone
taken more care of himself, especially in the matter of
food and cooking, in all probability he would have been
alive now, and have accomplished his life's work. In
his latter days he was too much of the Mary and too
little of the Martha.

From Tshibisa's, on the Shire, Dr. Kirk and Mr. Rae
made a plucky march overland to Tete, which, however,
proved one of the most trying experiences of the whole
period of their services on the Zambezi, owing to the
want of water and the frightful heat of the sun.
Livingstone in the meantime ran down the Shire-
Zambezi to the Kongoni mouth, where the wretched
little *Ma-Robert* had once more to be beached for repairs. Further misfortunes pursued the ill-fated expedition here, misfortunes of a heart-breaking character
at the time to poor exiles in Africa. H.M.S *Lynx*
arrived off the Kongoni with supplies and mails. In
sending two of her boats in across the bar one of them
was capsized by the heavy breakers, and although the
officer in charge of the other boat most skilfully and
gallantly succeeded in rescuing every one of the first
boat's crew, the stores they were bringing to Livingstone, and, above all, the mail-bags, were totally lost.
This meant that the unfortunate travellers would be
twenty months without other news from home. However, they resigned themselves to this misfortune, and
having repaired their crazy little steamer, they left once

more for Tete, which they reached on the 2nd February 1860, after a most distressing passage up the river, wherein the *Ma-Robert* constantly broke down.   At Tete, about this time, Mr. Thornton rejoined the expedition, having agreed to let bygones be bygones.   In the interval between his former dismissal and his return he had made a remarkable journey up to and beyond Zumbo ; then, leaving the Zambezi, he joined the expedition of Baron von der Decken, and in company with him explored and mapped the surroundings of Mount Kilma-njaro. His differences with Livingstone were made up, and the salary which had been stopped was restored to him.

Finding that it would be better to defer their journey with the Makololo up the Zambezi until the rains were over and the harvest gathered in, Livingstone decided that he would run down the river once more to the Kongoni mouth, in the hope of receiving letters and despatches from an expected man-of-war.   On the way down he heard that his lost mails had been picked up on the beach by the natives, carried to Quilimane, sent thence to Sena, and crossing him somewhere on the river, had passed on to Tete.

On their arrival at the Kongoni they found their friend, Major Sicard, hard at work building a fort and a custom-house, and making good the Portuguese claims to this part of the Delta, to which attention had been, in the first case, directed by Livingstone's exploration of it.   Before reaching the Kongoni, however, Livingstone had stopped at a place near the modern station of Vicente, and had despatched Mr. George Rae (the engineer of the expedition) overland to the Kwa-kwa River, with instructions to proceed thence to Quilimane, and at Quilimane to embark for England.   Living-

R

stone's idea in sending Rae home was that, as he could
be of no further use on the wretched "Asthmatic" (as
they called the *Ma-Robert*), he would be better at home
advising the Admiralty in the construction of the new
vessel asked for. With Mr. Rae were sent five boxes
of botanical specimens, carefully collected and prepared
by Dr. John Kirk, and destined for examination at the
Kew Herbarium. These were eventually entrusted to
the naval authorities for forwarding to Kew, but in
some undiscoverable way they were shunted into a naval
store or depôt at Portsmouth, and were never delivered
at their destination. Livingstone and Kirk therefore
believed them to be lost, and grieved greatly over such
a disappointing result of nearly two years' hard work.[1]

Having returned to Tete in the month of May 1860,
Dr. Livingstone obtained a small plot of ground to form a
garden for the two English sailors[2] who were to remain
in charge of the expedition stores during his absence.

On the 15th May he made a start from Tete for the
interior, assisted, as usual, by the much-abused Portuguese, who lent him a couple of donkeys and several
porters to supply the places of certain Makololo
deserters; for when it came to the test of marching,
the Makololo evinced much less enthusiasm about returning home than had been expected. Not a few of
them had cohabited with the native women of Tete, and
as many as fourteen children had been born to them;
they were therefore somewhat loth to leave the comfort

---

[1] After an interval of nearly *thirty* years, these collections were eventually discovered in some naval pigeon-hole, and were forwarded on to
Kew, having suffered, strange to say, but little for their long detention.

[2] These two men—Rowe and Hutchins—appear to have done very
well throughout the expedition, and deserve to have their names
recorded,

and security of this Portuguese settlement, where a living was easily made and money easily spent in European luxuries; so that a number of them refused to go, and others deserted after the first day's march and returned to Tete.

Little incident of note occurred to the party [1] on their journey up the Zambezi to the Makololo country. They visited the Victoria Falls and made an examination of them more thorough and complete than Dr. Livingstone was able to undertake at the time he discovered them. On the 18th August 1860 they entered the new town of Sesheke, which was built on a site somewhat removed from the old place that Livingstone had visited on his previous journey. They arrived there, however, to be somewhat disappointed in the Makololo chief, Sekeletu, of whom Livingstone had hoped such great things. During the four years which had elapsed since he had left Sekeletu to return to England, the latter had been stricken with leprosy, and believing himself to be bewitched, had put a number of persons to death, and lived apart from his people in sulky sickness and retirement. The country was suffering grievously, and Sebituane's great Barotse empire was crumbling to pieces. Already large sections of the Barotse and Batoka tribes had obtained their independence, and the Makololo power was visibly passing away. [2]

Livingstone and Kirk applied themselves industriously

[1] Which consisted of Dr. Livingstone, Charles Livingstone, and Dr. Kirk.

[2] I have already related how Sekeletu died in 1864, and that his death was eventually followed by a civil war, which resulted in the expulsion of most of the Makololo and the re-creation of a native Barotse kingdom, which remains under the Barotse rule to the present time of writing, although the district has now come under British protection.

to Sekeletu's needs, and treated his leprosy with a local application of lunar caustic and internal doses of hydriodate of potash. A decided temporary improvement was noticed in the chief's health as the result of this assiduity on the part of two medical men of such marked medical attainments as Livingstone and Kirk. Unfortunately, these two doctors incurred, as the result of their attentions to Sekeletu, a slight touch of something like leprosy themselves on their hands, but this was stopped and removed by prompt applications of lunar caustic.

Before leaving Sesheke's to return to the coast, Livingstone and his party were implored to bring about an English settlement on the Batoka Highlands. Sekeletu had taken an especial fancy to Dr. Kirk, and wanted him to reside with him in perpetuity. He offered to cut off a large section of the country for the use of the English, and even proposed to go over with his guests to a district called "Pori," to point out to them a likely site for a residence.

Livingstone and his party left Sesheke on the 17th September 1860, and were accompanied for a certain distance by two Makololo head-men, called Pitsane and Leshore, and an escort of men who were to go with them as far as the end of the Makololo territory. There further went with them two young Makololo gentlemen, named Moloka and Ramakukane,[1] and half-a-dozen canoe-men. Their return journey was mainly by water, in canoes bought from the Batoka, and thus they were able to put to the test the navigability of the Central Zambezi. They passed the Kariba Rapids with little

---

[1] Ramakukane settled on the Shire, where he became a great and powerful chief. He remained a firm friend of the English, and died a few years ago.

difficulty, but very nearly came to grief near those of Karivua, some distance farther on, which are nearly opposite the mountains of Mburuma, and not far from the confluence of the Loangwa. However, the disaster was confined to the wetting of their goods, the fright experienced from the narrow escape from drowning of their canoe-men, and did not result in the loss of anything. But when they came to the Kebra-basa Rapids, Dr. Livingstone's obstinacy and tenacity in persisting in the oft-repeated attempt to navigate these impassable cataracts nearly resulted in the drowning of Dr. Kirk, for his canoe was raised by the boiling swell of the water (which in some of the rapids rises and falls, so to speak, in a sort of pulsating whirlpool) and capsized against a ledge of rock. By great good fortune Dr. Kirk managed to clutch the ledge with his hands, and in spite of the sucking-down action of the water, scrambled on to it and saved himself from drowning, while his steersman holding on to the same rocks saved the canoe. But nearly all its contents, including a chronometer, a barometer, and Kirk's notes and drawings of the botany of the Upper Zambezi, were lost.

After this decisive experience they landed and walked the rest of the way to Tete, which they reached on the 23rd November, having spent on this journey a little over six months. Here they found the two English sailors who were left in charge of the steamer in good health, and with an excellent record as regards their conduct. Their garden had not been a success, as it had been plundered by monkeys and hippopotamuses, but they had behaved exceedingly well to the natives, whose liking they had won, and with whom quite a flourishing little trade had been created.

Livingstone, his brother Charles, Kirk, Rowe, and Hutchins left Tete on the 3rd December for the Kongoni in the wretched *Ma-Robert*. In spite of the sailors' repairs which had been carried out during Livingstone's journey to Sesheke, the *Ma-Robert* was in a hopeless condition. New leaks broke out every day; the engine-pump gave way; the bridge broke down; three compartments filled at night, and except the cabin and front compartment, all was flooded. At length, on the morning of the 21st December, the "Asthmatic" grounded on a sandbank and filled. She could neither be emptied nor got off. The river rose during the night, and all that was visible of the worn-out craft the next day was about six feet of her two masts. Most of the property of the expedition was saved, but Livingstone and his party had to spend the Christmas of 1860 encamped on the island of Tshimba, a little above Sena. Here again the "wicked" Portuguese acted with a certain amount of Christianity, for they sent canoes from Sena and transported Livingstone and his party to that place, where they were hospitably entertained. In these canoes they afterwards descended the river to the Kongoni mouth, which they reached on the 4th January 1861. Here they were permitted to lodge in the newly-built Portuguese station. Their stores were practically at an end. They had to make imitation tea and coffee out of roasted millet. But the large marshy islands of the Zambezi Delta were simply swarming with game, and by using their guns they easily kept themselves supplied with fresh meat.

On the 31st January 1861 the long-expected new steamer for the Zambezi, the *Pioneer*, arrived from England and anchored outside the bar, but she was not able to cross until the 4th February. Two of Her

Majesty's cruisers arrived at the same time, bringing with them Bishop Mackenzie and six missionaries, who had been sent out by the Universities' Mission, which Livingstone had initiated at Oxford and Cambridge, to evangelise the tribes of the Shire and Lake Nyasa.

The Bishop and his party were naturally anxious to proceed at once to Tshibisa's, on the Shire, and commence work, but Livingstone was equally determined to explore the Rovuma River without delay. This latter plan was consistent with the orders given to the *Pioneer*, and Livingstone was anxious to examine that river without delay, because he believed it might afford a navigable channel to the heart of Nyasaland which would not be under the control of the Portuguese, who at that time did not own any part of its estuary, and could not pretend to interfere with its navigation. Livingstone was getting a little heart-sick about the Zambezi. The Portuguese seemed resolved to adopt a "dog-in-the-manger" policy. They were unable to develop the Zambezi themselves, but they would not allow its development by other European nations except under such restrictions and with such profit to the Portuguese Government as would interfere with remunerative commerce. Their personal conduct towards himself and his party had certainly been of the kindest, but their authorities, especially of the Home Government, refused to permit the free navigation of the Zambezi, and had shown on one or two occasions when it had been sought to use the river without their permission that they had many effective means, without recurrence to actual force of arms, of preventing this; one of these means being the prohibition of the cutting of firewood for the fuel of steamers, a means the Portuguese authorities at the present day not infrequently employ when on bad terms with the English. Livingstone had therefore decided that, unless the Zambezi-Shire should be declared a free waterway, an attempt on the part of the English to open up this region must be attended with almost insuperable difficulties. Before endeavouring to force on this throwing-open of the Zambezi to the world,[1] Livingstone resolved first to see what could be done with the Rovuma.[2]

Accordingly it was decided, after some discussion, that the Bishop and his party should be conveyed to the island of Johanna, one of the Comoro group, that the Mission party should reside for a short time in that delicious tropical paradise[3] whilst Bishop Mackenzie

[1] This consummation of Livingstone's hopes has only been effected at the close of the year 1890 by Lord Salisbury's influence with the Portuguese Government.

[2] Although this latter river turned out a great disappointment as far as its navigability was concerned, still its valley was and is a natural highway from the coast to Nyasa, and Livingstone was instinctively right in wishing to open it up. Following this tradition, Sir John Kirk never lost sight of the same idea, and as soon as he was able, induced a former Sultan of Zanzibar to send Mr. Joseph Thomson thither to create a kind of satrapy along the Rovuma, which, although nominally under the Sultan of Zanzibar, would have been as much British in its results and bearing as was Sir Samuel Baker's work on the White Nile. But Mr. Thomson did not view the project with much enthusiasm, and soon relinquished his post in the Sultan's service. Four years later the Rovuma was within the scope of German influence, and a British highway to Nyasa along its banks was relegated to the limbo of impossibilities.

[3] At that time Johanna Island and most of the Comoros were as much under British influence as Zanzibar, and, as they possessed a much healthier climate, would have proved far more favourable as *sanitoria* for our fleet in the Indian Ocean. But, instead of clinging to them as tenaciously as other European powers would have done, we allowed them to be taken by the French. And yet foreign nations speak of us as greedy !

rejoined Livingstone at the mouth of the Rovuma and accompanied him in his exploration of that river.

Accordingly the *Pioneer* proceeded straight to the mouth of the Rovuma, which she entered without difficulty, as there was then apparently no bar. Here, at the entrance to the river, Livingstone awaited the arrival of Bishop Mackenzie, who finally joined him on the 9th March. Two days after, they proceeded up the Rovuma.

They were only able, however, to ascend the Rovuma for a distance of thirty miles from the sea, as the water was rapidly falling and the rainy season had drawn to a close. Livingstone longed to leave the ship and journey with his now well-seasoned companions overland to Lake Nyasa, but he was fettered by his somewhat unwilling connection with the Mission, a connection which was purely that of sympathy. He felt that he was more or less responsible for their having come out to East Africa, and that it was his duty to see them first of all established on the Shire before he resumed the explorations for which his soul longed. Accordingly, though inwardly pishing and pshawing, he turned his steamer southwards with a good grace. I write "*he* turned his steamer," because a severe outbreak of marsh-fever caught in the swamps of the Rovuma Delta had prostrated the naval officers of the *Pioneer*, and Livingstone was again obliged to undertake the duties of captain and navigating lieutenant. He took the *Pioneer* over to the Comoro Islands, picked up the missionaries, re-entered the Zambezi through the Kongone mouth, and passed rapidly up it to the Shire.

In their third ascent of this latter river they found that disappointment still dogged the unfortunate expedi-

tion.   The *Pioneer* was an admirable vessel, and had a
long life, afterwards doing very good service in the
West African Oil Rivers, but she drew far too much
water for the Zambezi, and especially for the Shire.
She was originally designed for a draught of only three
feet,[1] but the weight of her machinery and coal brought
her down two feet more, so that she drew five feet of
water when she attempted to ascend the Shire.   The
result of this was, that a terrible amount of time and
temper were expended in perpetually toiling at capstans
and laying out anchors to get her off sandbanks.

After a great deal of difficulty, the *Pioneer* reached
Tshibisa's [2] in the middle of July.   Here bad news
awaited them—rumours of approaching raids of the
Wa-yao or A-jawa, who were beginning to attack the
unfortunate Mañanja for the object of procuring slaves
to sell to the Portuguese at Tete.   Livingstone and the
Bishop, however, resolved to explore the Shire Highlands to choose a suitable site for the establishment of
the Mission.   Shortly after they started they encountered a slave-party on its way to Tete, and recognised
as its leader a slave belonging to a former commandant
of Tete.   Eighty-four of these slaves were liberated, and
as they had nowhere to go to, were attached to the
Mission as a nucleus of its colony.   On the road more
slaves were freed as the party continued its journey
inland and encountered the caravans returning to Tete.
But little violence was used in these proceedings—hardly
any, in fact, for as soon as the slave-drivers perceived

---

[1] One foot eight inches is the supposed draught of the modern gunboats recently placed on the Zambezi by the British Government.

[2] It may be as well to remind my readers that Tshibisa's is close to
the modern Katunga, which is the headquarters of our new gunboats
on the Shire.

tho English they bolted into tho bush, and it required nothing more to be done than to strike the fetters off tho slaves and set them free.[1]

Bishop Mackenzie having decided to accept the invitation of a Mañanja chief to settle at a place called Magomero, to the cast of the Shire Highlands, the party were proceeding thither, when they were attacked by a large body of the Wa-yao slave-raiders. In self-defence they had to fire a volley from their rifles, which had the effect of dispersing the enemy. After this skirmish a council was held among the members of the expedition and the Mission as to what course should be taken, whether they should pursue the offending Wa-yao and recapture the wretched Mañanja they had enslaved, or whether they should leave them alone and continue their journey to Magomero. The latter course was decided on, and accordingly the Bishop and his party soon reached that place, and Dr. Livingstone having seen them safely established there, turned with his expedition to the west, engaged a number of porters, and carried his boat round the Murchison Cataracts to the navigable part of the Upper Shire.

On the 2nd September they sailed into the waters of Lake Nyasa, and proceeded to explore its western coast. Rounding a fine mountain promontory, which Livingstone named " Cape Maclear " after his friend the Astronomer-Royal at the Cape of Good Hope, they caught a glimpse of the south-western gulf of Nyasa, and thence proceeded along its western shore towards the north, pursued and persecuted by the furious storms

---

[1] A number of the descendants of these freed slaves are now living in tho Shire Highlands, forming quite a civilised little community there.

which prevail on that most stormy lake. Dr. Livingstone had left the boat at a place somewhere on the
south-west coast, and had proceeded with a party overland to lighten the boat, and to endeavour to see something of the country along the lake-shores, pausing for
the rest of the party for four days, during which time
Kirk and Charles Livingstone journeyed in the boat
along the west coast of the lake until they got to about
11° 18′ S. latitude. From this point they believed that
they were able to see some twenty miles farther, and the
land-party from a height of about a thousand feet also
looked ahead and thought that they saw the high mountains bordering the lake closing in to the north and
terminating its extent in that direction.[1] During this
short land-journey Livingstone met with more and more
evidences of the horrible wrongs that the negro inflicts
on the negro. He passed through a country raided
and ravished by the Angoni-Zulus of Western Nyasa,
who there and at that time went by the local name of
Mazitu. In the course of his walk he met six boastful
young warriors of this tribe, who accosted him insolently
and attempted to scare him and his party into flight, or
at any rate into handing over a large present, but their
bounce had no effect on him. They gradually reduced
their demands to the presentation of a goat, but when
Livingstone refused them even that, and asked sarcas-
tically how many of his party they had killed, the bullies
turned into cowards, and actually fled from the people
they had intended to rob.

[1] Livingstone's conjecture that Lake Nyasa terminated in about 10°
S. latitude was a wrong one, for the subsequent explorations of Mr.
Edward Young show that it extended some sixty miles farther. The
boat-party under Dr. Kirk probably ascended the lake as far as Kuta
Bay, about forty miles north of the modern settlement of Bandawe.

The two sections of the expedition having been happily reunited, it was resolved to return, lest their goods should be expended before they rejoined the *Pioneer*. On their journey back, while detained by a storm, they visited the Arab settlement of Kota-kota, since better known as the headquarters of a powerful Arab sultan, Jumbe, who was afterwards constituted a sort of viceroy in those regions by the Sultan of Zanzibar. As they re-entered the Shire they witnessed the most terrible results of the Wa-yao slave-raids ; and what shocked them as much as anything was the utter want of union among the Mañanja people, who, instead of making common cause against the Wa-yao, who have blighted that district of late years (and who, if they were dealt with in Mosaic justice, would be simply exterminated), were equally ready to enslave and sell the people of their own tribe who were fugitives from the Yao raids.

They rejoined the *Pioneer* on the 8th December 1861, in a weak condition, having suffered much from hunger. Bishop Mackenzie visited them at Tshibisa's on the 14th of that month, with some of the *Pioneer's* men who had been visiting Magomero for the benefit of their health, and for the purpose of assisting the Mission. At that time the prospects of the Mission settlement seemed bright enough. The Wa-yao had been driven off, and had sent word that they desired to live at peace with the English. Many of the Mañanja had settled round Magomero in order to be under the protection of the Bishop, and as agriculture was taken up vigorously, it was hoped that the little colony might become self-supporting, and not have to rely on supplies from Quilimane.

As it was resolved not to bring the *Pioneer* on

her next voyage higher than the confluence of the Ruo
(her draught being too much for the upper part of the
river), the Bishop and his companions decided to explore
the country between Magomero and the mouth of the
Ruo, so that they might be able to meet the ship at that
place in the following January, by which date the Bishop's
sisters and the wife of one of the missionaries would have
arrived.   Bishop Mackenzie and his energetic young
companion, Mr. Burrup, then bade what was to be a last
farewell to Livingstone, and saluted the departure of the
Pioneer with three hearty cheers.

On the way down, shoals and sandbanks again checked
their progress in the most disheartening manner.   The
Pioneer re-entered the Zambezi on the 11th January, and
steamed down towards the coast, frequently grounding,
however, on the way.   On these occasions, whenever the
Pioneer ran aground in the vicinity of a Portuguese
settlement, prompt help was always rendered by the
Portuguese, none of whom seemed to bear any malice
on account of Livingstone having dispersed the slave-
caravans and freed the slaves that were on their way
to Tete.

On the 30th January the *Pioneer* met H.M.S. *Gorgon*
at the Luabo mouth of the Zambezi.   This vessel was
towing a brig, on board of which were Mrs. Livingstone,
the ladies about to join the Universities' Mission, and a
new iron steamer in twenty-four sections for the navigation of Lake Nyasa.   This steamer was afterwards called
the *Lady Nyassa*.[1]   Having towed this brig into the
Kongone harbour, the *Pioneer* started back for the Ruo,

---

[1] I retain in this name Livingstone's spelling. On the principle of
never doubling a consonant unless it is twice pronounced (as in the
Italian word *Bas'so*), I spell Nyasa with one *s*, because only one is
pronounced. All the missionaries on the lake do the same.

accompanied by two steam-launches belonging to the
Gorgon, and having on board Captain Wilson of that
ship, with a number of his officers and men to help in
discharging the cargo.   Their progress up-river, however, was so distressingly slow, and the engines of the
Pioneer had been so entirely neglected of late by the
engineer who was supposed to attend to them, that the
party were actually delayed six months in the Delta,
instead of, as they anticipated, six days.   Therefore,
finding it impossible to carry the sections up to the Ruo
without further loss of time, it was thought better to
land them at Shupanga, and put the hull of the *Lady
Nyassa* together there, and then tow her up to the
Murchison Cataracts.

A few days before the *Pioneer* reached Shupanga's,
Captain Wilson, seeing the hopeless state of her engines,
had generously resolved to hasten with the Mission ladies
up the Shire.   He therefore started in his gig for the
Ruo, taking with him Miss Mackenzie, Mrs. Burrup,
and his surgeon, Dr. Ramsay.   They were accompanied
by Dr. Kirk and Mr. Sewell, paymaster of the *Gorgon*,
in the whale-boat of the *Lady Nyassa*.   After a terribly
difficult journey, pulling against the Shire in the full
force of its flood-tide, they reached Tshibisa's (getting
no news of the Bishop at the Ruo), and here met with
the sad tidings of the death of Bishop Mackenzie and
Mr. Burrup.   Hearing further bad news of the condition
of the Mission at Magomero, Captain Wilson and Dr.
Kirk walked up to that place, and met some of the Mission
party half-way at the village of Sotshe.   The privations
to which Captain Wilson and Dr. Kirk on this forced
march were subjected were such that they both very
nearly died of fever, and Captain Wilson was only saved

by his cockswain—who must have been a splendid fellow
—carrying him on his back when he was too weak to
walk. He, however, survived, and returned to Tshibisa's
with the remaining missionaries, who, together with the
bereaved ladies, returned to the *Pioneer* at Shupanga.
The death of Bishop Mackenzie and Mr. Burrup is one
of the saddest episodes which ever occurred in the history
of a pioneering enterprise, and the account of the causes
of this disaster is one which it is difficult to read with
patience, because it is simply an illustration of the stupi-
dity of attempting to travel about Tropical Africa in a
haphazard manner, and of doing things in "rushes" and
unreflecting hurries.

Soon after the Universities' Mission had established
itself at Magomero the Wa-yao had recommenced their
raids on the Mañanja in the vicinity of the Mission
station. They had been beaten off, and it was ascertained, and probably with truth, that the missionaries
themselves had taken an active part in the defence of
their flock, taking up arms on purpose.[1] Some little
while after this action on their part the Bishop sent two
of the missionaries, Messrs. Proctor and Scudamore, to
explore the country between Magomero and the junction
of the Ruo. Their guides, however, led them uninten-
tionally or purposely to an Anguro village near the
upper waters of the Ruo where slave-trading was going
on. They were landed, in fact, among a nest of slave-
raiders, who looked upon them as their natural enemies.
On their leaving the village the Anguro people followed
them and shot arrows after the retreating party. Two
of their carriers were captured and all their goods
taken away. The two missionaries, barely escaping with

[1] For which no one but a perverse fanatic can blame them.

their lives, swam the Ruo at night and returned to
Magomero famished. The wives of the captured carriers
besought the Bishop to rescue their husbands from
slavery, and he, feeling that the men had been caught
while in his service, and that there was no power at
hand to whom an appeal could be made for assistance,
resolved to go and rescue these kidnapped porters. He
invited the Makololo, whom Livingstone had left behind
in the Shire, to go with him. Nothing could have been
proposed to them which they would have liked better,
and they joined his party with alacrity. Had the
matter been left entirely in their hands, they would
have made a clean sweep of that part of the country
(says Livingstone), but the Bishop restrained them,
and went in an open manner in order to commend the
matter to all the natives as one of justice. This deliberation of procedure, however, gave the delinquents a
chance to escape.

The expedition was fairly successful; the offending village was burned, and a few sheep and goats were secured,
which, it must be admitted, was not a very severe punishment, considering that the original caravan of the Mission
had been robbed of all its goods. The head-man of the
offending village, scared by these unlooked-for reprisals,
liberated the prisoners, who returned to their homes,
while the other missionaries made their way back to
Magomero, whence the Bishop immediately started again
for Tshibisa's, in order to descend the Shire and reach
the mouth of the Ruo by water. Yet at this time
both the Bishop and Mr. Burrup were suffering from
diarrhœa in consequence of the wet and hunger endured
on their punitive expedition to the Anguro village; and
so little had they realised the necessity of taking the

s

utmost care of themselves in Africa, that on leaving
Magomero to descend to Tshibisa's, the Bishop waded
through every stream he met with on the road, instead
of having himself carried across, or, if he could get no
one to carry him, undressing before entering the water,
and donning his dry clothes when he had passed through
the stream.   The two unfortunate men took five days
to reach Tshibisa's, a journey which would otherwise
have occupied only two days and a half.   Their meals
were never properly cooked, and were always of some
indigestible substance, such as roasted maize.

When they reached the Shire the river was in flood,
and none of the Mañanja were willing, under the circumstances, to take them down the stream.   Three of
the Makololo, however, volunteered, and they started
with these people in a small canoe.   Instead of stopping
to rest at night (they had no tents, no beds, and no
mosquito-curtains with them), they were compelled to
go on through the darkness because the mosquitoes were
unendurable on the shore.   In the middle of the night
the canoe, badly steered, was upset in a whirlpool, and
although the Bishop and his companions and their three
canoe-men reached the shore without difficulty and even
saved their canoe, their spare clothing, their medicines,
and provisions were all lost.   The next morning they
reached what is now called the island of Tshiromo, at
the mouth of the Ruo, and here the Bishop, wet through
to the skin, unfed, and worn out with fatigue, was
seized with strong fever.   He took refuge in the village
of a disagreeable chief who grudged him the use of a hut.
Here day after day for three weeks the Makololo tended
the slowly-dying Bishop with affectionate solicitude, but
without the means of healing him.   At length, worn out

with fever, with no medicines and no proper food, he died. His companion, Mr. Burrup, all this time far gone with dysentery, staggered from the hut in which the Bishop had expired and read the burial-service over him as the Makololo placed his body in the grave they had dug—a grave which should now be surrounded by some more fitting memorial than the crazy paling which at present marks its site. Then, when all was over, the Makololo, with the utmost difficulty, but with the tenderest care, conveyed Mr. Burrup on a litter of branches back to Magomero, which he reached just in time to die among his brethren.

On the 15th March the *Pioneer* steamed down the Kongoni with Captain Wilson, Miss Mackenzie, Mrs. Burrup, and all the surviving missionaries, except Messrs. Horace Waller and Hugh Rowley, who decided to remain. At the mouth of the river they were disappointed to find that the *Gorgon* had left on account of bad weather; but she returned on the 2nd April, and departed again on the 4th, taking away the unhappy Mission party.

Livingstone was almost broken-hearted at this deplorable catastrophe of the death of Mr. Burrup and of the man whom he affectionately calls the " good Bishop." Not only did he grieve at the personal loss he had sustained by their decease, but he felt that, argue it as he might, this was a staggering blow to his aspirations for forming a successful establishment of British civilisation on the Shire. Up to this time he had been full of enthusiasm in contemplating the formation of British colonies in this direction ; now he found it hard to battle against the discouragement which was creeping over his own mind and over that of his associates.

Dr. James Stewart had been brought to the Zambezi by H.M.S. *Gorgon*. He had been sent out by the Free Church of Scotland to inspect the lands of the Zambezi and report on the probable formation of a Scotch Mission in those regions. He made a careful examination of the river as far as Kebra-basa, and of the Shire up to the Murchison Cataracts, but the time of his coming here was inopportune; the disasters which had befallen the Universities' Mission had such a depressing effect, and the Shire countries which it was proposed to evangelise were at that time being so ravaged and laid waste by Yao raiders, that Dr. Stewart was fain to decide it was not a propitious time for his Church to adventure in that direction. He therefore returned to the Cape of Good Hope, and the project of the Free Church Mission in Nyasaland was allowed to stand over.[1]

But at the time Dr. Stewart left the Zambezi to return with his unfavourable report, Livingstone could not foresee the bright future which was to attend his frustrated plans, and Dr. Stewart's negative decision in the matter of founding a Scotch Mission was another disappointment to the heart-sick Livingstone.

Yet a further blow was to come. He left Kongone to return to Shupanga with several more sections of the *Lady Nyassa* on the 11th April. Everywhere along his journey up the river he found people, even the

[1] Dr. Stewart, on his return to South Africa, created the great Missionary College of Lovedale, but he was always hankering to return to the Shire and carry out Livingstone's wishes. Eventually he did so in 1875, and assisted in putting the first steamer, the *Ilala*, on the lake. He established on the west shore of Nyasa that flourishing "Livingstonia" Mission which has since prospered so markedly under the able guidance of Dr. Robert Laws.

natives, suffering from fever, and at Shupanga the season was more than usually unhealthy. About the middle of April Mrs. Livingstone was prostrated by that severe form of bilious remittent which I have described in a foregoing chapter on African fever. She received the most sedulous attention from her husband and from Dr. Kirk, but nothing was of any avail, and she died on the 27th April 1862. Dr. Stewart, who had not yet left the Zambezi, read the burial-service over her, and

MRS. LIVINGSTONE.

the seamen of the *Pioneer* mounted guard for some nights at the place where she was buried, which was under the branches of a baobab-tree at Shupanga. A temporary paling and a wooden cross were erected over her grave, and these were subsequently replaced by a stone cross and slab, and iron railings have recently been put up in place of the iron paling.

The latter years of this poor lady were not happy. In fact, it may be said that the happiness went out of

her life from the day that she parted with her husband
at Cape Town in 1852, she to return to Scotland, and he
to commence his great series of explorations. It was
more than four years before they came together again, and
during those four years Mrs. Livingstone had led a weary,
dreary, narrow life in Scotland, worried and persecuted
by tiresome pietistic friends who were always bothering
her about her religious beliefs. Because she was the
wife of a great missionary it was considered that she
ought to be always gushing about religion, and as she
had not the gift of glib expression, she disappointed the
severely good people around her, much in the same way
that her husband had done when a youth, because he
was not an adept at mouth-religion. Mrs. Livingstone
was always being told that she was in a state of much
"spiritual darkness;" others of her friends seem to
have made her unhappy by hinting that her husband's
long separation from her arose from his "not being
comfortable at home." When Livingstone returned
home at the end of 1856 she thought her troubles were
at an end, and a happy interval ensued until they both
of them started for Africa in 1858. Then they were
once more separated, and Mrs. Livingstone did not
rejoin her husband until 1861. She was not, from what
we know, up to her husband's level of intellect, but in
many respects she was an ideal missionary's wife in her
practical understanding of how to make life civilised
and comfortable in the wilderness.

Livingstone bore this last calamity with a quiet
resignation and absence of all ostentatious display in
public, which of course gained for him from the excellent
people who were always longing to find flaws in his
character an accusation of not having sufficiently cared

for his wife ; but concurrently with these allegations we find him expressing in private letters the deep and bitter grief with which he regarded the loss which had befallen him.   Still, he would not allow private sorrows to interfere with his dogged determination to carry on his work in Nyasaland.   Dr. Kirk and Charles Livingstone were sent to Tete to bring away the remaining stores and other property of the expedition, and the preparations for the launch of the *Lady Nyassa* were continued with vigour.   The *Pioneer* went backwards and forwards to Kongone, bringing up the remaining sections, and on the 23rd June 1862 the *Lady Nyassa* was safely launched on the Zambezi.   As, however, the waters of the Zambezi and the Shire had fallen so low that no attempt could be made to reach the Murchison Falls before the December rains, and as Livingstone fancied the Portuguese were throwing impediments in the way of trade on the Zambezi, he resolved to make another attempt on the Rovuma.   Accordingly he left Kongone in the *Pioneer* on the 6th August, and proceeded to the island of Johanna, to arrange for the purchase of oxen for use on the Shire, and thence crossed to the mouth of the Rovuma in the beginning of September.   Livingstone was somewhat disappointed with the appearance of this river, and the bar at its mouth was not found to be so simple in the dry season as at other times of the year. They journeyed up the Rovuma in their boats to a distance of 160 miles from the sea, measured by the course of the river.   At this point they found it narrow and full of rocks, and it was considered unnecessary to go any farther, as more impassable places were reported a little farther on, and Livingstone was soon convinced that a greater interval of land-carriage would intervene from

the farthest navigable point of the Rovuma to the shores
of Nyasa than existed round the cataracts of the Shire.
The natives, moreover, were quarrelsome and hostile,
and Livingstone therefore decided to give up the Rovuma
for a while [1] and return to the Zambezi, which he reached
at the end of November, having first called in at Quilimane, finding the river so low, however, that he did
not get up to Shupanga until the 19th December,
which they left again on the 10th January 1863, with
the *Lady Nyassa* in tow.   On their way up the river
they saw the most sickening scenes of destruction due
to the slave-raids of that vile being Mariano, one of
those black Portuguese who are a disgrace to humanity.
For miles and miles nothing but burnt villages, stinking
corpses, and white skeletons could be seen, together with
a few wretched survivors slowly starving to death in the
absence of the food which the slave-raiders had taken
away or destroyed.[2]

Unfortunately, the *Pioneer* stuck again in a shallow
part of the river above the Ruo, and whilst waiting here
Mr. Thornton rejoined the expedition.   He too was
doomed to leave his bones in this land.   The remaining
missionaries at Magomero had, after the death of Bishop

[1] There was one pleasing feature about this last Rovuma expedition
in agreeable contrast to all the other work which had taken place on
the Zambezi, and that was the excellent health that prevailed amongst
all concerned in this journey.

[2] Throughout the Zambezi expedition Livingstone recounts numerous
instances of these destructive ravages due to the slave-raids of the
black Portuguese.   In allowing these horrors to take place and to
continue, the Portuguese Government was certainly to blame in its
pusillanimity and indifference.   It did not seem able to take stronger
measures to keep these half-caste scum under better control; but, at
the same time, it should be clearly understood that no *white* Portuguese
were concerned in these slave-hunts.   They were only so far to blame
in that they did not actively put a stop to them.

Mackenzie, fled from that place down to Tshibisa's, on
the Shire, and Thornton, finding that they were suffering
from want of animal food, volunteered to go across to
Tete and bring thence a supply of goats and sheep.   He
was anxious at the same time to connect, by a survey,
his former work at Tete and that in the mountainous
Shire district.   But the toil of this terrible journey,
which had once very nearly killed Dr. Kirk and Mr.
Rae, proved too much for his strength ; for when he
returned from Tete to the *Pioneer* he fell ill with dysentery and fever, and died on the 21st April 1863, adding
another grave to the number which dot the banks of the
Shire with English bones.

Having at last got up to the vicinity of the cataracts,
Livingstone and his party unscrewed the *Lady Nyassa*,
and began to make a road over the forty odd miles of
land porterage round the Murchison Falls.   But the
task proved too much for their strength.   The fact was,
they were all in a state of despair.   All the native labour
being swept away by the slave-raids, the country was in
a condition of utter desolation ; no food could be procured but what they shot themselves, and over and above
this, the worry, anxiety, and hard work under a tropical
sun had laid low nearly every member of the expedition
with dysentery.   From this terrible disease Dr. Kirk
and Charles Livingstone suffered so severely that they
were ordered to return home ; but just as they were
about to start Livingstone himself fell ill with the same
disease, and Dr. Kirk was obliged to remain in attendance
till the worst was past, and he was nursed back again to
convalescence.   Kirk finally left him on the 9th May
1863.

A few miles of road had been completed, and the oxen

had been broken in, so when Livingstone recovered he resolved to go to the Upper Shire and endeavour to recover and patch up the boat which he had left behind him above the cataracts, and reach in her the southern shore of Lake Nyasa, where he would be able to buy a large quantity of provisions, that would render his expedition independent of the Portuguese settlements for a while. Accordingly he started, accompanied by Mr. Edward Rae (who had returned to the Zambezi in the *Pioneer*), and drove part of the way in a cart; but on arriving at the upper portion of the river, they found their boat had been burned by the Mañanja about three months previously.

On returning to the *Pioneer* on the 2nd July, Livingstone found awaiting him a despatch from Earl Russell, containing instructions for the withdrawal of the expedition. In view of the many disasters which had occurred, it is not to be wondered at that the British Ministry considered the expenditure caused by the expedition to be already so large that it was felt it could not be allowed to go on with so little prospect of a favourable result. While concurring in the inevitable necessity for this action on the part of the Secretary of State for Foreign Affairs, Livingstone, with his indomitable perseverance, resolved not to have done with Nyasaland before he had seen a little more of the lake, and taking advantage of the excuse that it was quite impossible for the *Pioneer* to go down to the sea until the floods of December, he made arrangements to have the *Lady Nyassa* screwed together once more, and then, while this was doing, he determined to have a boat carried past the cataracts for the second time, and to effect, if it were possible, the circumnavigation of Lake Nyasa. Fate was not tired of spiting him yet. His boat, which he had attempted to get past the cataracts, was wrecked by the carelessness of his men, and dashed down the Falls, everything in her being lost. Bitter as was his vexation, however, Livingstone organised a little caravan of seamen from the *Pioneer* whose health required a change to the breezy highlands, and started off for the Upper Shire, with the intention of crossing it and proceeding to the south-west of Lake Nyasa, to obtain information about the slave-routes in that direction. Passing through a country to a great extent deserted by its inhabitants, they eventually reached Kota-kota, on the shores of Lake Nyasa, where they were kindly received by the Arabs. After a short stay here, and the acquisition of much information about the slave-trade, they turned due west along the great route to Central Africa which leads to Lake Bangweolo and the Upper Congo. In this direction they travelled as far as a place called Tshimanga, in the vicinity of the Loangwa River. Here Livingstone was told, and not untruly, that he was only ten days' journey from Lake Bemba or Bangweolo. But here they had to turn back, because it had been made clear to them, in a manner more public than was pleasing to Livingstone's feelings, that the pay of all members of the expedition would positively cease on the 31st December, and Livingstone felt that it would be unfair to the men to delay them any longer, as he had received orders to take the *Pioneer* down to the sea in the preceding April, and had delayed doing so until the following December. Accordingly, with bitter regret at having to turn back within smell, almost, of new lakes and rivers, he gave the order to retrace their steps to Lake Nyasa, the shores of which they

reached on the 8th October. His little party finally
arrived at the *Pioneer* on the 1st November. The river,
however, did not rise sufficiently for their departure
until the 19th January 1864. They were not, of course,
permitted by the ill-luck which dogged their progress
to descend the river even on their homeward journey
without some mishap. The *Pioneer* carried away her
rudder in passing suddenly round a bank, which delayed
them from reaching Morambala till the 2nd February.
At this place they stopped to pick up the remaining
members of the Universities' Mission.

Bishop Mackenzie had been succeeded, after a considerable delay, by Bishop Tozer, who viewed the Shire
Mission in a very different light to his enthusiastic
predecessor. He had no great liking for the natives,
and the appearance of the country, the awful ill-health
which prevailed amongst such missionaries as were remaining, and the terrible desolation which was brought
about by the raids of the Wa-yao and the black Portuguese, filled him with disgust, and he had left the Shire
for Quilimane before Livingstone had arrived at Morambala to take away the remnant of the Universities'
Mission who were awaiting him there.

Bishop Tozer's conduct is rather severely animadverted
on by Livingstone in his account of the Zambezi expedition, but there is little doubt he acted wisely under
the circumstances, and his petulant remarks about
" black people " were very likely due to worry, vexation,
and ill-health. The continuance of the Universities'
Mission work on the Shire under the circumstances which
then prevailed would probably have only led to fresh
disasters. The subsequent history of the Universities'
Mission has shown that Bishop Tozer acted prudently

in removing its headquarters to Zanzibar.   At Zanzibar the Mission began to get at Central Africa through the intelligent Swahili race.   Bishop Tozer was succeeded by that justly-famed man Bishop Steere, whose practical genius established the Mission on a firm basis.   Dr. Steere's patient study of East African languages enabled him to produce grammars and vocabularies of the Ki-

BISHOP STEERE.

(From a photograph by Barraud, by permission of the Universities Mission to Central Africa.)

swahili, which remain the standard text-books of that language to this day.

In after-years, and under Bishop Steere's directions, the Universities' Mission in Nyasaland was re-established,[1] and has grown and flourished ever since.   During the interval of time which ensued between the two

[1] In 1881.

attempts, our missionaries had learnt much as to the
requirements of white men in Tropical Africa, and
although a few among this second batch of pioneers have
died from fatigue, exposure, and the severe discomfort
incidental to the evolution of such a work, still there have
been many bright episodes in the history of the Mission
to counterbalance its first few losses, and a much better
standard of health has since been maintained among its
members.

After a hurried visit to Sena in order to settle out-
standing accounts for supplies with the kindly Portuguese
at that place, Livingstone proceeded with the *Pioneer* and
Lady Nyassa to the mouth of the Zambezi, which he
reached on the 13th February 1864. Here he was met
by H.M. ships *Orestes* and *Ariel*, which severally towed
the *Lady Nyassa* and the *Pioneer* to Moçambique.

On their way thither they were most severely tried
by the elements. Indeed, an irreverent person reviewing
the history of the Zambezi expedition would almost
come to the conclusion that Providence was on the side
of the Portuguese and determined to thwart it. A
terrible hurricane struck the *Ariel*, which was towing
the *Lady Nyassa*, and again and again it seemed inevitable that the latter vessel must be destroyed by the
plunging backwards and forwards of the man-of-war.
"When the *Ariel* pitched forward," writes Livingstone,
" we could see a large part of her bottom, and when her
stern went down we could see all her deck. A boat
hung on her stern davits was stove in by the waves.
The officers on board the *Ariel* thought it was all over
with us." . . . During the whole of this hurricane, in
which three towing hawsers were snapped one after the
other, the *Lady Nyassa* behaved admirably, and never

shipped a single green sea. During the same gale the *Orestes*, which was towing the *Pioneer*, split eighteen sails, some of the *Pioneer's* cargo had to be thrown overboard, her roundhouse was washed away, and the cabin was frequently knee-deep in water. The *Orestes* and the *Pioneer* did not arrive at Moçambique until nine days after the *Ariel* and the *Lady Nyassa*. The cool-headed pluck and admirable seamanship of the British navy had baffled the spite of the powers of the air who are for ever plaguing the martyr-man, and will continue to do so until he acquires the knowledge which will bring them under his control.

CHAPTER XVI.

LAST VISIT TO ENGLAND.

At Moçambique the Zambezi expedition came to an end. The *Pioneer* returned to the Cape with the Rev. Horace Waller and the remnant of the Mission pupils. The other ships dispersed, and Livingstone proceeded in the *Lady Nyassa* to Zanzibar to endeavour to dispose of her there. But no one being willing or able to buy her, he made a most plucky journey across the Indian Ocean to Bombay in this tiny little craft. At Bombay he was received with much kindness by Sir Bartle Frere (the Governor), and failing to sell the *Lady Nyassa* here, he left her at this place pending his possible return, and made the best of his way to England *viâ* Egypt and France. He reached Charing Cross Station on July 23, 1864.

On the same day that he returned to London he called on Sir Roderick Murchison early in the evening, and was taken by him straight away to a reception at Lady Palmerston's, where London society treated him with a certain amount of condescending politeness. Two or three days afterwards he went to the Foreign Office to see the Secretary of State for Foreign Affairs, but he was not over well received by Earl Russell, whose manner, he notes in his diary, "was very cold, as is that of all the Russells."

However, outside the Government offices, the great hearty British public of prosperous merchants, busy clerics, good-natured dukes, and simple-minded, earnest scientific men—still more, perhaps, the intelligent arti-zans, who had read about Livingstone, and made him into a popular hero—was kind enough, and to some extent made him their lion for the summer season of 1864. He attended a meeting of the British Associa-tion, he assisted at the launching of an ironclad, he planted trees at the Duke of Argyll's, and figured in other public functions wherein he was always welcomed with enthusiasm, and not only retained his old friends, but made new ones by the modest, deprecating way in which he received the applause of the populace. In the autumn he set to work writing his book, "The Zambezi and its Tributaries," which is compiled from his own and Charles Livingstone's Journals. This book was written at Newstead Abbey, in Nottinghamshire, the residence of his friend and old companion, Mr. Webb. He had originally gone there with some reluctance and intending to spend but a few days, for he had wished to surround himself with some of his children and retire into privacy, so that he might give undivided attention to his book; but when his kind hosts, Mr. and Mrs. Webb, learnt the reasons of his reluctance to make a long stay with them, they invited down his daughter Agnes to join him, and made such arrangements for his accommodation that he might have all the seclusion and facilities for writing which he desired. The result was, that his intended stay of a few days expanded into a residence of eight months at Newstead Abbey; perhaps, all things considered, the eight happiest months of his life, for his was a nature which was peculiarly sensitive and expansive to kindness.

T

Through the efforts of Sir Roderick Murchison, Livingstone's brother Charles had been appointed Consul at Fernando-Po. Livingstone had also advocated the claims of Dr. Kirk for recognition at the hands of the Government.[1] As regards himself, it is a strange thing, and one not easily explained by the information which has come down to us, that, whereas most of Livingstone's associates in his Zambezi expedition were fairly well provided for, Livingstone himself got nothing of the substance and very little of the shadow. Dr. Blaikie informs us that during the early part of 1865 Mr. Hayward, the Queen's Council and essayist, was the bearer to Livingstone at Newstead of a vague verbal desire from Lord Palmerston "to do something for Livingstone," but nothing came of this, because Livingstone declined to have anything done on his behalf, unless it were the conclusion of a treaty with Portugal for the opening of the Zambezi. About the same period a movement was set on foot by Sir Roderick Murchison for Livingstone's return to the exploration of Africa.

Sir Roderick's idea was that Livingstone should proceed *via* the Rovuma to the south end of Tanganyika, and endeavour afterwards to solve the question of the southern limits of the Nile Basin. This idea did not

[1] Shortly afterwards Dr. (now Sir John) Kirk was offered an important post as Assistant Curator at the Royal Gardens, Kew; but his ambition tended steadily towards Africa, and, to the surprise of his friends, he declined this. He was ultimately offered the post of medical officer to the Zanzibar Consulate, which he accepted. Soon after he had established himself at Zanzibar he was made Vice-Consul in addition. During the absences of his superior officer, the Consul-General, Dr. Kirk acted in that capacity with distinction for several years, until, in 1873, he was promoted to be Consul-General, to which was added the function of Political Agent in 1880. He retired from the Consular service in 1887, but has since been employed by H.M. Government in various diplomatic negotiations respecting Africa.

at first coincide wholly with Livingstone's own wishes,
which were to devote himself more especially to the
opening up of Nyasaland, if not by the Zambezi, then
by the Rovuma. However, in time, he was brought to
see that the two projects might be combined. At any
rate, that strange longing to return to Africa, which
besets every one who has visited that continent, urged
him to seize the first opportunity that presented itself of
returning to Africa. Indeed, the conditions under which
he ultimately resumed his explorations were so unsatis-
factory and unjust, and so ludicrously inadequate to the
value of his work, that the disinterestedness of his desire
to devote himself to Africa is clearly apparent. No one,
in fact, can say that Livingstone "made Africa pay."
It will be remembered that his original salary as an
agent of the London Missionary Society was £100
a year. For the two books published in his lifetime he
received in all some £11,000 or £12,000, a public testi-
monial in Scotland brought him in about £2000, at the
Cape of Good Hope he was presented with 800 guineas
on his way back to the Zambezi, and a public subscription at Bombay brought in not quite £1000. His pay
during the six years in which he served Her Majesty's
Government on the Zambezi was £500 a year. And
when he returned for the last time to Central Africa,
holding the rank of Her Majesty's Consul to the chief
and tribes of Central Africa, his pay was—nothing, and
in addition he was distinctly told by the Foreign Office
that he would have no claim on them for a pension.[1]

[1] The total of Livingstone's earnings in Africa, and of the bounties
he received (not counting his £100 a year whilst he was in the service
of the Mission, which did not even suffice for his needs of food and
clothing and the maintenance of his family), may be set forth as
follows :—

Nor had the Royal Geographical Society much occasion to vaunt its goodness to Livingstone. He brought *it* a vast amount of renown and legions of fellows whose united subscriptions probably amounted to a thousand guineas annually. The Council of the Society had given him after his journey to Angola a gold medal. To the second Zambezi expedition they contributed nothing, as far as I am aware; and on the occasion of his third and last departure for Africa the Society contributed £500, and coupled their contribution with provisos and restrictions of the most stringent kind. To this insufficient donation on the part of the premier geographical society of the world Her Majesty's Government was induced to add £500; thus Livingstone started with a fund of £1000 to explore about half Central Africa, to discover

Aggregate of money awards, testimonials, and subscriptions, say £5,000
Total pay from Government for six years' services on the Zambezi at £500 a year 3,000
Total received from publication of books, say . . . 12,000
Government grant for last expedition 500
Grant from Royal Geographical Society 500
_____
£21,000

On the other hand, he spent on the *Lady Nyassa* . . £6,000
He gave various grants and allowances to fellow-missionaries, and gratuities to some of the men who were with him on the Zambezi expedition which amounted altogether to about 1,000

And he, further, bore himself the expenses of his first great African journey from the Cape to Angola, and Angola to the Indian Ocean, and about two-thirds of his expenditure in Africa during the last eight years of his life. As two items in remarkable contrast to Livingstone's financial straits, it may be mentioned that the Royal Geographical Society expended (partly out of funds subscribed) £11,000 on Commander Cameron's expedition across Africa, and Stanley is calculated to have received from his publishers for all the books he has written on Africa about £80,000.

three or four lakes of sufficient magnitude for each one to be as good as a knighthood to the explorers of a later day, to determine the true sources of the Nile, and represent Her Majesty among the chiefs and tribes of the interior. We are, however, informed that a private friend [1] gave a subscription of £1000 to help him in his projects of exploration, and relieve him of any financial embarrassment that he might be in at the time of his departure, for the maintenance of his family during his absence.

Livingstone could not wait for the publication of his book on the Zambezi (which did not come out until the autumn of 1865), but left London on the 13th August in that year, and stopping a day or two at Paris in order to place his daughter Agnes [2] at a school, he reached Marseilles on the 19th August, and left by steamer for Alexandria. In Egypt he spent a few days on his way overland to Suez, and visited a portion of Lesseps' Canal. He finally reached Bombay on the 11th September.

At this place he sold the *Lady Nyassa* (which had cost him £6000) for £2300. He invested this money in shares of an Indian bank, which failed a year or two afterwards, and thus the *Lady Nyassa* proved a dead loss to him from first to last. He made a pleasant little stay in India from the middle of September 1865 till the middle of January 1866. His old friend the Governor, Sir Bartle Frere, kindly arranged that his arrival at Zanzibar should be associated with as much prestige as he could confer on it. So he killed two birds with one

---

[1] James Young of Glasgow, who was a true friend to Livingstone, and would have placed half his fortune at the explorer's disposal had the latter consented to accept more than was barely necessary. Livingstone's *real* friends were the aforesaid James Young, William C. Oswell, and William F. Webb (of Newstead Abbey).

[2] Now Mrs. Bruce.

stone by giving Livingstone a passage in the *Thule*, a Government steamer, and at the same time commissioned him to present this steamer to the Sultan of Zanzibar as a gift from the Bombay Government.

Arrived at Zanzibar, he received, as might be imagined under the circumstances, a most friendly reception from the Sultan, and was furnished with letters of recom-

MRS. LIVINGSTONE BRUCE.
(*From a photograph by John Fergus.*)

mendation to the Arabs of the interior.   He had brought with him from India a number of boys from the Nassick Mission as a nucleus for his expedition to the interior. In the high-lands behind Bombay there had been established an educational mission by the Church Missionary Society, to which most of the slaves captured on the

Indian Ocean by our cruisers were sent. It was Livingstone's idea to utilise some of these educated Africans in the opening up of Africa. Unfortunately, neither with him nor with others did they prove a success.[1] He had also brought with him from India thirteen sepoys, and at Zanzibar he further engaged ten Johanna men, several of whom had been in his service before, and four natives of Nyasaland whom he had originally brought to Zanzibar. In Zanzibar he bought six camels, four buffaloes, two mules, and four donkeys. The buffaloes, of course, were the domesticated buffalo of India. These he was desirous of experimenting with on the African continent in the hope that they might prove able to resist the bite of the tsetse fly. He hoped also to show that camels, mules, and donkeys might be used for transport in East African countries. These animals were embarked in an Arab dau, whilst Livingstone and his men went on board H.M. ship *Penguin*, which had been commissioned to transport him to the mouth of the Rovuma.

He arrived off this river on the 22nd March, but owing to the difficulty of entering it (for many alterations seem to have taken place in the position of the shoals and the nature of the bar since he had visited the river previously), he was unable to land his menagerie of transport animals. Accordingly it was thought better to proceed a little distance to the north and land in the Bay of Mikindani. This was effected without any difficulty, and the *Penguin* steamed off, leaving Livingstone to set out on his third and last African journey.

[1] The present writer has had several old Nassick boys in his service in Africa, chiefly as cooks. They are generally well taught in whatever may be their trade, but are somewhat inclined to drunkenness. The Christian negro is too apt to lose the restraint on indulgence in alcohol which Mohammedanism imposes on him.

CHAPTER XVII.

FOUR GREAT LAKES AND A MIGHTY RIVER.

On the 4th April 1866 Livingstone and his party started from Mikindani for the Rovuma, with the intention of following that river as far as they might towards Nyasa. The expedition, at the commencement, consisted of Livingstone, thirteen sepoys (Mohammedan Indians from Bombay), ten Johanna men, nine negroes from the Nassick Mission, two men from Tshupanga, on the Zambezi, named Susi and Amoda, and two Wayao, Wekatani and Tshuma (Chuma), who were originally slaves whom Livingstone had freed in the Shire Highlands on the occasion of his first Zambezi expedition, and whom he had afterwards conveyed to Zanzibar. The expedition possessed, as beasts of burden, six camels, three Indian buffaloes and a calf, two mules, four donkeys, and a poodle-dog named Chitane.[1] Just at starting, one of the buffaloes gored one of the donkeys so badly that it had to be shot. This was misfortune

[1] Of this pet Livingstone writes: "He had more go in him than a hundred dogs of the country, took charge of the whole line of march, ran to see the first man in the line, and then back to the last, and barked to hasten him up ; and then, when he knew what hut I occupied, would not let a country cur come in sight of it, and never stole anything himself." This poodle was afterwards, to Livingstone's great grief, drowned in a marsh on the road between Nyasa and Tanganyika.

number one. On their way south to the Rovuma their camels and buffaloes were bitten by the tsetse fly, and already Livingstone noticed how badly the camels were treated by the sepoys, who overloaded and maltreated them.

On approaching the Rovuma they passed through dense thickets of trees growing closely together, but not of any great height. Having struck the river, they marched along its north bank as far as the town of Mtarika, on the banks of the Rovuma, in the northern part of the Yao country. On the way neither the mules nor the donkeys were annoyed by the tsetse. The camels and buffaloes, however, were incessantly bitten by this noxious fly, which would only leave them gorged with their blood, and with small streams flowing down the animals' bodies from the bites. Nevertheless, what worried Livingstone more than the attacks of the tsetse was the abominable cruelty on the part of the sepoys to these unfortunate animals. They overloaded them, prodded them with sharp sticks until there were large holes in their bodies, left them standing loaded in the sun, and often neglected to see that they were fed. By the 7th May, a little more than a month after starting, two camels and one buffalo were dead, and on the next day, the 8th, Livingstone writes : " One mule is very ill, one buffalo drowsy and exhausted, one camel a mere skeleton from bad sores, and another has a small hole at the point of the pelvis which sticks out at the side. I suspect that this was made maliciously, for he came from the field bleeding profusely." Thinking to give the animals the benefit of a few days' rest, he resolved to push on ahead with his Johanna men and local carriers, leaving the sepoys and Nassick Mission

boys—who were about on a par for rotten badness,
laziness, and cruelty—behind to tend the animals and
rejoin him later. This was certainly not a very wise
thing to do, for if these men treated the animals badly
when checked with Livingstone's presence, they were
not likely to amend their conduct when removed from
his scrutiny. Ultimately the *havildar* of the sepoys
and one of the Nassick boys caught them up in the
Matambwe country, reporting that a second buffalo was
dead, and another camel and a mule had been left behind
ill. It was afterwards reported to Livingstone that
they had killed one camel with the butt-end of their
muskets, beating it till it died. On the 3rd June a
third buffalo died, and its calf soon afterwards followed
it. Apparently, in spite of the incessant way in which
they had been attacked by the tsetse, their death was
not due to the poison of that fly, but to the maltreatment they had suffered at the hands of the sepoys. On
the rest of the way to Mtarika's the sepoys caught
them up one by one, but behaved abominably. Most of
the Nassick boys re-joined the expedition, but one or
two had been left behind ill—and these finally died.

On their way to Mtarika's the expedition passed first
through a country harassed by the raids of the Magwangwara, the roving Zulu robbers of whom I have written
in previous chapters, and then through a district which
exhibited the most distressing evidences of the slave-
raiding of the Wa-yao and Swahili Arabs. Livingstone
here saw many ghastly scenes of slave-women stabbed
or shot through the body and left lying on the path
because they were unable to walk any longer; in other
places slaves were lying starving with the slave-sticks
round their necks, abandoned by their masters from

want of food. " They were too weak to be able to speak
or to say where they had come from ; some were quite
young." At Mtarika's place,[1] on the south bank of the
Rovuma River, it was decided to turn to the south-west,
because by striking straight across to Nyasa along the
Upper Rovuma they would have to pass through a
country ravaged by the Magwangwara and in a state
of famine. They therefore obtained guides and started
for the town of Mataka,[2] an important Yao chieftain
dwelling in the mountains near the south-east coast of
Nyasa. On the way the behaviour of the sepoys became
intolerable. They dawdled behind, picking up wild fruit,
and took from fourteen to twenty-two days performing
a march which Livingstone accomplished in one morning.
Livingstone had lent to their sergeant or *havildar* the
remaining donkey to carry his things, and this unfortunate brute was killed by striking it on the head whenever it stuck in any marshy place along the road. They
killed the last young buffalo calf and ate it, but when
questioned about this by Livingstone, they declared it
had been carried away and devoured by a tiger ; in fact,
they *saw* the tiger. Livingstone asked them if they saw
its stripes,[3] and they all declared that they had seen them
distinctly. Their *havildar* had no authority over them,
and the men wore the sulky look of people who were
going where they were compelled but did not wish to
go. On one occasion, when Livingstone allowed some
of them to sleep at the fire in his house, they plundered

[1] This must not be confounded with another Mtarika much farther
to the south, on the River Lujenda. It is a common Yao name.

[2] The son and successor of this man, also called Mataka, has recently
been brought into prominence from having caused to be killed two
young Portuguese officials, Senhores Valadim and Almeida.

[3] I need hardly remind my readers that there are no tigers in Africa.

him of everything they could sell, such as cartridges,
cloth, and meat. They threatened three times to shoot
his interpreter for exposing their thefts, and endeavoured repeatedly to bribe his men to desert him
and break up the expedition. Their talk was of the
filthiest character, and their evil communications corrupted the Johanna men and Nassick boys. At Mataka's, Livingstone resolved to endure their wickedness
no longer, so he paid them off, and made arrangements
for their returning to the coast with an Arab trader.
The *havildar*, however, entreated for permission to go
on with Livingstone, and he unwillingly consented, not
liking to repulse the man's expressions of attachment.[1]
In all his dealings with these sepoys and with his
Nassick boys and Johanna men one cannot fail to be
struck with the great want of discipline and firmness
which characterised Livingstone's third expedition. It
seemed somehow to lack organisation. There was a
"go-as-you-please" air about it, and it was fortunate
that Livingstone was received in a friendly way by the
natives; otherwise his party might have been exterminated with the greatest ease. Although, in all, the
permanent men of the expedition only numbered some
thirty-six (not counting the occasional native porters
hired from village to village), they were at times distributed over a hundred miles of country; one man at
this village, another couple staying with that chief, four
or five with Livingstone, and so on. Little effort seems
to have been made to keep the men together on the
march, and although Livingstone complains bitterly of
the maltreatment of the animals, he apparently took no
measures to prevent it, but was content to push on along

[1] This man returned to the coast later on with the Johanna men.

the road in feverish haste far in advance of his lagging
sepoys and slowly dying beasts. The admirable manner
in which he handled his Makololo in his former expeditions seems to have deserted him.

On the 29th July 1866 Livingstone made a start from
Mataka's for Nyasa, having been very hospitably treated
by this Yao chief. He reached Nyasa without any
difficulty on the 8th August, and sent word to Jumbe,[1]
the important Arab chief of Kota-kota on the opposite
coast, of his arrival, asking that a *dau* might be sent to
ferry him across, forwarding at the same time his letter
of introduction from the Sultan of Zanzibar to the Arabs
of the interior. His message, however, was apparently
not delivered, and after waiting a little while and seeing
no *dau* coming, he started off with his men and marched
round the south end of the lake, crossing the Shire
River at the entrance to its lake-like widening of
Pamalombwe. When on the south side of the Shire
he proceeded to the settlement formed by Mponda,[2] a
big Mohammedanised chief who had settled in this
country some years before, and had made himself king
among the timid A-nyanja people. At Mponda's one
of his Yao servants, Wekatani, found himself among
relations, and wished to stop with them. Accordingly
Livingstone paid him off, and commended him to
Mponda's care, to see that he should not again be sold
into slavery.

From Mponda's, Livingstone marched across the mountainous peninsula of Cape Maclear, and continued his
journey round the south-western gulf of Lake Nyasa.

---

[1] Predecessor of the present Jumbe, Sultan of Marimba.
[2] The Mponda who rules there to-day is the son of the man with
whom Livingstone stayed.

Here, however, he was to meet with some troubles from
his rascally men. At the town of a chief called Marenga,
at the south-west angle of the lake, there were rumours
that the country in front of them was being raided by
the Angoni-Zulus (whom Livingstone speaks of as the
" Mazitu "), and that forty-four Arabs and their followers
had been killed by these marauders at a place in the
interior called Kazungu.   The Johanna men, therefore,
became scared at this news, and Musa, their spokesman, said that they would go no farther, but wished
to return.   Livingstone took these men with him to
the chief Marenga and asked for an explanation of
the tales about the Mazitu.   The chief explained them
away, and Livingstone attempted to show his men
that on the road they were taking they would incur
no danger of meeting these robbers.   Musa and the
Johanna men, however, refused to believe either Livingstone or the chief Marenga, and when the former
attempted to continue his journey, the Johanna men
threw down their loads and walked off.   Their departure did not cause Livingstone any particular grief, as
he found them to be such inveterate thieves that he
could not even trust them with flints in their guns
(which they would sell to the natives) or allow them
to remain behind, for their object was invariably to
plunder their loads.   When they had left him he
obtained canoes from the friendly chief Marenga, and
in this way passed round the heel of Lake Nyasa and
landed at the town of another very friendly chief,
named Kimsusa, who showed him the most thorough-
going hospitality, and after escorting him for some
distance on his march northwards, handed him over
to another chief equally hospitable.   Livingstone and

his party, now consisting of a few Nassick boys, one
Yao and one Zambezi man (Susi and Chuma), crossed
the end of the long range called the " Kirk Mountains,"
at a height of over 4000 feet, and pursuing a very zigzag
track north-westwards through the Matshewa country
(disturbed by occasional scares of Zulus, but never seeing them, and meeting with no hindrance or event of
importance), they reached the Loangwa River on the
16th December 1866.

In the meantime the runaway Johanna men had
journeyed back rapidly to the coast, and finally reached
Zanzibar.   It is wonderful that they were not enslaved
on the way, and shows the respect with which Livingstone must have been regarded by even the Wa-yao, from
the fact that they allowed a handful of his men to pass
back unhindered through their country.   As they were
returning, however, the wily Johannas resolved to con-
coct such a tale as should excuse their return and not
prevent the payment of their wages.   On arriving at
Zanzibar, therefore, they related to Dr. Seward and Dr.
Kirk[1] a most cleverly constructed tale, which was so
well told that it was not to be wondered that some
believed it, though there were one or two small dis-
crepancies which those who knew the country were able
to detect.   The Johanna men, through their spokesman,
Musa, related that Dr. Livingstone had crossed Lake
Nyasa to its western shore, and was pushing on towards
the north-west, when beyond Marenga's village he was
met by a band of Zulus, who charged his small party of
twenty men with a rush.   Livingstone (they said) fired
at the advancing Zulus and killed two of them, but

[1] These gentlemen were at that time respectively Acting Consul-
General and Vice-Consul at Zanzibar.

before he could fire again he was felled to the ground with the blow of an axe, which nearly severed his head from his body. His Johanna men had then fled into the dense bush, and not being followed up by the "Maviti,"[1] had escaped. Not liking, however, to leave without absolute certainty of Livingstone's death, they went on to relate how they had returned to the place where he had been killed, and finding his body there, they dug a grave with sticks and buried him. Musa was repeatedly cross-examined by Dr. Seward and Dr. Kirk, but he stuck to the one version of his tale.

In England public opinion was divided as to the truth of Musa's statements. The press generally considered that the story was true in the main, and that Livingstone was really dead, and most of the newspapers hastened to publish his obituary notice. In various books issued at the time and dealing with African subjects one frequently meets with passages bewailing Livingstone's untimely end at the outset of his exploration.

However, Mr. Edward Young, the gunner of the *Pioneer* (of whose work with the Zambezi expedition Livingstone writes so favourably) had had Musa working under him in the *Pioneer*, and knew what a liar he was, and he for one declared that this history of Livingstone's death was false. The Rev. Horace Waller also expressed incredulity, as some of Musa's statements connected with the geography of the lake and of the Shire were known to him to be inconsistent with actuality. Sir Roderick Murchison, President of the Royal Geographical Society, also, in a speech delivered on one of his last appearances in public, declared his disbelief in

1 Mazitu, Mavitu, Maviti, are convertible terms given to the invading Zulus by the indigenous inhabitants of East-Central Africa,

this news of Livingstone's death; but in his case the reasons for his refusal to believe it were rather of the heart than of the head. However, public opinion was so far stirred on the subject that the Geographical Society determined to organise a search expedition, and they appointed Mr. Edward Young to command it. Judged by the results, a better choice of a leader could scarcely have been made. "The Livingstone Search Expedition" was one of the most brilliant feats ever recorded in African travel. Mr. Young left England in the middle of May 1867, and was accompanied by Mr. Faulkner,[1] John Reid (the excellent seaman who had sailed with Livingstone in the *Lady Nyassa* from Zanzibar to Bombay), and Patrick Buckley. They reached the mouth of the Zambezi on the 25th July, having brought out with them a steel boat which was named *The Search*. In this, with their baggage in a flotilla of smaller boats and canoes, they journeyed up the Zambezi and the Shire to the Murchison Cataracts. On this part of the Shire below the falls they found that the remnant of Livingstone's Makololo, who had chosen to remain behind in Nyasaland, had gradually become chiefs among the timid and servile A-nyanja, whom they were protecting to a certain extent from the raids of the Wa-yao and the Angoni. They received Mr. Young with enthusiasm, and together with their A-nyanja people assisted him to carry his loads round the Murchison Cataracts to the upper reaches of the navigable Shire. *The Search* was taken to pieces below the falls and skilfully reconstructed on the Upper Shire, and then was navigated up the river to the south end of

[1] Who afterwards returned to Nyasaland as a sportsman, and was eventually killed by the natives.

U

Lake Nyasa. Here Mr. Young proceeded to examine the people at Mponda's, and in this way collected a mass of information which conclusively proved the Johanna men to be liars, for the whole circumstances respecting their desertion of Livingstone were related by eye-witnesses, like Marenga. Having thus obtained satisfactory proof of the falseness of Musa's story, together with all the news obtainable of Livingstone's further journeys in the interior, Mr. Young and his party returned, and reached England in the very beginning of 1868, having been absent exactly and *only* eight months. *The Search,* under another name, still plies to and fro on the Upper Shire.

In the meantime Livingstone was plodding steadily on through the country of the Ba-bisa towards Lake Tanganyika. The rainy season had come on in all its force, and the land was beautiful in the springtide which the rain, supervening on the drought, produces. Livingstone gives in his Journal a pretty description of this vernal aspect of Central Africa : " The country now exhibits the extreme of leafiness, and the undulations are masses of green leaves ; as far as the eye can reach with distinctness it rests on a mantle of that hue, and beyond the scene becomes dark blue. Near at hand many gay flowers peep out. Here and there the scarlet martagon (*Lilium chalcedonicum*), bright blue or yellow gingers ; [1] red, orange, yellow, and pure white orchids ; pale lobelias, &c. ; but they do not mar the general greenness. As we ascended higher on the plateau, grasses, which have pink and reddish-brown seed-vessels, imparted distant shades of their colours to the lawns, and were grateful to the eye."

[1] *Amomum.*

The Bisa, or, as they are sometimes called, the Mushinga Mountains, over which he passed, were found to
be of pink and white dolomite, beautifully covered with
trees and upland vegetation.   In crossing the Tshimbwe
river or marsh, his poor little dog, Chitane, was drowned,
as already related in a footnote.   They found the Bisa
country a hungry land, owing to the slave-raids, which
caused famine everywhere, but the trees at this season
of the year bore so many edible fruits that his men
were saved from starvation.[1]   Some of the altitudes to
which Livingstone ascended in crossing the mountains
of the Bisa country reached to nearly 6000 feet, and he
seemed to have struck on one of those splendid healthy
regions of Central Africa which, by their altitude, are
raised to an almost temperate climate.

On the 20th January 1867, near a place called Lisunga,
a disaster happened to Livingstone of the greatest
magnitude.   He had engaged, some distance back along
the road, two Wa-yao porters, who were useful as in-
terpreters.   They, for some inexplicable reason, after
having done excellent service up to this date, deserted
Livingstone's expedition as it was passing through a
forest, and disappeared with the loads they were carrying.   One of the loads happened to be Livingstone's
medicine-chest, in which were placed all his drugs
without exception.   Although he stopped on the road
and made anxious search and inquiry, no trace could be
found either of the deserters or of the medicine-chest
they had stolen.   This was a terrible blow, because not

---

[1] Especially one called Masuko, which, in the right condition of
ripeness, is delicious. It has a thick brittle rind, and a sweet salmon-
coloured pulp with a taste of honey, and two large seeds in the pulp.
I have recently sent a number of these seeds to Kew, in the hope that
we may be able to try the Masuko under cultivation.

only would Livingstone have no means of checking
illness in himself or in his people, but the mental shock
was severe inasmuch as he now began to despair, feeling
that he had no safeguard against sickness.   It was unfortunate that he had put all his eggs in one basket (so
to speak), that he had stored all his medicines in one
receptacle instead of distributing them through several
loads; but he thought they would be best kept from
injury and breakage in the carefully constructed medicine-chest, and having entrusted this to the most careful of his personal attendants to carry, he thought he
had taken sufficient precaution against loss.   But this
attendant, Baraka, had exchanged it with one of the
runaway Yao porters for a lighter load, and thus Livingstone was stranded in the heart of Africa without
medicines, and this at a very unhealthy part of the year,
when he was daily soused by heavy rains.   Of this
calamity he writes in his Journal: "It is difficult to say
from the heart, 'Thy will be done;' but I shall try. . . .
Yet this loss of the medicine-box gnaws at the heart
terribly."

On the 28th January Livingstone crossed the Tshambezi, which may almost be regarded as the upper waters
of the Congo.   This river rises along the eastern edge
of the Nyasa-Tanganyika plateau, and flows south-west-
wards in a very gentle descent (expanding frequently
into wide marshes) till it reaches Lake Bangweolo.   It
then passes in a visible current through the southern
end of that lake, and on flowing out of it to the westward receives the name of Luapula, under which appellation it flows through Lake Moero, and eventually joins
with the Lualaba, thus forming the main stream of the
Congo.

All this land seemed to Livingstone a vast sponge, on account of the incessant rain and the dense, matted vegetation under foot. He describes the character of the Lobemba country at this season of the year as being " dripping forests and oozing bogs." On the 31st January he arrived at the town of Tshitapangwa, the then chief of the Ba-bemba. Here he was at first received with great friendliness ; the chief gave him five oxen and several large tusks of ivory. At this place they found staying for a few days a party of Swahili slave-traders who were on their way back to the coast. For ten rupees their leader consented to take a packet of letters to Zanzibar, which letters, it is to be noted, reached England safely. In this way Livingstone was able to send an order for stores and medicines to meet him at Ujiji.

After a few days, however, Tshitapangwa's covetousness (which had been excited by the descriptions given to him by an old Swahili follower of Burton and Speke of the generosity of those explorers) began to grow troublesome. He asked for all sorts of things, and on being refused vaguely threatened to place obstacles in Livingstone's path. Their unfriendly relations were rather caused by the stupid behaviour of Livingstone's boys, especially the Nassick boys, who were the most abject cowards, and never interpreted honestly between Livingstone and the chief, telling each in turn not what the other had said, but what was pleasant for either to hear. They also, apparently, were wanting in their knowledge of the Ki-bemba tongue, and not liking to confess their ignorance, made up statements on their own account to represent conversations which they did not properly understand. However, Livingstone's

patient, dignified manner soon began to prevail over
the chief's petulance and greediness, and eventually they
parted very good friends, Tshitapangwa having pretty
well returned the value of Livingstone's presents in fat
oxen and implements and curiosities of the country.

In this district Livingstone notes that the camwood
(*Baphia nitida*) grows abundantly. Its local name is
Molombwa. The people take the bark, boil and grind
it fine. It then makes a splendid blood-red pigment,
which they smear over their bodies, their heads of hair,
and the bark-cloths which they wear. It is prepared
in the shape of large balls, which are a most common
article of local trade all over the Congo Basin and right
away to the Niger Delta.

After three weeks' stay with Tshitapangwa he started
again on his journey northwards towards Lake Tanganyika. In the high plateau to which he ascended
from the valley of the Tshambezi he noticed a quantity
of the gum-copal tree (*Trachylobium*), which, " when perforated by a grub, exudes from branches no thicker than
one's arm masses of soft, gluey-looking gum, brownish-
yellow and light grey, as much as would fill a soup-
plate." A short distance beyond Tshitapangwa's his
porters insisted on deflecting their march to the village
of a chief called Moamba, lest they should offend him
by passing him by unvisited. However, this individual,
whom Livingstone describes as "a big, stout, public-
house-looking person, with a slight outward cast in his
left eye," proved intelligent and hearty. He gave them
plenty of food, and plied them with many questions as
to their reasons for travelling. Like most of the chiefs
in this region, he was greatly given to drinking "beer,"
which is really a kind of fermented gruel made from the

grain of millet. A young wife was specially told off to supply him with this mild intoxicant, which was to him both food and drink in one. Indeed, many of the chiefs in these countries of Nyasaland live wholly on this millet beer, taking no other kind of nourishment, and yet looking remarkably fat and jolly in appearance. I have noticed, however, that these men have very poor constitutions, and easily succumb to a slight illness.

On the 10th March they had entered the Ulungu country, and Livingstone notes in his diary how ill he has been with fever for some time past, how every step he took " jars in his chest," and how he could scarcely keep up with his people in the march. At length, on the 1st April, he came within sight of the south end of Tanganyika, or, as he calls it, " Lake Liemba." Here, at a place called Pambete, near the modern station of Niamkolo, he spent more than a fortnight, being too ill with fever to move, falling down in fits of insensibility, and sometimes suffering from temporary paralysis in his limbs. Nevertheless he does not fail to record his impressions of the beautiful scenery around him. This lake appears to him to be one of surprising loveliness : " Its peacefulness is remarkable, though at times it is said to be lashed up by storms. It lies in a deep basin whose sides are perpendicular, but covered well with trees ; the rocks which appear are bright-red argillaceous schist ; the trees at present all green : down some of these rocks come beautiful cascades, and buffaloes, elephants, and antelopes wander and graze on the more level spots, while lions roar by night. The level place below is not two miles from the perpendicular. The village (Pambete), at which we first touched the lake, is surrounded by palm-oil trees—not the stunted ones of

Lake Nyasa, but the real west coast palm-oil tree, requiring two men to carry a bunch of the ripe fruit. In the morning and evening huge crocodiles may be observed quietly making their way to their feeding-grounds; hippopotami snort by night and at early morning."

Going westwards of Pambete, Livingstone crossed a high range of mountains and came down into the valley of the Lofu. Here he met a large party of Arabs, who, as usual, received him with great kindness. On the Lofu, at Tshitimbwa's town, he was delayed for some time owing to a war which had occurred to the westward between the Arabs and a native chief of Itawa called Nsama. Whilst residing at Tshitimbwa's with the Arabs, and awaiting the course of events before deciding on his route, he made the acquaintance of a personage whom he mentions somewhat casually as "an Arab named Hamidi bin Muhammad, nicknamed by the natives 'Tipo-Tipo.'" This was none other than the celebrated "Tippoo-Tib,"[1] afterwards renowned as the friend of Cameron, Stanley, Wissmann, and other African travellers; as the great slave-raider of the Upper Congo; and, finally, as an official of the Congo Free State.

The three months and ten days' delay which occurred to Livingstone in this town of Tshitimbwa was far from being unpleasantly spent. The Arabs were exceedingly kind and affable. The rest and good food enabled him to regain his health and strength, and he obtained a vast amount of information about Central Africa from conversations with the Arabs, information which, read in

---

[1] The proper spelling of the word is Tipu-Tipu. He, however, is offended if addressed by his nickname *tout court*, and desires to be known by the Arab name, Hamid bin Muhammad.

the fuller light of to-day, appears singularly correct, although its full purport was not grasped by Livingstone at the time he wrote it down.

At length negotiations were satisfactorily concluded with Nsama, peace was made, and Livingstone, with the help of the Arabs, passed through the country of Itawa without any trouble, in the wake of a very large Arab caravan. Of the Arabs he writes repeatedly, "They have been extremely kind," and they certainly seem to have behaved towards him with generosity and studied courtesy. In spite of Lake Moero being reported to be nearly three days from Nsama's, Livingstone occupied all the time between the 22nd September and the 8th November (1867) in getting there. He reached the shores of the lake, however, on the last-named date, his health having again become bad on the way. From the north-east shores of Moero, Livingstone turned south and entered the country of the chief Kazembe.[1] This personage he describes as having a heavy, uninteresting countenance, without beard or whiskers, and somewhat of the Chinese type. His eyes had an outward squint; he smiled but once during the day, and that was pleasant enough, though the cropped ears and lopped hands of many of

---

[1] Kazembe, it will be noticed, is a very common title for a chief in East-Central Africa. It really means general, satrap, or lieutenant, and in most cases originates as a rank held under a supreme monarch by some minor chieftain, who in time becomes independent and retains the title of Kazembe, much as the Bey of Tunis, though practically an independent sovereign, continues to be known by the title of a Turkish officer. The Kazembe of Lake Moero was originally a lieutenant of the great Lunda empire under Mwato-yanvo. He has nowadays, however, shrunk to the position of an independent but almost powerless chief, alternately swayed by Arabs and Ba-bemba. I have already related that in the early part of this century he was rather an important personage in South-Central Africa, and received at different times two Portuguese missions.

his people, and the human skulls posted at the gate,[1] made Livingstone indisposed to look on him with any-think like favour. Kazembe's smiles were elicited by the antics of an uncouth dwarf, three feet nine inches in height, who was a kind of court jester. His executioner also came forward to look at Livingstone, with a broad Lunda sword on his arm, and a curious scissor-like instrument at his neck for cropping ears. On Living-stone saying to him that this was nasty work, he smiled ; so did many present who were not sure of their ears for a moment. Indeed, Livingstone noticed that many people of great respectability at Kazembe's court had been thus punished.

Kazembe's country was found to be an exceedingly fertile, pleasant land, with abundance of food. Oil-palms were common, the ground-nuts (*Arachis* and *Voandzeia*) were the largest he had ever seen, and the cassava or manioc the finest of its kind.

Livingstone had arrived at Kazembe's on the 21st November, and he left this town on the 22nd December for another visit to Lake Moero, the eastern shores of which he again explored. He then rejoined the Arabs, and stayed for some time in a large Arab settlement at Kabwabwata. While residing here, during the spring of 1868, he decided to start to explore Lake Bangweolo, but the Arabs endeavoured to dissuade him from this project, as they declared that he would meet with insuperable diffi-culties. They advised him to accompany them to Ujiji. However, on the 13th April, when he was about to leave Kabwabwata to return to Kazembe's in order to pass

---

[1] This custom of decorating the approach or the ramparts of a chief's town with human heads is common throughout South-Central Africa.

through that country to the reported Lake Bemba or
Bangweolo, his people, especially the whining Nassick
boys, refused to accompany him. It is curious to note
how, in spite of Livingstone's extraordinary kindness to
these supposed Christians, for a mere trifle they would
throw him over, desert him, steal from him, betray
him, and thwart him. However, nothing daunted,
Livingstone started the next day with only five attendants, leaving most of his baggage with Muhammad bin
Saleh, a friendly Arab. The next day another of his
men, Amoda, a Yao, ran away. Yet Livingstone viewed
this conduct on the part of his men with extraordinary
forbearance. "They were tired of tramping, and so
verily am I. . . . Consciousness of my own defects
makes me lenient."

On the borders of Kazembe's country, however, he
was stopped by a number of indignant crop-eared officials,
who declaimed excitedly against his entering the country
a second time. He patiently waited while the matter
was referred to Kazembe, who, to the great surprise of
his officious frontier-guards, sent a gracious permission
to Livingstone to re-enter his country, where he accorded
him an unusually kind reception. At Kazembe's town
Livingstone again remained for some weeks, and passed
much of his time in the company of an important Arab,
Muhammad Bogharib.

On the 11th June (1868) he started once more towards
the south for Lake Bangweolo, which he discovered on
the 18th July. On his journey thither he speaks of a
small variety of lion called by the natives the "lions of
niasi" or long grass, which particularly affected the dense
beds of reeds in Kazembe's country, and which would
appear to be a distinct variety of lion without a mane,

and scarcely exceeding three feet in height. At the village of Masantu he hired a canoe and crossed an arm of Lake Bangweolo to the peninsula called Mpambala or Bawara.

Whilst Livingstone explored the upper part of Lake Bangweolo [1] considerable confusion had occurred in Kazembe's country. It had been invaded by a number of the roving Zulus or Ba-tuta, and the Arabs and the Nyamwezi traders in this country had joined together to drive back these raiders. To do so they had built

[1] A considerable discrepancy was afterwards found between the maps of Bangweolo compiled from Livingstone's observations and notes, and the outline of the lake resulting from the more complete survey of the French explorer, Lieutenant Giraud. A careful examina tion of the facts attending Livingstone's visits to Bangweolo will explain away this discrepancy without damage to either traveller's work. Livingstone, though he went twice to Bangweolo and died close to its shores, only actually *saw* and navigated the lake *once*, and on that occasion merely explored its northern end. No doubt at that period —about fifteen years before Lieutenant Giraud's visit—Bangweolo was wider and larger in its expanse of open water, for the lake, like Nyasa and Tanganyika, is evidently shrinking in extent. The islands and coast-line which Livingstone actually visited he laid down correctly, but one, if not two, of his islands—Tshirue or Tshirubi and Mpambala or Bawara—have since, by the shrinkage of the lake, become penin- sulas. Livingstone never visited the outlet of the Luapula, nor ever actually saw the eastern or southern shores of the lake, so that these features were simply laid down by pure conjecture in his sketch-maps. On his second journey to Bangweolo—or rather to the east of it—he never actually saw the lake ; he travelled merely through the vast marshes which skirt its eastern side and render its eastern coast-line so very indefinite. On this journey, too, he was so harassed and so extremely ill that he kept but little record of distances, and so his route-survey cannot be depended on. Neither can the return journey of his men round the west shores of Bangweolo be considered of much value as geographical evidence. What Livingstone actually saw of the north end of Bangweolo he mapped correctly. What he did not see, but what he and his cartographers hypothetically drew to com- plete the outline of the lake, cannot be regarded as founded on suf- ficiently accurate observations to be set up in rivalry to the careful survey of Lieutenant Giraud.

LAKE BANGWEOLO.

L. Moero

Kazembe

Mbereze

Moene Mpundu

Mlundu

BAMB OZH

Kombokombo

Mwegge

Kahmbi

Tshana

Masantu

Kalasa

Kusunwa

Miombo

Mpambala

Tshatwende

Capello & Ivens

Kinyama

KASENGA

MereMere

Kalasa

Kisamba

SUNGA

IRAMBA

Mambirima Falls

Jiwande

Luapula

Mokoso

Mcosa

Jitilu

Kitebe

Kambalala

Bridge

Tshungu

Nhitunkubre

Kizinga

Tshinpa

Mguro Ashinto

Bridge

Kabaia

Senets Buga

Zapura

Tamatese

Lifungo

Lotovinza I.

Kizi

Inama

Moero

Mampa

Tshirube

Kawende P.

Kobinga

Bulungu

Kibya

Mapapa

Tshinama

Lolotikila

Lavusi Hills

Msiri

Tshitumba

ILALA

Open Lake.
Choked with Rushes &c.
Flooded during Rainy Season (Nov. to April)

Moero
Okata

Cazembe

LUNDA

Chibue's

Moambwa's

Malemba

LO BEMBA

Chibanda's

KABENDE

Lifunge Kisi

Moeria

Chirube

Mudholi

Masanga

L. Bemba
or
Bangweolo

M's of Bisa or Lokinga 5000-7000

L. BANGWEOLO.

From a MS. by Dr. Livingstone.
(1868)

George Philip & Son

stockades, and then, when they had finally repulsed the
Zulus, Kazembe and his chiefs began to fear that, by
means of the stockades the coast people had built, they
would themselves hold and possess the country ; accordingly Kazembe attacked one of the Nyamwezi strong-
holds called Kombo-kombo. In the meantime the Wa-
nyamwezi had certainly given some cause for this action
on Kazembe's part by attacking two tribes, the Bausi
and the Bambozhwa, dwelling to the south of Kazembe's
country. In one village Livingstone himself was nearly
killed by these people because they identified him with
the cause of his Arab friends. But one or two friendly
natives, intervening, explained matters and helped him
away. He finally joined the Arabs and got safely out
of Kazembe's country, re-entered Itawa towards the end
of October, and remained some time at Kabwabwata,
where he spent his time nursing himself through an
attack of fever and reflecting on the sources of the Nile.
It was just about this time that he began to be possessed
with the idea that the two great lakes he had found to
the west of Tanganyika and the great river that flows
through them might possibly prove to be the Upper Nile.

It almost goes without saying that, on his return to
Kabwabwata, he was soon induced to forgive the Nassick
boys, for whose conduct in deserting him he was fertile
in finding excuses. So he took them back into his
service, and almost began to persuade himself that it
was he who was wrong in wishing to go to Bangweolo
against their desire.

The delays of the Arabs—always the most dilatory of
men—in starting for Tanganyika began to vex Livingstone very much, as he was desirous of getting to Ujiji.
Again and again he was on the point of starting without

them, but they begged him to accord further delay, and
it must be admitted that all this time they were treating
him with unvarying kindness and cordiality, and provided
him with food every day.   His stay with them also had
an excellent effect in preventing them from making
slave-raids, for he had begun to inspire them with
extraordinary respect for his feelings, and they frequently ceased to do things he disliked, or refrained
from repeating evil actions so that they might avoid
wounding his feelings.   Just as the Arabs, however,
had decided to start and they were about to leave
Kabwabwata, their encampment was suddenly attacked
by the Ba-bemba.   Some quarrel had arisen between an
Arab and the head-man of a Bemba village, and a skirmish
between the two had aroused the whole country.   A
large number of people attacked the Arab settlement
in which Livingstone was residing.   Both defence and
attack were equally gallant.   Livingstone remained in
his house holding aloof from the fight, only resolved to
defend himself if he were personally attacked.   About
ten of the Ba-bemba were killed.   The attack was
renewed during several days, but eventually the Ba-
bemba sued for peace.   After fluctuating negotiations
some kind of peace was patched up with the Ba-bemba,
and Livingstone managed to start with the Arabs who
were bound for Ujiji :—

" It is a motley group, composed of Muhammad and
his friends, a gang of Wa-nyamwezi hangers-on, and
strings of wretched slaves yoked together in their heavy
slave-sticks.   Some carry ivory, others copper, or food
for the march, whilst hope and fear, misery and villainy,
may be read off on the various faces that pass in line
out of this country, like a serpent dragging its accursed

folds away from the victim it has paralysed with its fangs."

During the latter part of 1868 and the beginning of 1869 Livingstone's health was extremely bad. He took less and less care of himself, got wet through again and again in the rain, and persistently crossed brooks and rivers by wading through them up to the waist. His wretched health is shown by the dismal entries in his diary during the month of January 1869.

The Arabs were very kind to him, as usual, and nursed him as well as lay in their power, having him carried along in a kind of swinging cot made of boughs. On the 14th February he arrived on the west shore of Tanganyika. Here he obtained canoes from an Arab, and after coasting the lake a little towards the north, struck across to the east side, and so on to Ujiji, which he reached on the 14th March. Here disappointment awaited him, for the goods which had been sent to him overland from Zanzibar had been made away with in all directions, and only a poor remnant of them had actually reached Ujiji. Sixty-two out of eighty pieces of cloth had been stolen, and nearly all the beads. The buffaloes which were to be despatched to him had all died on the way. Fortunately, however, a little tea and coffee remained among the plundered stores, and some flannel, which, when made into vests, did him a great deal of good, and his cough ceased through wearing warmer clothing. He found considerable difficulty in persuading the Arabs to carry his letters from Ujiji to the coast, because they feared that he would report their slave-raids in the Bemba country; and, indeed, such letters as they consented to take they never delivered.

After making many inquiries about a route to the

north of Tanganyika, and deciding that it would be too
difficult to attempt it at that juncture, on account of
the impossibility of getting porters to enter the Ruanda
country, where the Arabs had hitherto been fiercely
repulsed, Livingstone finally settled that he would cross
Manyemaland to the west of Tanganyika, and endeavour
to find that great river of which the Arabs brought
him word. He therefore left Ujiji on the 12th July
1869, sailed over to the other side of the lake, joined
a large party of Arabs and Swahilis, and with them
passed through the Guha and Bambare countries north-
westward to the village of Moenekus,[1] a Manyema
chieftain, who had recently died. Here he remained
till the 5th November, resting and endeavouring to
recover his health, which he did partially. He then
pushed on towards that Lualaba River of which he had
heard so much to excite his curiosity. He travelled on
almost incessantly; his health soon failing again after
he had started, for the reckless way in which he got
wet through day after day, either by walking through
the rain or wading torrents, had reduced him to a
terrible condition of illness and exhaustion. As he was
compelled to travel with the Arabs and follow them in
their erratic course, he zigzagged through the Manyema
country until he got to a point as far north as the
Binanga Hills (about 3° 30′ S. latitude). He then
turned southwards again with the Arabs, and after more
than a year's wandering and waiting in Manyema, he
finally reached the banks of the Lualaba, at Nyangwe,
on the 1st March 1871. During this period the Nassick
boys were very troublesome; they were constantly de-

---

[1] This name should really be spelt Moenckusu, which means "Lord
of the Parrot," or " Owner of the Parrot."

serting or threatening to desert, and often he was left
with only three attendants, amongst them the peculiarly
faithful Susi and Chuma.   Once, during his residence
at the Arab settlement in Bambare, a worthless lot of
porters reached him from the coast with letters and a
few stores.

During his long stay at Nyangwe a dreadful massacre
of Manyema women occurred in the market-place of that
town, arising from a squabble about a fowl.   In this
slaughter the Arabs themselves estimated the loss of life
among the unarmed Manyema men, women, and children
at 330 to 400, killed by shooting, stabbing, or drowning.
The chief among the Swahili scoundrels concerned in
these atrocities was named Tagamoio.   Livingstone's first
impulse was to shoot the murderers with a pistol, but a
friendly Arab, who had been his host, protested against
his getting into a blood-feud.   " I was thankful afterwards that I took his advice " (he writes in his Journal).
"Two wretched Moslems asserted 'that the firing was
done by the people of the English.'   I asked one of
them why he lied so, and he could utter no excuse; no
other falsehood came to his aid as he stood abashed
before me, and so telling him not to tell palpable false-
hoods, I left him gaping."   Livingstone used all his
efforts with the leading Arab of Nyangwe, Dugumbe, to
have these murderers caught and hanged up in the
market-place as a visible protest in the eyes of the
Manyema against the " bloody deeds of the Wa-swahili ; "
but although Dugumbe attempted to appease Livingstone
by vague promises, he performed nothing, except re-
storing to liberty such of the Manyema as had taken
refuge in his house.   Eventually, through Livingstone's intervention, a sort of peace was patched up

between the wretched Manyema and the Arabs; but
Livingstone decided to return to Ujiji, being so filled
with horror at the crimes of the Arab slave-raiders
that he felt he could no longer travel under their escort.
Unfortunately, the porters who had been sent him from
Zanzibar, and who had reached him in Manyema, were an
extremely bad lot of men. He speaks of them always
as "the Banian's slaves;" and, indeed, it would appear
that the Hindi merchants with whom Dr. (now Sir
John) Kirk had contracted for a supply of goods and
porters to be sent to Livingstone, had simply chosen the
porters to convey these goods from among their own
slaves, and had picked out the worst men to boot. When
these people had been staying with Livingstone a short
time at Manyema, they refused to go with him along
the course of the unknown Lualaba, and would only
consent to carry for him as far as the Arab settlement
on the Lomami, a little distance to the west of Nyangwe.
Moreover, they were strongly inclined to leave Livingstone and attach themselves to Tagamoio, the Swahili-
Arab who had been the main agent in that unprovoked
slaughter of the Manyema in the market-place, being
attracted by the idea of sharing in his slave-captures.
Livingstone, therefore, could see no way out of his difficulty but to return to Ujiji and procure other men.

On the 20th July 1871 he started for Ujiji, Dugumbe
loading him with presents and provisions, no doubt with
the desire to conciliate him, as he was already beginning
to feel considerable apprehension as to how this raid on
the Manyema would be viewed at Zanzibar. On the
way back through the Manyema country large parties
of Arabs joined the caravan, with the desire of protecting him, for it was thought probable that the Manyema

might attack them in the forest, out of revenge for the slaughter at Nyangwe. Their apprehensions were justified by after-events. On the road to Bambare they were surprised by the Manyema on the 8th August, and three times during the course of the day Livingstone escaped death by a few seconds of time or a few inches of space. For five hours his caravan had to run the gauntlet of invisible enemies hidden in the dense vegetation. Spear after spear hurtled across the narrow path, sometimes almost grazing Livingstone's back as they just missed him. Great trees were burnt or chopped through at the base, and crashed down as he passed by, the smaller branches snapping off around him, and only his rapid instinctive ducks forward saving him from being smashed. At last, however, they got out of the forest into an open clearing, and were met by the Manyema chief of the district, who coolly sauntered up unarmed and asked what was the matter. When he realised who and what Livingstone was, and how utterly foreign he had been to the raids at Nyangwe, he accorded him his protection, and offered to make good some of his losses ; but Livingstone waived the compensation, and passed on dejectedly, having lost all his remaining cloth, a telescope, an umbrella, and most of the Manyema curiosities which he had been carrying away from Nyangwe. His route through this country, of such natural beauty, but so full of ghastly scenes of man's war on man, led him among some of the most thorough-going cannibals in the world, and his remarks on the eating of man's flesh, as practised by the Manyema, recall vividly the horrors revealed by Stanley's recent journey.

"Very ill with bowels;" "I rested half a day, as I am still ill;" "obliged to rest from weakness;" "ill all night, and remain," are phrases which frequently recur in Livingstone's diary during his journey back to Tanganyika, and convey some idea of his relapse into ill-health from fatigue, frequent wettings in the crossing of rivers, and heart-sickness at the horrors going on around him. As he nears the coast of Tanganyika he writes : "I was sorely knocked up by this march from Nyangwe to Ujiji ; in the latter part of it I felt as if dying on my feet. Almost every step was in pain, the appetite failed, and a little bit of meat caused violent diarrhœa, whilst the mind, sorely depressed, reacted on the body."

On his return to the west shore of Tanganyika he propounds the first hint that the outlet of Tanganyika is through the Rukuga [1] River to the Lualaba.

On the 23rd October he reached Ujiji, in such a condition that he was scarcely more than a living skeleton. The Arabs welcomed him with effusion, but he was perfectly aghast on finding that the leading Arab of Ujiji, a man known as the "Shereef" (Sharif), had sold off all the goods which had been sent to that place for him from the coast ; he had not left a single yard of calico out of three thousand, nor a string of beads out of 700 lbs. The Arab who had done this he describes as "a moral idiot," for he came without shame to shake hands with Livingstone, and when his proffered hand was rejected he assumed an air of displeasure, but nevertheless did not desist from coming twice a day to give the stereotyped salutation of "Sabah-'l-kheir ;" [2] after which he would say, in irritating sanctimoniousness, "And now I'm going to say my prayers," until the exasperated Livingstone expelled him from his house.

----

1 Livingstone calls this river Loñgumba.
2 "The best of the morning to you."

One of the better class of Arabs had begged Livingstone to accept goods from him to meet his immediate needs, but Livingstone would not receive his charity until he should be quite destitute, for he had still a few trade goods left which had been taken care of by an old Arab friend, Muhammad bin Saleh.

Just as he was in the sorest need and deepest mental depression, his faithful Susi came running up to him one morning and gasped out that he could see an Englishman coming.   Livingstone looked out and beheld a big caravan filing into the Arab settlement at Ujiji, loaded with all the elaborate paraphernalia of a well-equipped European expedition, but with a man in front carrying high the flag of the United States of America.   The sole white man who was leading the caravan was Henry Moreton Stanley, who had been sent by the *New York Herald* " to find Dr. Livingstone, living or dead."

CHAPTER XVIII.

THE MANYEMA AND THEIR LAND.

BEFORE continuing a review of Livingstone's further journeys, I will do here as I have done before—pause and describe the character of the country of Manyema, which was the scene of Livingstone's explorations in 1869–70 and 1871.

The Manyema country[1] is practically West Africa. Indeed, as I have already pointed out, the West African *flora* and *fauna* extend to the west shores of Tanganyika, but partly owing to the action of man in provoking forest fires and clearing the ground for plantations, and also owing in part to the more rocky nature of the soil, the luxuriant forests of West Africa do not show themselves until the *versant* of the western shores of Tanganyika is crossed and the traveller begins to descend towards the basin of the Lualaba-Congo. Then he enters upon a densely-wooded country similar in character to all the great forests of the Congo which stretch away to the Niger Delta with scarcely a break. In Manyema, however, even as far back as Livingstone's day, when the opening-up of the country by Arabs was of quite a recent date, the forest no longer usurped the

[1] Livingstone spells this word constantly Manyuema, but most other authorities, Manyema. I have questioned not a few of its people who are brought to Zanzibar as slaves, and they all pronounce it in the same way—Manyema.

whole surface of the land. The Manyema seem to have already made much more progress towards laying bare the country to the sky and thinning the woods than the more scattered Bantu tribes to the north. The forest is cleared by them partly by burning, but still more by cutting down the trees with their small iron axes. The white-ants in time consume the fallen trunks and reduce them to the most fertile vegetable soil. These clearings therefore form plantations of splendid fertility. Where-ever the forest has been cleared away in a wholesale manner, it never seems to grow up again in the same way or composed of the same ingredients as the primeval woodland. Gigantic grasses immediately replace the fallen trees as the occupants of the soil, unless man has already set to work to plant his crops ; and if the clearing is still further neglected and unutilised, there grows up among the grass a stunted *Copaifera* tree, or else a closely allied shrub of the genus *Bauhinia*. This style of debased forest—long grass and *Copaifera* trees—is characteristic of enormous tracts of Africa. The dense forest, however, is seldom wholly expelled from the river-valleys, and no doubt extent of moisture has much to do with the extinction or maintenance of the old forests, with their gigantic trees and luxuriant undergrowth ; for the clearing away of the woods and the laying bare of the ground not only drives away the rain to a consider-able degree, but what rain does fall is rapidly drained off or evaporates under the action of the sun; whereas where the rain-drops percolate through a dense forest, the soil remains full of moisture. In some parts of the Manyema country an occasional big tree resists the sharp, short blaze of the annual grass-burnings, or if seared with the flames up to a certain point, nevertheless sends

out new shoots and suckers from its roots, so that a
number of nearly straight but more slender masts grow
with great rapidity alongside their parent trunk.   Many
trees growing like this are protected by the natives from
the further action of the fire by cutting a bare space
of sufficient circumference around them, so that in the
grass-fires they may not be further scorched.   The
natives (the Manyema) interlace this natural scaffolding
with rope ladders made of creepers, and so can ascend
to a considerable height.   In other parts of the forest
country it is even said that they construct houses or
shelters high up the tree, assisting themselves by these
supplementary and parallel stems.

In the Manyema country the natives are in the habit
of making elephant-traps, which Livingstone describes
as follows: "A log of heavy wood, about twenty feet
long, has a hole at one end for a climbing plant to be
passed through to suspend it; at the lower end a mortice
is cut out of the side, and a wooden lance about two
inches broad by one and a half inches thick, and about
four feet long, is inserted firmly in the mortice; a latch
down on the ground, when touched by the animal's foot,
lets the beam run down on to his body, and the great
weight of the wood drives in the lance and kills the
animal.   I saw one lance which had accidentally fallen,
and it had gone into the stiff clay soil two feet."

As I have already reminded my readers, all this
country is thoroughly within the West African sub-
region as regards its *flora* and *fauna*.   The big-game
animals of East Africa are absent, with the exception
of the elephant and one or two tragelaphine antelopes.
There is no lion, but the leopard is abundant.   The
grey parrot—one of the most distinctly West African

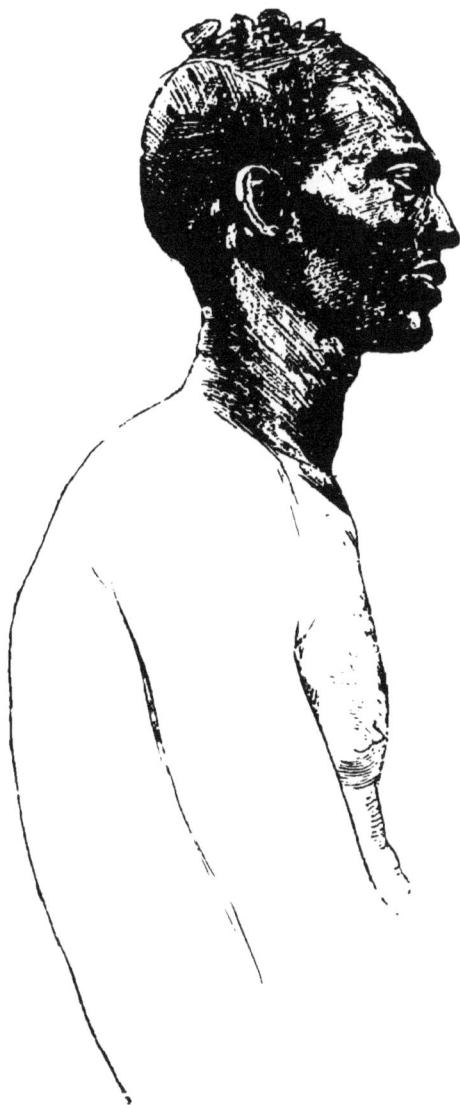

A MANYEMA CANNIBAL.

(From an Original Drawing by H. H. Johnston, C.B.)

types—is exceedingly common, and is a great pet among the Manyema people, who obtain them young from the nest and train them up to be perfectly tame and to become household pets. There is also present in these forests an anthropoid ape, which Livingstone describes under its Manyema name of *Soko*. From all we know about this interesting beast, it would seem to be either a somewhat larger variety of the common chimpanzee or a very closely allied species.[1]

[1] The colour of the skin is a pale yellow, as in the common chimpanzee, and not black, as it is among the other species of anthropoid ape in West Africa. The *Soko*, which is probably identical with that form of chimpanzee found by Emin Pacha farther north in the Mombutu country, is also said to extend its range southwards to the vicinity of Lake Moero and along the banks of the Upper Congo. According to Livingstone, these creatures often walk in an erect position, but steadying their bodies by placing the hands on the back of the head. He represents this beast as being of great intelligence, and so cunning that it is difficult to stalk him in front without being seen, and therefore when he is killed it is usually from behind. The Manyema people frequently string a number of nets round some enclosure in the forest and drive the *Sokos* into them and spear them. Brought to bay like this, they will frequently turn on their assailants, and will snatch their spears from them and break them, and perhaps also bite off the ends of the men's fingers. As a general rule, however, they seem to be far from ferocious ; indeed, there is a strong element of playfulness in their nature. They will stalk the men and women who are at work in the forest or in the plantations, and occasionally seize them, but after grinning and giving vent to a shrieking kind of laugh, will leave them unharmed. They will also kidnap children and run up the trees with them, but can be lured down, however, by being tempted with bananas. The ape scrambles down the tree to seize the bananas, and in doing so looses its hold on the child, who is then recovered. Occasionally the children they catch are pinched and scratched, and swung backwards and forwards by one arm, but not seriously hurt. If a *Soko* encounters a man who is unarmed, he grabs hold of him possibly, but does him no injury. Should the man fight with him, however, or wound him, he will seize his wrists and bite off his fingers (which he spits out), buffet his cheeks with back-handed slaps, and scratch him. If the *Soko* has been wounded in his encounter with the man, he endeavours to stuff leaves

A young *Soko* which was given to Livingstone as a
pet seemed instinctively to take to him as a friend, and
would sit quietly on the mat beside him. If he went
for a walk she insisted on coming too, and would hold
up her hand to him that he might take her with him.
If refused, she hung down her head and made grimaces
of the most pathetic human-like sorrow. She would not
only wring her hands, but sometimes her feet too, to
make it appear more touching. She would gather grass
and leaves around her to make a nest, and resented any
one meddling with her property. She would endeavour
to untie a knot in the cord which bound her to a post, and
when interfered with by a man, raged at him, and tried
to beat him with her hands. In attacking him, she put
her back against Livingstone's legs, looking upon him
instinctively as a friend. She covered herself with a
mat on going to sleep, and would wipe her hands, when
dirty, with a leaf.

The Manyema people appear to belong to the same
Bantu group as the Ba-kusu on the Lomami, the Ba-
songo on the west bank of the Lualaba, and all the
tribes along the Lualaba-Congo and the Lomami up to
the Aruwimi; and judging by an interesting vocabulary

into the wound to stanch the blood. These chimpanzees live in communities of about ten, and are monogamous. If one male *Soko*
attempts to seize the female of another, the rest of the community
all unite in punishing him with buffets and bites. The female *Soko*
occasionally brings forth twins. Both father and mother show great
affection for their offspring, and if the parents are crossing a bit of
dangerous open country with their child, the father carries it until
they have arrived at a safe place, and then hands it over to the
mother. Their food is principally wild fruits, and they are peculiarly
fond of bananas. At times the *Sokos* collect together and drum with
their fists on the trunks of hollow trees, and accompany this perform-
ance with loud yells and screams, which seemed to Livingstone to offer
some resemblance to the singing of the Manyema.

of the language of the Aruwimi people published by Dr.
Sims, it would seem as though they too belong to the
same racial and linguistic group. In fact, the peoples of
the Congo Basin may be summarised into the following
groups, according to the affinities of their dialects.
Starting from the upper waters of the Congo where it
leaves the Nyasa-Tanganyika plateau and flows through
Lake Bangweolo, there is the Bisa-bemba group; then
the Rua or Lunda people, who extend northwards from
the southern limits of the Congo watershed to about the
fifth degree of north latitude, and westward from the
shores of Tanganyika to the Upper Kwango. North of
the A-rua comes the Manyema group, which apparently
extends right down the course of the Lualaba-Congo as
far as its confluence with the River Loika to the north
of the Aruwimi. Westwards of Manyema, in that great
bend of the Congo you have the far-stretching Balolo-
Bateke group, which extends from the Lomami River
westwards right across the Lower Congo to the Ogowe
watershed. Along the Congo in its most northern
reaches, and in the valley of its great affluent, the
Mubangi River, there is the Babangi-Bangala group;
and, finally, along the course of the extreme Lower
Congo, from Stanley Pool to the sea, and inland from
Stanley Pool to the River Kwango, there is the Kongo
group, which is the best studied of all.

The language of the Manyema is a very degraded
type of Bantu tongue with several of the prefixes miss-
ing, and others reduced to a vowel. The vocabularies
I have been able to collect show how lopped and abbre-
viated most of the words are from the original Bantu
type.

The Manyema are a decidedly handsome people; in

fact, one of the few tribes of pure negro race who can be called really good-looking, with delicate features, and bodies and limbs proportioned according to our European canons of beauty.[1] Nor, in spite of their cannibalism, can they be looked upon as savages. They are much less given to nudity than the tribes farther south.[2] The men usually wear long kilts of many folds or flounces, either made of cloth procured from the Arabs, or else of the bark-cloth which they beat out themselves. Until the advent of the Arabs they possessed no cattle, but had the usual domestic sheep of Africa—that kind with the long mane and thin tail—goats, dogs, pigs, and fowls. They cultivate tobacco, maize, ground-nuts, bananas, *Pennisetum* or millet, and *Holcus sorghum* or Durha grain; and Livingstone mentions that in the Ba-kusu country pine-apples are cultivated, and coffee also, and that, still more remarkable, they make an infusion of its berries and drink it flavoured with some species of vanilla orchid ! This, if true, is very remarkable, because no African race yet has been known to use coffee for making a beverage until taught by Arabs or Portuguese, or other Europeans; and, according to Livingstone's account, the Ba-kusu must have known the use of coffee before the Arabs came amongst them. The same people are said to bathe regularly twice a day, and to build houses of two storeys, and to smelt copper from the ore.

The houses built by the Manyema are of the rect-

---

[1] The accompanying engraving is from a drawing of mine made from a Manyema slave belonging to a Tanganyika Arab.

[2] The women, however, among the Manyema (according to Livingstone) are less particular about clothing than is the other sex. As a rule (to which, however, there are several marked exceptions), the men among African savages have no regard for decency, while the women are modest and sufficiently clothed.

angular Congo style. They are fairly large, the walls are
of well-beaten clay, and the leaf-stalks of palms[1] split
in two make capital rafters for the sloping roofs, which
are thatched usually with the dried fronds of the banana
or an allied zingiberaceous plant. The inside of their
dwellings is clean and comfortable. Before the Arabs
came bugs were utterly unknown, though now they are
beginning to infest the native villages. The houses
are generally in a line; the streets are broad, and run
east and west in order that the sun may rapidly dry
them. There is generally a large public meeting-house
at each end of the broad street, and here guests arriving
are usually required to take up their residence. The
people form hedges round their gardens, often eighteen
feet in height, by cutting off portions of the stems of a
species of *Dracæna* or *Hibiscus,* and planting them in
the ground, like a lot of stout staves close together.
These rapidly sprout, and soon form an almost impene-
trable fence. At some height from the ground lianas
or " bush-ropes " are tied along the poles horizontally,
and from these are suspended maize cobs of a variety
that bends its fruit-stalk round into a hook. These
hedges thus become a regular upright open-air granary
surrounding the villages and the gardens.

The Manyema, in spite of their being far removed
from savagery by their skill as potters and smiths and
cultivators, are yet much given to bloodshed, and are
undoubtedly outrageous cannibals. Their rage for eating human flesh is utterly inexcusable, because it would
appear to be simply a matter of *gourmandise.* Their
soil is singularly fertile, and foods of all kinds abound.
Livingstone thinks that their love of man's flesh arose

[1] Chiefly got from the immense fronds of the *Raphia vinifera.*

from their practice of eating chimpanzees, for the Manyema are as fond of the flesh of these apes as they are
of that of their own species; but I doubt whether he is
right in this deduction. I should think it likely that
the Manyema have been anthropophagic from time im-
memorial, and quite independently of a local taste for
the flesh of apes or monkeys. As in other parts of
Western-Equatorial Africa, and indeed of other portions of the globe, two kinds of cannibalism seem to
exist, one which is merely the eating of man's flesh
because its taste is liked, and the other springing from
a religious custom. Thus, Livingstone ascertained that
in the case of chiefs, or the head-men of villages, their
bodies were eaten after death, and all the flesh removed
from the head and eaten too, the skull being preserved
as a kind of fetish, a relic of the dead person which in
some sense enshrouds the spirit. But there are other
causes and excuses for cannibalism; thus, Livingstone
relates "that a quarrel with a wife often ends in the
husband killing her and eating her heart mixed up in a
huge mess of goat's flesh."

In conversation with Livingstone the Manyema referred to their acts of cannibalism with but little reserve.
His guides conducting him through the forest would
casually remark at some camping-place, " Here we killed
a man and ate his body." At one place, after a great
fight amongst the Manyema, the Arabs saw the meat of
the slain being cut up to be cooked with bananas. " The
Manyema were annoyed at having these proceedings
watched" (writes Livingstone), "and said, ' Go on, and
let our feast alone.' They did not want to be sneered
at. They seem to eat their foes to inspire courage, or
in revenge. One point is very remarkable; it is not

want that has led to the custom, for the country is full of food; they have maize, durha, *Pennisetum*, cassava, and sweet potatoes; and for fatty ingredients of diet, the palm-oil, ground-nuts, sessamum, and a tree whose fruit yields a fine sweet oil: the saccharine materials needed are found in the sugar-cane, bananas, and plantains. . . . Goats, sheep, fowls, dogs, pigs, abound in the villages; whilst the forest affords elephants, zebras, buffaloes, antelopes, and in the streams there are many varieties of fish. The nitrogenous ingredients are abundant, and they have dainties in palm-toddy, tobacco, or Bange (hemp): the soil is so fruitful that mere scraping off the weeds is as good as ploughing, so that the reason for cannibalism does not lie in starvation or in want of animal matter, as was said to be the case with the New Zealanders. The only plausible reason I can discover is a depraved appetite, giving an extraordinary craving for meat which we call 'high.' They are said to bury a dead body for a couple of days in the soil in a forest, and in that time, owing to the climate, it soon becomes putrid enough for the strongest stomachs."

In a market-place one day, when Livingstone went to buy provisions, a Manyema man came up to him with ten human under-jaw bones hung by a string over his shoulder. On Livingstone questioning him as to how he obtained these horrible ornaments, " he professed to have killed and eaten the owners, and showed with his knife how he had cut up the victims." When Livingstone expressed disgust at this, the man and those around him laughed. Livingstone also comments much on their strange alternations of heartlessness, ferocity, and loving-kindness. " They are the lowest of the low,"

Y

he writes, "and especially in bloodiness: when a man had killed a woman without cause he was going about free, but he offered his grandmother to be killed in his stead! After a good deal of talk, nothing was done to him." Yet he frequently observes the affection between husband and wife, father and son (which is rare in Africa), mother and child, and even between the hunted, harassed Manyema and a friendly stranger like himself —how the women would bid him eat and rest in their huts as he dragged himself wearily along the road, and how they would rush out with presents of bananas, and on occasions make him the most beautiful, touching, and tender remarks about death and heaven and brotherly kindness one toward another. They were also exceedingly honest, though very untruthful.

Since Livingstone's day the Manyema have become almost as much Arabised as the Wa-nyamwezi and the Wa-yao. They are now entirely identified with the rule of Tipu-Tipu and the Arabs who exercise sway over the Upper Congo; and from among the Manyema (as the Stanley expedition showed) the bulk of the Arabs' fighting forces is recruited. The Arabs have turned their ferocity to terrible account in raiding the Aruwimi and Lomami countries. It is to be hoped that in course of time a civilised government in the Congo territories may wean them from Arab influences and bring out their better qualities. There would seem (from the accounts of those that know them) to be a strange charm about the handsome faces and bright, vivacious manners of the Manyema, a charm which cannot even be wholly effaced by a contemplation of the scenes of frantic ferocity and ghoul-like cannibalism in which they indulge.

CHAPTER XIX.

The long absence from civilisation of Dr. Livingstone, the scarcity of news about his movements, owing to the loss and interception of his letters on their way to the coast, caused many people in England and in America to be anxious as to his fate. The expedition of Mr. Edward Young in 1868 had proved with tolerable certainty that Livingstone had not perished at the hands of the Angoni-Zulus; news also had been received about Livingstone's arrival on Tanganyika and discovery of Lake Bangweolo; but the long, long pause which ensued owing to his three years' wanderings in Manyema had been quite sufficient for those croakers in our society who like to predict bad news to declare Dr. Livingstone dead. The *bon gros public*, however, refused to give up their hero so easily, and there began to be vague suggestions set afloat of search and relief expeditions. But whilst people in England were merely talking and writing letters to the *Times* and making philanthropic speeches at the fag-end of Royal Geographical Society's meetings and Lord Mayor's dinners, an American newspaper proprietor resolved to do something towards finding Livingstone, and did it. No doubt the owner of the *New York Herald* was not actuated, or did not profess to be actuated, by high-flown philanthropy; he wanted a new sensation and startling copy for his journal. But that little matters. He had, at any rate, the sense to do the thing well, and the immediate outcome of his journalistic inspiration was probably the addition of two more years to Livingstone's life ; while the far-reaching effect of the resolution taken by Mr. James Gordon Bennett in some tawdry chamber of that tawdriest of hotels—the Grand—in Paris has been the discovery of the whole Congo Basin, the founding of the Congo Free State, the intervention of all the European Powers in Africa in place of the monopoly enjoyed by England, France, and Portugal, and a host of other things, good and bad, but all attendant on the advance of civilisation.

Mr. Bennett had been much struck by the ability and daring of a young man named Stanley who had been connected as a travelling correspondent with the *New York Herald* ever since the American Civil War, in which he had served, first on the Southern and then on the Northern side. He had been through our Abyssinian war as correspondent for the same paper, and was following the Carlist struggle in Spain when he received a telegram from Mr. Bennett telling him to come to Paris. There, in the course of a conversation in Mr. Bennett's bedroom at the Grand Hotel, he was asked if he had any idea of Livingstone's whereabouts, and whether he could discover him. Stanley did not know, but was quite willing to try. He was accordingly despatched by Mr. Bennett to do this as well as—and after—a number of other commissions, which were to include visits to Constantinople, the Levant, Persia, and India.

Stanley arrived at Zanzibar on the 6th of January 1871, and made preparations for an expedition to Ujiji, on Lake Tanganyika, where it was thought probable he would encounter Livingstone or get reliable news of him. He kept up, however, a considerable amount of mystery about his object in undertaking this journey. He feared that if he announced it was for the relief of Dr. Livingstone a hundred jealousies would be aroused and fifty rivalries spring up. In this motive for veiling his plans he may have been right, but I think he would have acted with greater wisdom had he made a confidant of Sir John (then Dr.) Kirk, the British representative at the court of Zanzibar. In the face of the political rivalries and intrigues which were already beginning to spring up in connection with the Zanzibar dominions, it is hardly to be wondered at that Dr. Kirk—the jealous guardian of British interests in East Africa—should have viewed with some coldness and distrust the mysterious expedition of an unknown American.

Worried with refractory porters and hindered rather than helped by his two demoralised and useless European companions (Farquhar and Shaw, two British seamen), Stanley soon began to experience to the full the difficulties of African exploration. Shaw and Farquhar both died eventually, and neither got any farther than Unyanyembe. Stanley became involved in the war between the Arabs of Tabora and the Nyamwezi chief, Mirambo (who afterwards swelled into a powerful African monarch, able to close the road to Tanganyika at his will); and sharing in the severe defeat of the Arabs, was delayed some time in Unyanyembe, only getting away by taking a circuitous southern route through trackless thorn forests, and then, when at a safe distance from Mirambo, turning his steps once more toward Ujiji. After much difficulty in the Uha country, he finally reached Tanganyika on October 28, 1871, and found himself face to face with Dr. Livingstone. The juncture at which he arrived was a crisis in Livingstone's life. Robbed of nearly all his goods by the rascally slave porters sent him from Zanzibar, without stores, medicines, news from the outside world, letters from his children, or any assurance that the world had not forgotten him, Livingstone was as near despair as his nature and religion permitted. Stanley appeared to him in the light of a saviour. He had found Livingstone's letter-bags lying about at Bagamoio, while the idle slaves who were to have transported them to Ujiji were living in that African Capua. Stanley had brought on the letters with him, and he was, moreover, himself a living newspaper in the full stock of universal information he had been trained to carry in his head of the current history of the world's doings. Owing to the troubles in Unyanyembe, he had been obliged to leave Livingstone's stores behind at that place, but that was a small matter compared to the poor old man being without stores at all, for his immediate needs were satisfied, and the mere contact with a bright, intelligent man, full of admiration and appreciation of his deeds, revived Livingstone's spirits, and this revival imparted a stimulus to his worn-out body.

The Royal Geographical Society, in the letters which Stanley conveyed to Livingstone, had suggested that the great traveller might profitably explore the north end of Lake Tanganyika to satisfy himself by ocular testimony that there was no outlet to the lake in that direction. Accordingly, Livingstone and Stanley made a boat-journey round the north end of Tanganyika, which settled the question once and for all. The Rusizi

River, which enters the lake in a small delta at the north end, was proved conclusively to be flowing into and not out of Tanganyika. Thence they returned to Ujiji, and after delays, consequent on severe fevers which attacked Stanley, and through which Livingstone nursed him with assiduity, they journeyed together to Unyanyembe, where they finally parted.

Once more in Unyanyembe, as on the shores of Tanganyika, Stanley urged Livingstone to return with him to Europe; and posterity can only heave a sigh of vain regret over Livingstone's obstinacy in rejecting Stanley's advice. He was, however, mad with the idea of finding the Nile sources. It had indeed almost become a monomania with him that the Lualaba must be the Upper Nile. He was so absolutely sure in his own mind—the wish being father to the thought—that he scarcely contemplated the necessity of proving it by descending the stream until he reached the Albert Nyanza; he thought, on the contrary, that his task ought to be the discovery and mapping of its actual sources in Lake Bangweolo and on the Katanga Highlands. That having been done, he was ready to return to Europe. About the Congo he cared little. The reports of the Arabs, that the Lualaba flowed considerably to the west, of course raised the fear in his mind that it might be the Congo after all, but he would not allow himself to believe this; he repeatedly assured himself that it *must* be the Nile. But the monomaniac obstinacy which Africa creates in every one, the extraordinary fascination she exerts over all Europeans who fall into her meshes (as if she hypnotised them), acted on Livingstone as it did on Gordon, and as it has done on Emin in inducing them to remain or return against their better judgment, against menace of death and the snapping of family ties. Had Livingstone returned to Europe with Stanley, we should have been no less rich in geographical information, for his after-journeys were unproductive; and he would have received that full reward of appreciatory praise which was never his in his lifetime. Skilful dentists would have replaced his loosened, decaying teeth with an artificial set which would have enabled him to masticate his food, and thus improve his digestion. Comfort and kindness would have restored his health and cured his despondency. He might have lived many years longer, even to the present day of writing, have died a baronet and president of the Royal Geographical Society. But no; he would listen to none of these reasonings, none of these tempting prospects baited with common sense. He *would* go back to the west, finish his work, and *then* return. Stanley was forced to let the wilful man have his way, but resolving that that way should be made as easy for him as possible, he agreed with Dr. Livingstone to organise for him a body of reliable carriers, and send them back from Zanzibar to Unyanyembe with a further complement of stores. Accordingly the two friends parted, not without emotion, for Livingstone felt grateful to Stanley from the bottom of his heart, and Stanley seems to have been led captive by the nobility of Livingstone's disposition.

Stanley reached Zanzibar on the 7th of May 1872, but before he had crossed over to the island he had met on the mainland the vanguard of an imposing expedition got up by the Royal Geographical Society, and subscribed to by Her Majesty's Government, for the relief of Livingstone. This expedition was officered by Lieutenants

STANLEY RELIEVES LIVINGSTONE.   345

Dawson and Henn, and Livingstone's son Oswell; and
there was attached to it, as interpreter and general
adviser, the Rev. Charles New, of Kilima-njaro fame.[1]
All these gentlemen, as soon as the result of Stanley's
journey was made known, promptly resigned. All the
carefully prepared equipment of the expedition was sold,
or some portion of it handed over to Stanley to trans-
mit to Livingstone.[2]

Finding that none of the gentlemen who had come
out with this relief expedition were willing to conduct
the porters back to Livingstone at Unyanyembe, Stanley
was forced to make the best arrangements possible for
forwarding the goods and men, under the charge of a
young Arab, who did not turn out remarkably well, but
who, nevertheless, led the fifty-seven porters in safety

---

[1] Mr. New was the first to ascend Kilima-njaro to the snow-line.
He afterwards returned to the mountain, was robbed by the chief
Mandara of all his goods, and died of a broken heart.

[2] The Royal Geographical Society sent round a circular in 1872
inviting subscriptions from the British public towards a fund for de-
spatching an expedition to find and relieve Livingstone. To this fund
the Geographical Society itself subscribed £500. In 1870 Her Majesty's
Government, through Lord Clarendon, had granted a sum of £1000
to be expended on behalf of Livingstone, the balance of which, in
1872, was £557, 7s. 10d. This also was transferred to the Relief Fund,
together with another small amount of about £30, the interest on
some Exchequer Bills. This made a total, therefore, of about £1088,
which the public subscription increased to £5770, 3s. 1d. So soon
as this amount had been collected, the Royal Geographical Society
despatched an expedition on the 7th February 1872, under the command of Lieutenants Llewellyn, Dawson, and William Henn, and of
Mr. Oswell Livingstone. The final cost of this abortive expedition
amounted to £2359, 6s. 6d., but a portion of this sum was expended
in providing stores to be sent up to Livingstone by the porters whom
Stanley had engaged. However, it reduced the Livingstone Relief
Fund to about £3175, 16s. 6d., an amount which was afterwards
spent in fitting out an expedition under Lieutenant (now Commander)
Cameron.

to Unyanyembe, and only lost three donkeys, two loads of cloth, and some tins of cocoa on the way.

Meanwhile, as soon as he had despatched these supplies and men to Dr. Livingstone, Stanley took a passage in a German steamer for Seychelles, together with the ex-members of the relief expedition. At the Seychelles he was compelled to remain a month, till the French mail came from Mauritius, and thus he proceeded to England *viâ* Aden and Marseilles, calling at Paris on the way, and entrusting Livingstone's Journal and despatches to Her Majesty's Ambassador at that place, to be trans-mitted to the Foreign Office. His reception in England, however, was somewhat disappointing. It is a well-worn subject, and has been much commented on. There were perhaps faults of manner on both sides ; but, at the same time, there is no doubt that Stanley was unkindly dealt with by those who, in their bitterness of disappointment that Dr. Livingstone had been relieved by one who was not a British subject, attempted at first to dispute the authenticity of the discovery, and, secondly, to minimise its value, in asserting that " Dr. Livingstone had dis-covered Stanley, rather than that Stanley had relieved Livingstone." This hasty judgment has long, long since been rescinded, and the amplest amends made by such geographical authorities as may have wounded Mr. Stan-ley's feelings by their hypercritical remarks. Perhaps, I dare say, too, if the Stanley of to-day looks back on his early manner of 1873, and the way in which he spoke of, and to, certain persons whom he too rashly and sweepingly condemned, he will acknowledge that the injustice and the faults of temper were not wholly on the other side. But it is really unnecessary to rake up these old ashes of a quarrel long since grown cold. The

British nation, from their ruler downwards, as soon as they realised the greatness and importance of Stanley's exploit, afforded him ample reward and recognition. When it came out that Stanley was a Britisher born, and merely one of our errant children, who had placed himself for a while under the protection of a scarcely foreign flag, public satisfaction at his great deeds increased continually, until it culminated in that almost regal triumph accorded him in the summer of 1890.

CHAPTER XX.

Dr. Livingstone left Unyanyembe on the 25th August 1872 to resume his exploration of what he imagined to be the Nile sources. He started with probably the best-equipped expedition that had ever yet accompanied him in his African journeys. He had nearly sixty good men, several riding-donkeys, and some cows. A reserve of stores was left behind in charge of an Arab at Tabora, and by the usual unfortunate accidents which seemed always to attend Livingstone, among the things left behind by mistake was a case of desiccated milk, which would have been of the greatest service to him as nourishment during his attacks of dysentery.

He embarked on this fresh journey with his old eagerness, and with renewed hopes, greatly cheered by the unusual comfort which attended his journeys and the excellent character of the men whom Stanley had sent him. But a few days' travel on the road showed him that he was unfit for any more African journeys. He suffered acutely, not only from his old complaint of hæmorrhoids, but with a renewal of that dysenteric affection that had become rooted in his sytem by his awful trials in Manyema. After a severe bout which occurred on the 18th September there are constant entries in his Journal noting the loss of blood through both these

348

maladies combined, while the pain he suffered at times
was frightful. Nevertheless he managed somehow to
ride his donkey, and reached the shores of Tanganyika
on the 14th October. He skirted the south-east coast
of the lake through the Fipa and Ulungu countries, and
then turned south and west till he reached the Kalon-
gosi River, which flows into Lake Moero. Crossing
this stream and the high range of mountains beyond,
he descended into the terribly marshy region north of
Lake Bangweolo, which is intersected by innumerable
streams and is one vast sponge.

Thenceforward the journey became terrible. One
looking on would have seen Livingstone literally dying
by degrees day by day. The rainy season was at its
height, the land was an endless swamp, the inhabitants
were scattered and suspicious from the remembrance of
old Arab raids, starvation was constantly menacing the
expedition, chiefs promised canoes, but did not send
them, and one reads in the diary which Livingstone
kept accounts of the dull grey skies, the incessant downpour of rain, the oozy, spongy soil of the villages in
which they stayed (a soil which stank with the rotten-
ness of a soaked manure-heap), of the filthy huts, and
the attacks of that dreadful species of bug (which
Livingstone misnames tick) that is so prevalent in parts
of East-Central Africa.

He crossed the Tshambezi River on the 4th April
1873, and continued his course along the east shores
of Bangweolo, if shores they could be called, for it was
difficult to say where the solid land ended and the lake
began. All this country through which they had been
passing since crossing the Liposhosi River, which flows
into the north end of Bangweolo, was a vast swamp of

shallow water overgrown with giant reeds with great white heads of blossom, and luxuriant papyrus eight feet high and sometimes as much as three feet across its crowns of filaments. The marsh was further covered with four varieties of rushes, the two species of African water-lily, and various arums. The water in these swamps was about four to six feet deep. Here and there small islands of firm soil rose above that sea of rustling reeds which extended illimitably all round them. On these mounds villages were established, but owing to the incessant rains their sites could scarcely be called dry land, and the accumulation of refuse round the habitations, rotting in the wet, gave out a fearful stench. Millions of mosquitoes swarmed; there were poisonous spiders and stinging ants. Yet, amid all his misery and the attacks of sickening pain which his dysentery brought on, Livingstone could record flashes of humour and delicious little bits of natural-history observation in his Journal. He describes the natives hunting the water-antelopes,[1] and the sound of these beasts plunging through the reeds and dashing and splashing through the shallow water; and farther on writes about a lion "which had wandered into this world of water and ant-hills, and roared night and morning as if very much disgusted: we could sympathise with him!"

On the 15th March 1873 Livingstone had addressed his last despatch to Lord Granville. On the 9th April he took his last observations for latitude. From the middle of that month he was so ill through loss of blood that he was obliged to be carried by his men in a litter made of boughs. On the 27th April he made the last

_____

[1] *Tragelaphus spekii.*

entry in his note-book. This runs : " Knocked up quite, and remain = recover. Sent to buy milch-goats. We are on the banks of the River Molilamo." A few days before that he writes : " Tried to write, but was forced to lie down, and they carried me back to vil. (village) exhausted."

The milch-goats, however, that might have provided the sustenance of which Livingstone stood so sorely in need, were not procurable. The hateful Zulu raiders had swept the country of nearly all its flocks. Poor Livingstone, as he lay sick, thought that he could eat some millet-seed pounded up with ground-nuts,[1] and he gave instructions that it should be prepared for him, but he was not able to take it when it was brought to him.

Still he would not stop. As he was too weak to move from his bed to the door of his tiny little hut to reach the litter in which he was carried, he asked the men to break down one side of the little house, and so bring the litter to his bed-side. This was done ; he was gently placed on it and borne out of the village. On their route to Tshitambo's town, on the southern end of Bangweolo, another river had to be crossed, the one which he speaks of as the Molilamo, but the name of which is Lulimalo. Livingstone was too weak to sit in the canoe, as he had hitherto done. His men, therefore, laid his mattress along the bottom of the biggest canoe, and tried to lift him on to it, but he could not bear the pain of a hand being passed under his back. Beckoning to his faithful Chuma, he asked him in a faint voice to bend his head over him as low as possible, so that he might clasp his hands round his neck, and thus the

[1] A ghastly diet for a dysenteric man !

greatest leverage would be exerted without hurting his
loins.   At the same time the other men gently lifted
him by the legs, and in this way he was laid in the
bottom of the canoe, and with the utmost care lifted out
of it on the other side of the river and conveyed to
Tshitambo's village, where he arrived in a dying condition.   Even during the short distance from the marshy
borders of the Lulimalo to Tshitambo's, Livingstone's
sufferings were so great that his men were every now
and then implored to stop and lay his litter on the
ground.   The pain and weakness which he endured on
this last day of his travels rendered him unable to stand,
and if he were lifted bodily for a few yards, he fell into
a state of faintness which came dangerously near death.
Then at times he would become conscious, and complain
of terrible thirst and ask for water, but by a cruel irony
of fate they had just left the leagues and leagues of
water behind them, and nothing could be given him to
drink until he arrived at the village.   With pathetic
assiduity and thoughtfulness, the bulk of his men had
rushed on in front, and had prepared and built—that is
to say, modified an existing hut—a suitable house for
him, had constructed a bed of poles covered with dry
grass and raised above the ground, and had lit a bright
fire in the centre of the hut.   As soon as might be he
was placed within, and with the relative comfort and
the blessed rest he regained full consciousness.   On the
next day, which was, as far as can be reckoned, the 30th
April, the chief Tshitambo came early to pay a visit of
courtesy, but Livingstone was obliged to feebly waive the
greeting and beg him to come on the morrow instead,
when he hoped to have more strength to talk with him.
In the afternoon of that day he explained to his man

Susi how to hold his watch and wind it up. In the middle of ensuing night Susi went to his master, who had inquired for him, having heard loud shouts in the distance. Livingstone asked whether it was his men that were making that noise, but Susi told him it was the cries of the natives scaring away a buffalo from their corn-fields. A few minutes afterwards, as though half delirious, he asked, " Is this the Luapula ? " Susi replied, " No ; we are in Tshitambo's village, near the Lulimalo." After another silence, Livingstone, who had apparently spoken in English before, now asked Susi in Ki-swahili, " *Siku ngapi kwenda, Luapula ?* " ("How many days to go to the Luapula ? ") Susi replied, " *Nathani siku tatu, Bwana* " (" I think three days, master"). Livingstone to this only answered, with a sigh of pain, " Oh dear, dear ! " Then he dozed off a while, but afterwards called for Susi again, and asked him to boil some water and bring him his medicine-chest. With great difficulty, from this Livingstone took out the calomel and placed it by his side ; then directing his man to pour a little water into a cup, and to put another empty one by it, he said in a feeble voice, " All right; you can go out now." These were the last words which Livingstone was heard to speak.

At four o'clock the next morning, Majiwara, Livingstone's personal attendant, rushed out of the hut and summoned Susi to come and look at his master. The boy had suddenly awaked, and had found Livingstone out of bed and no longer living. Susi and Majiwara ran into the hut with four other men, lit a candle, and looked towards the bed. Their master was not lying on it, but was kneeling by the side of the bed, his body stretched forward and his head buried in his hands upon

z

the pillow. He had probably got out of bed with the intention of mixing his medicine, or it may have been with the idea of putting up one more agonised prayer for recovery, and the exertion had stopped the feeble action of his heart. At the time the men advanced to him and placed their hands on his cheeks they found him cold.

From the fact that his servants had spoken with him shortly before midnight, it is probable that he did not die until the turn of the new day. It may, therefore, be concluded that he expired on the 1st May 1873. Some of his men have placed the date later, on the 4th May, and have even said that they were obliged to remove him from Tshitambo's village owing to the horror which most Africans feel of a stranger dying in their midst, but this account does not tally with the description of events given by the majority, and it is difficult to reconcile it with the known kindness of Tshitambo. I therefore agree with the Rev. Horace Waller, that the 1st May 1873 was the date on which the greatest and best man who ever explored Africa yielded up his life, as much a martyr to a sense of duty as Gordon, but in his sublime obstinacy sacrificing but his own life and not involving the death of thousands.

From the vague accounts which are given of Livingstone's maladies, owing to the mistaken idea that the details of a hero's sickness should be lightly passed over, lest in some way they detract from the heroic character (though why, I cannot see), it is not easy to decide what Livingstone actually died of. Although no doubt a certain amount of fever ensued on the disorganisation of his system, it was not the ordinary marsh fever or the severe bilious remittent which killed him. From early middle age he had shown a tendency to suffer from hæmorrhoids, and, indeed, on the occasion of his last stay in England, from 1864 to 1865, he was counselled to submit to an operation, but, on reflection, would not do so. In his last African journeys this complaint caused him frightful agony—so excruciating, in fact, was the pain, that he seems to have welcomed the severe discharge of blood which for the time relieved it. This constant hæmorrhage, however, slowly killed him; in fact, he bled to death by degrees. Coupled with this malady was a great derangement of the bowels, which apparently was dysenteric. It would seem, therefore, as though he had two causes for the frequent loss of blood. It is probable that he actually died of exhaustion, of that sudden syncope—failure of the heart's action—which is so commonly the way in which African diseases terminate. Few people in Africa die actually of fever or pneumonia or dysentery; the immediate cause of death is failure of the heart's action through weakness, and this often occurs during early convalescence, when the patient is thought to be progressing favourably, and the disease from which he has suffered is cured. He sits up in bed suddenly, or attempts to get out of bed, and in the unusual exertion faints away. If consciousness is not immediately restored by strong measures, the syncope rapidly passes into death.

It has pleased many of Livingstone's commentators and biographers to surmise that he died in prayer, and that the prayer was one offered up for Africa and the woes of the enslaved and wretched continent. It is an idea which is pleasing to the fancy, but with all due tenderness for the wish that is father to the thought, I do not think it is consistent with actuality. The

approach of death in Africa is preceded by a singular
numbing of the mental faculties. Dying people appear
to think of nothing but their immediate physical
requirements. They drowse and drowse, and express
neither fear, joy, anxiety, nor interest. I have leant
over the beds of several dying men to catch the sentence
that the poor whitened lips were trying to form, but it
has been no last words to those they loved at home, and
no reference to the death that was creeping over them;
merely some inquiry as to the time or a request for
water, or some wandering thought or recollection of a
trivial kind, such as—"Forgot to tell you that I owe
so-and-so half-a-crown." In an interesting address recently delivered by Archdeacon Maples of Nyasa, he
expresses the same opinion as to the ignorance of approaching death and lack of all beautiful "last words"
among all those who die in Africa. It therefore seems
to me more probable that Livingstone expired in the
mere effort to get out of bed and mix his medicine. And
why should we wish it otherwise? Thirty years of his
life were one long prayer for Africa. Does it matter
whether or not that prayer was continued to the last
few hours of consciousness?

Livingstone's men behaved admirably in the circumstances which followed his death. They made a most
careful inventory of all his effects, and packed them in
tin boxes where they would be safe from the attacks of
white ants or from damp. They decided that, come
what might, his body must be conveyed to Zanzibar,
for they knew with what importance he was regarded
among white men, and how necessary it would be to
prove his death by the identity of the corpse. Yet this
proceeding was attended with the utmost difficulty,

because of the superstitious horror that all Africans have of a dead body. A council of all the porters was called, and those men who had recently come from Zanzibar voluntarily placed themselves under the command of Livingstone's two most faithful old followers, Susi and Chuma.

At first it was arranged that the body should be prepared secretly for conveyance to the coast, but the news of Livingstone's death having leaked out and reached Tshitambo's ears, he came at once to inquire into the matter. He said to Chuma, " Why did you not tell me the truth ? I know that your master died last night. You were afraid to let me know, but do not fear any longer. I too have travelled, and more than once have been to Pwani (the coast), before the country along the road was destroyed by the Mazitu.[1] I know that you have no bad object in coming to our land, and death often happens to travellers in their journeys." Reassured by this speech, the men set to work to carry out their intentions of preparing the corpse for its long journey, and gave Livingstone such obsequies as they, poor souls ! judged fitting. A handsome present was given to Tshitambo in order that he might help in paying honours to the dead. At the appointed time, the chief, accompanied by his wives and people, came to the little settlement where Livingstone had died. Tshitambo was arrayed in his best raiment, and his followers carried bows, arrows, and spears, but no guns. Two of his people who were " special mourners " raised the loud, wailing lamentations with which death is greeted in Africa. At the same time Livingstone's servants fired volley after volley into the air, after the manner of the Arabs and the half-caste Portuguese.

[1] Zulus.

One of the native mourners wore anklets composed of hollow seed-vessels filled with tiny pebbles, which rattled as he danced in circles. He sang in a low monotonous chant words which have been translated, "To-day the Englishman is dead, who has different hair from ours : come round to see the Englishman."[1] Whilst these proceedings were going on one of the native boys, named Jacob Wainwright, read the burial-service from the English Prayer-book.

Having built a special settlement apart from the village, surrounded by an exceedingly strong stockade, to prevent any attempts of wild beasts to break through, Livingstone's men conveyed his corpse into a hut which was open to the air at the top, and surrounded by their own temporary dwellings, and then they set to work to prepare the body with a rough embalming. They had with them a quantity of salt, and out of their master's stores they obtained some brandy. With these materials they hoped to preserve the body from decay. One of the men, named Farijala, was appointed to remove the viscera, and in their place was inserted a quantity of salt. Brandy was poured down the mouth and over the hair of the head. The poor frame of the long-suffering man was found to be little more than skin and bone.

The heart and the rest of the viscera were placed in a tin box and buried in a hole dug some four feet deep in the centre of this little settlement.[2] Jacob Wain-

---

[1] This is Mr. Waller's translation. From the native words he records I make it out to be as follows :—"To-day died the English-man, the child of hair (*i.e.*, possessing long hair) and of the coast : let us come forward to see the Englishman."

[2] Tshitambo was charged by the men before they left to keep the place sacred where Livingstone's heart had been buried. He faithfully did so, and to this day Livingstone's grave in Africa remains carefully

wright then once more read the burial-service in the presence of all the men. The body was placed for fourteen days to dry in the sun, the men watching round it all the time. When thoroughly dry it was wrapped round with calico, the legs being bent inwards at the knees to shorten the package. In order to disguise the character of their load as far as possible, they ingeniously constructed a cylinder of bark, which was obtained by stripping a stout tree. In this the body of their master was placed, and the package completely enveloped in a piece of sail-cloth and lashed to a pole, so that it might be carried by two men. A day or two afterwards they further added to their precaution for preserving the remains from the action of moisture by tarring the whole package outside, Livingstone having carried about a small cask of tar with him which had been left behind at Tshitambo's village.

They then set out on their march to the coast through the country of Ilala (which was the name of the land in which Livingstone died). Remembering keenly the frightful difficulties of their previous march round the eastern shores of Bangweolo, they resolved to take a western route and complete the circuit of the lake. Three days after starting, however, they were all down with some rheumatic affection which completely prostrated them. It was supposed that this was the ultimate result of their terrible experiences in the marshes on the east of Bangweolo. However, the chief in whose village they fell ill was a brother of Tshitambo's, and treated them with great kindness. As soon as they

guarded from desecration or obliteration by Tshitambo, to whom the Royal Geographical Society recently sent a handsome present as a mark of the good feeling entertained for him by the British people.

were sufficiently restored to health they continued their march across the Luapula, the cynosure of Livingstone's eyes which he was fated never to see, and journeyed thence to the north, skirting the western shores of swampy Bangweolo. On the other side of the Luapula, Livingstone's pet-donkey was killed by a lion. In the country of the cantankerous Ba-usi people, on the west of Bangweolo, the natives picked a quarrel with them, and the men of the expedition therefore boldly assaulted their town and carried it by storm, resolving to show no sign of weakness in the absence of their white leader, for they felt instinctively that if they gave in to extortion and violence thus early on the road they would none of them reach the coast with their precious burden. At the captured town of Tshatwende they obtained a great quantity of food, which proved most useful to them, as they were able to stay here and recruit and thoroughly prepare themselves for the long journey ahead of them.

From Bangweolo they passed with little difficulty to the south shores of Tanganyika, and not wishing to incur the difficulties with extortionate chiefs and the waste of time which would be involved in following Livingstone's old route along its eastern shores, they resolved to strike boldly across the Fipa country, near Lake Rukwa, to Wunyamwezi, which country they entered without any serious mishaps about the 20th October 1873. At the settlement of Kwihara, near Tabora, they encountered the second Livingstone relief expedition which had been sent out by the Royal Geographical Society, that under the command of Lieutenant Cameron.[1] Here they were all compelled to pause whilst the officers in charge of this expedition considered what further course should be

[1] Now Commander Cameron, C.B.

taken in the matter of conveying Livingstone's body to the coast. It appeared to these gentlemen that, in view of the considerable risk attending the transport of the corpse through the Ugogo country, it would almost be better to bury it at Kwihara. But Livingstone's men were obstinate on this point; they were resolved that their master's body should be taken to the coast with the view of its being sent to England, and in the face of this resolution on their part the English officers wisely deferred to the men's ardent wishes. The boxes of Livingstone's effects which the men had carefully packed at Tshitambo's were gone over, and those amongst Livingstone's instruments which were thought likely to be useful to that section of the new expedition which was proceeding westwards were taken charge of by Lieutenant Cameron. The remainder of the things were then packed, and the four bales of cloth that had been left behind as a reserve with the Arabs were handed over to Livingstone's men.

Lieutenant Murphy and Dr. Dillon, members of Cameron's party, had been so persistently ill on their journey from Zanzibar to Unyamwezi, that it was decided they should return to the coast, whilst Lieutenant Cameron pursued his way to Ujiji with the intention of recovering further papers of Dr. Livingstone's which were said to have been left there, and with the hope of completing some of his discoveries. No doubt Cameron, on his way to Wunyamwezi, had discovered, what most African explorers have found out, that it is best for white men to work singly in Africa; and the remarkable journey which he subsequently made all round Tanganyika and across the lower part of the Congo watershed to the Atlantic Ocean was in striking contrast to the dismal record of his expedition on the march from Bagamoio to

Tabora, with the unavoidable hindrances caused by the constant sickness, and in one case the sad death, of the white men who accompanied him.

Accordingly Livingstone's little band of sixty men resumed their journey to the coast, with the additional charge of escorting Lieutenant Murphy and Dr. Dillon. Soon after their start, however, from Tabora they realised that some strategy must be resorted to to disguise the fact that they were carrying Livingstone's dead body; otherwise the superstitious and greedy natives of the countries that lay before them would oppose their progress at every turn, so as to exact enormous payments as an indemnification for this outrage on their superstitions about dead bodies. The men therefore devised one of those clever ruses which are such a fertile product of the African brain. At Kasekera, a town lying some distance to the south of Tabora, they came to a full stop, and told the villagers that they had given up as a bad job the attempt to carry Livingstone's body any farther, and they had decided it was to be buried at Tabora. What they really did was to take the body out of the bark cylinder in which it had been packed, and repack it in the middle of a bale of cloth. An imitation corpse was then made out of corn-stalks, put into the old bark cylinder, and sent back on the road to Tabora, with a letter in a cleft stick. As soon as the men who carried this fictitious Livingstone had travelled well out of sight and hearing of Kasekera they destroyed their burden and effaced the track of their footsteps, and rejoined the main caravan (which had already started coastwards) some distance farther on the road. Before they left Kasekera, however, a sad event had occurred in the suicide of Dr. Dillon, who had been suffering from dementia

consequent upon an exhausting attack of dysentery.   A
little farther on another tragedy occurred.   A child who
was travelling with Livingstone's caravan, a daughter of
one of the men, was suddenly attacked by an immense
snake as she travelled along the path carrying a water-
jar upon her head.   The snake started out of the jungle,
bit her in the thigh, and darted back to its hole.   The
child died ten minutes after having been bitten.

No further incident of note affected the expedition until
it reached Bagamoio, whither came the acting Consul-
General, Captain Prideaux, from Zanzibar, to meet the
body of Dr. Livingstone.   His faithful men handed over
their precious burden, which was coolly taken from them
without a word of acknowledgment for their great services,
or even a passage offered them across to the island of
Zanzibar.   How extraordinary it is that so many Englishmen are so utterly failing in tact, especially with black
men, and do not know that a few kind words of appreciation would gladden the hearts of men who have done
splendid work !   Susi and Chuma would probably have
remained ignored and forgotten, disappointed and deceived as to the character of white men, had it not been
for that most generous creature, that true friend of Dr.
Livingstone, James Young, who had the men forwarded
to Zanzibar and to England at his own expense, in order
that they might assist at Livingstone's funeral obsequies.   Had these men not thus been brought over to
England and placed at the disposal of Mr. Waller to
assist him in his task of editing Livingstone's " Last
Journals," we should have lost a considerable amount of
elucidatory information which has greatly enabled us to
understand obscure references and apparent contradic-
tions in the scattered records which Livingstone wrote

with a trembling hand during his last days. The Royal
Geographical Society, I believe, rewarded these men, and
they afterwards returned to Zanzibar and did good work
there in the service of other European explorers and
missionaries.

Nor should it be forgotten that Susi and Chuma were
only two among seven nearly equally faithful servants
of Livingstone's. The other five consisted of Amoda
(who, together with Susi and Chuma, had been a follower
of Livingstone's in the old days of the first Zambezi
expedition); then Abraham [1] and Mabruki, the only two
among the Nassick boys that started with Livingstone
in 1865, who turned out well; and after them must be
mentioned Ntoaika and Halima, two native women, ex-
slaves, who had married Susi and Amoda in Manyema.
Halima was usually Livingstone's cook, and, with one
or two occasional outbursts of temper, to which all good
cooks are addicted, she bears an excellent record. *Of
course*, directly people in England heard that Livingstone
had a female cook, that large section of us which delights
to find their own faults and failings in greater men,
hinted and whispered and suggested that Halima was
to Livingstone what the French would call *une servante-
maitresse*. It is hardly worth while to waste space and
words in this book to point out the falseness of this suggestion. Livingstone's life is quite beyond reproach.
African travellers little realise how completely their
reputations in Africa are at the mercy of their negro
followers. Every single little thing that a white man
does, whether he cleans his teeth with red tooth-paste or
white powder, whether he takes a bath once a day or

[1] This man's full name would seem to have been Abraham, or Abram,
Gardner.

only once a week, how often he changes his under-shirt, how much alcohol he drinks and what kind of alcohol, whether he is devout in public and loose-mannered in private, whether he is brave in sickness or too ready to despond—everything is known to these acute, sharp-eyed observers, who, by a kind of freemasonry, will rapidly impart all this information to the great con-fraternity of Zanzibar porters; and yet none of this gossip will reach the European who does not mix with the people and understand their language thoroughly. The present writer, being, however, conversant with the Wa-swahili and their tongue, has heard at times, with much detail, what So-and-So used to do in Africa, and the real conduct or misconduct of somebody else; and no doubt, in the same way, other African travellers who know Ki-swahili have been amused with an account of any little weaknesses of temper, eccentricities of tooth-wash, or fastidiousness of clean sheets and tablecloths in the wilderness which may have been displayed by the author of this book. I have, in fact, at different times and in many African experiences, on the hot, weary midday march, by the brookside, in the quiet grey moonlight round the camp-fire, in the gloomy forest, under the snows of Kilima-njaro, becalmed on the expanse of Tanganyika, or gliding rapidly down the Congo in a canoe, listened half idly, half attentively, to the discus-sions which would arise among the Wa-swahili carriers as to their view of the lives led in Africa by most great travellers. Of one thing, however, these gossips were all convinced (and among all the scandal they were talking there was little reason for them to exempt one man more than another), and that was, that Dr. Living-stone, who, according to their traditions, was sometimes

cross and even peevish, who was sometimes in their eyes
unreasonable and sometimes inexplicable in his actions,
was nevertheless absolutely pure from the least suspicion
of immorality. Had he been otherwise, had he been as
frail as are ninety-eight African travellers, and, for the
matter of that, other men, out of a hundred, I should
not have alluded to this subject, because it is one which
is better left undiscussed ; but as I have heard this
foolish slander half-gleefully hinted at by those who
derive some undefined pleasure by belittling great men,
I thought it better to refer to the rumour, and state
that, judged by the verdict of Livingstone's native followers, it is absolutely false.

Livingstone was buried in Westminster Abbey on
the 18th April 1874, and his pall-bearers were Henry
Moreton Stanley, John Kirk, Horace Waller, Edward
Young, William Oswell, Sir Thomas Steele, William
Webb, and Jacob Wainwright, the Nassick boy who
had read the burial-service over Livingstone in Ilala.
Among the mourners were Livingstone's surviving children, his brother and his sisters, sister-in-law, and
father-in-law, the venerable Robert Moffat. Then, further in attendance, a brilliant company of all who were
most distinguished in geographical exploration, or in
any way connected with Africa, either by interest, sympathy, employment, or experience. A graceful attention
on the part of the much-abused Portuguese may be
noticed in the presence of an official representative from
that Government, the Visconde Duprat. The Italian
Minister was there, and many members of Parliament
and representatives of the press.

On the widespread results of African exploration
and political development which ensued on Livingstone's

stately funeral I have already touched in different passages in this book. The opening-up of the Dark Continent has gone on unceasingly in wider and wider ripples of discovery and colonisation as the immediate and continuous result of the stirring manner in which he drew attention to the woes and needs and capabilities of Bantu Africa. In Zambezia and Nyasaland especially —in what will soon be called " British Central Africa " —Livingstone's work is rapidly nearing the fruition he longed for under the flag he loved. Almost in the centre of this newest addition to the Queen's vast Empire, near the southern shores of Lake Bangweolo, the heart and entrails of Livingstone were buried. To this shrine, it may be—unless all sentiment is repressed by a brannew civilisation—tribes of Africans will come to pay a pilgrimage of respect to the memory of their great advocate. Possibly over this spot we may raise a temple or place a statue; or it may be—and more likely—that in the gold-rush, in the land-grabbing, in the coffeeplanting, sugar-baking, and the prosaic prosperity that will undoubtedly some day fill this land, the local inhabitants will be too material-minded, too busy, too mean, to spend their money or thought on sentiment or statues or monuments; but, to quote the last stanza of the fine memorial verses which *Punch* offered up to the dead Livingstone—

" He needs no epitaph to guard a name
    Which men shall praise while worthy work is done ;
He lived and died for good—be that his fame :
    Let marble crumble : this is LIVING-STONE."

INDEX.

2 A

30'

Kasai

BA

L U N

Kashanjie

Ki...

Ka...

Batende
Kate

LUVA

Lutshaze Nva

Kuando

Kuando

Ri...

L.N
Ldi...

HO

K a l a h

K

A K W A

Schie

Roggeve

ant R.

CAPE

ua B.

e Town

20'

DR LIVINGSTONE'S
TRAVELS IN
SOUTH AFRICA

Scale 1:25 000 000.

Statute Miles

———— Missionary Journeys, 1849-56
———— Zambesi Expedition, 1858-64
------- Last Journey, 1866-73

☐ Highlands over 3000 ft above the Sea level

32 Fleet Street, London

The
World's Great Explorers and Explorations.

EDITED BY

J. Scott Keltie, Librarian, Royal Geographical
Society ;

H. J. Mackinder, M.A., Reader in Geography at the
University of Oxford ;

And E. G. Ravenstein, F.R.G.S.

UNDER this title Messrs. G. PHILIP & SON
are issuing a series of volumes dealing with
the life and work of those heroic adventurers through
whose exertions the face of the earth has been made
known to humanity.

Each volume will, so far as the ground covered
admits, deal mainly with one prominent name associated with some particular region, and will tell the
story of his life and adventures, and describe the work
which he accomplished in the service of geographical
discovery. The aim will be to do ample justice to
geographical results, while the personality of the ex-

2 B

plorer is never lost sight of. In a few cases in which the work of discovery cannot be possibly associated with the name of any single explorer, some departure from this plan may be unavoidable, but it will be followed as far as practicable. In each case the exact relation of the work accomplished by each explorer to what went before and what followed after, will be pointed out; so that each volume will be virtually an account of the exploration of the region with which it deals. Though it will not be sought to make the various volumes dovetail exactly into each other, it is hoped that when the series is concluded, it will form a fairly complete Biographical History of Geographical Discovery.

Each volume will be written by a recognised authority on his subject, and will be amply furnished with specially prepared maps, portraits, and other original illustrations.

While the names of the writers whose co-operation has been secured are an indication of the high standard aimed at from a literary and scientific point of view, the series will be essentially a popular one, appealing to the great mass of general readers, young and old, who have always shewn a keen interest in the story of the world's exploration, when well told. It is, moreover, believed that not a few of the volumes will be found adapted for use as reading books, or even text-books in schools.

Each volume will consist of about 300 pp. crown 8vo, and will be published in cloth extra, price 4s. 6d., in cloth gilt cover, specially designed by Lewis F. Day, gilt edges, price 5s., or in half polished morocco, marbled edges, price 7s. 6d.

The following volumes are either ready or are in an advanced state of preparation :—

JOHN DAVIS, Arctic Explorer and Early India Navigator. By CLEMENTS R. MARKHAM, C.B., F.R.S.

[*Ready.*]

PALESTINE. By MAJOR C. R. CONDER, R.E. Leader of the Palestine Exploring Expeditions.

[*Ready.*]

MUNGO PARK AND THE NIGER. By JOSEPH THOMSON, author of "Through Masai Land," &c.

[*Ready.*]

MAGELLAN AND THE PACIFIC. By DR. H. H. GUILLEMARD, author of "The Cruise of the Marchesa."

[*Ready.*]

JOHN FRANKLIN AND THE NORTH-WEST PASSAGE. By CAPTAIN ALBERT MARKHAM, R.N.

[*Ready.*]

LIVINGSTONE AND CENTRAL AFRICA. By H. H. JOHNSTON, H.B.M. Consul at Mozambique.

[*Shortly.*]

SAUSSURE AND THE ALPS. By DOUGLAS W. FRESHFIELD, Hon. Sec. Royal Geographical Society.

THE HIMALAYA. By LIEUT.-GENERAL R. STRACHEY, R.E., C.S.I., late President of the R.G.S.

ROSS AND THE ANTARCTIC. By H. J. MACKINDER, M.A., Reader in Geography at Oxford.

BRUCE AND THE NILE. By J. SCOTT KELTIE, Librarian R.G.S.

VASCO DA GAMA AND THE OCEAN HIGHWAY TO INDIA. By E. G. RAVENSTEIN, F.R.G.S.

Other volumes to follow will deal with—

HUMBOLDT AND SOUTH AMERICA.

BARENTS AND THE N.E. PASSAGE.

COLUMBUS AND HIS SUCCESSORS.

JACQUES CARTIER AND CANADA.

CAPTAIN COOK AND AUSTRALASIA.

MARCO POLO AND CENTRAL ASIA.

IBN BATUTA AND N. AFRICA.

LEIF ERIKSON AND GREENLAND.

DAMPIER AND THE BUCCANEERS.

&c.　　&c.　　&c.

www.ingramcontent.com/pod-product-compliance
Lightning Source LLC
Chambersburg PA
CBHW031350290326
41932CB00044B/863